SUCCESSFUL SCHOOLING:

Train Your Horse With Empathy

Karin Blignault

J. A. Allen
London

In Memory of Ina

British Library Cataloguing in Publication Data
A catalogue record for this book is available
from the British Library

ISBN 0.85131.628.X

Printed in Great Britain in 1997 by
J. A. Allen and Company Limited,
1 Lower Grosvenor Place,
Buckingham Palace Road,
London, SW1W OEL.

© J. A. Allen & Co. Ltd., 1997

Designed by Nancy Lawrence
Illustrations by Maryke Loubser

Typeset in Hong Kong by Setrite Typesetters Ltd
Printed in Hong Kong by Dah Hua Printing Press Co. Ltd.

CONTENTS

ACKNOWLEDGEMENTS

First and foremost I would like to thank the Lord. Without His guidance this work would not have been possible.

My dear and difficult thoroughbred, Making Eyes, made an enormous contribution to the book. In our fifteen years together he taught me to jump, to event and to do all the dressage movements. By trying every possible evasion he has also taught me some very exact horse language.

Special thanks go to my very supportive friends and pupils who helped by being sounding boards and guinea pigs. I would also like to thank my trainers, past and present. Through their teaching they enhanced my own knowledge.

Three friends deserve special mention: Maryke Loubser, whose beautiful illustrations enhance this book; Judith Moxon who, with great patience, took the photographs of the shoulder-in, half-pass and collected trot and Tessa Mills who edited the language of the original manuscript. I am most grateful for their efforts and assistance.

I would also like to thank my publishers and in particular Caroline Burt, Martin Diggle and Jane Lake for their expert editing, production and layout of the book.

Lastly I must thank my two sons, Jacques and Nico, and my husband. Their support made it a pleasure to write this book.

INTRODUCTION

The most important factor in training a horse is our ability to communicate with him. The better the communication, the quicker he will learn.

It has often been claimed that horse and rider do not share a common language. This, however, is not entirely correct – there exists a clear non-verbal language that both horse and rider can understand. This is the language by which movement is elicited through the use of the horse's automatic postural reactions. It is an exact language which is understood immediately by all horses. The book will endeavour to explain this language and make it available to all riders who aspire to become effective trainers.

There is no point in using a language that horses have difficulty in understanding. This will lead to confusion and anxiety in the horse and frustration in the rider. Frustration will lead to undue punishment of the horse and finally to a total breakdown of communication. All riders and trainers should therefore endeavour to become proficient in the language of movement as explained in this book. This language is scientifically proven, and was first described by Dr Carl Bobath and his physiotherapist wife, Berta, in the treatment method developed to help spastic children move more normally. Man, over the ages, has automatically been using this language to communicate with the horse. All the classical aids we are still using today are based on this facilitation of movement.

We have to work the horse correctly, using classical aids, to ensure that our end product will have all the attributes of an athlete. Through this training, the horse will become more comfortable to ride and will react effortlessly to all the aids. His balance will become perfect, leading to self-carriage, lightness and acceptance of the bit. He will move forwards freely with elastic, ground-covering strides. Transitions will be fluid, harmonious and effortless. Lateral movements and lengthening will become smooth and easy. His jumping ability will improve through the development of his balance, engagement of the hindquarters, straightness, suppleness and the ability to move forwards. He will do all this in rhythm, with energy and pure gaits.

This book explains, in simple and logical terms, how and why the aids we have been using for centuries are effective in producing the movements we desire. It also explains, in detail, how the rider can influence the automatic postural mechanisms of the horse to produce the required movements. Once riders understand these concepts and why they work, they will learn to ride or train their horses in a much shorter time, and therefore gain more enjoyment from their sport.

PART ONE

THE NEURO – MUSCULAR

BASIS OF TRAINING

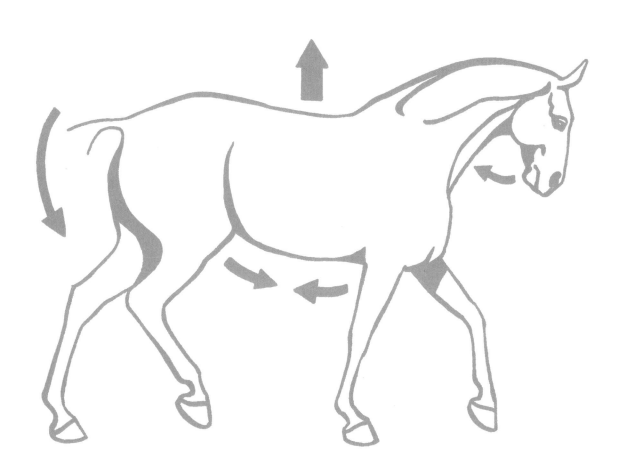

CHAPTER 1

THE PRINCIPLES OF

MOVEMENT

Training horses is not only an art, but also a science – the science of movement. Some riders have an inborn ability to use this science without really realising it. These are the naturally talented riders. The majority of riders, however, first need to understand what the aids are all about.

Riding a horse can be compared to leading a blind person. If a blind person being led is not prepared for turning a corner, they will more than likely lose their balance. The same applies to preparing horses for changes of direction. Also, if you should suddenly pull a blind person forwards, they will more than likely pull back. Similarly, if a horse's reins are pulled insensitively, he will lift his head and pull back against the rider's hands. Therefore, a horse should be carefully prepared for every movement so that he can use his balance reactions effectively without losing the harmony of the movement. The following chapters will explain how to use basic balance reactions to train a horse.

THE PROMOTION OF MOVEMENT: BASIC CONCEPTS

A horse has no idea why he should be doing all the things demanded by the rider. It will, therefore, be greatly to the rider's advantage to use a language that the horse can understand. This horse language is the language of:

1) Normal postural reactions to the disturbance of balance.

2) The effect of gravity on the muscles.

3) Movement of the head in relation to the body.

All the classical aids we use are based on facilitating these reactions.

Since the horse's reaction to (understanding of) the aids is entirely based on this science of movement, understanding the following basic concepts will greatly simplify the training of your horse.

THE MECHANICS OF MOTION IN HORSES

Voluntary and skilled movements in all mammals are based on postural reflex mechanisms. For the purpose of training the horse we can differentiate three groups of automatic reactions:

Balance reactions.

Righting reactions.

Automatic changes of muscle tone as a protection against the forces of gravity.

Balance reactions
In order to understand balance reactions, it is first important to understand the concepts of the centre of gravity and body schema.

The centre of gravity is the point in a body about which all the parts exactly balance. (In a perfect cube, the centre of gravity is located at its exact centre.) In a living body (a horse), the location of the centre of gravity depends on various factors: conformation; weight distribution; gait and posture at a specific moment and whether the horse is supporting external weights (saddle and rider). As we shall see, the horse's large neck plays an important part in the location of his centre of gravity.

In order to stay balanced, the horse has to keep his centre of gravity over his base of support (his four legs). Any movement, or change in position of a body part, will have an effect on the centre of gravity and lead to an automatic balance reaction.

Body schema is the automatic knowledge an animal possesses of where his body parts are at any moment. For example, when a horse steps over an object with his forelegs, he automatically knows where his hind legs are in relation to the object, even though he is not able to *see* the position of his hind legs. This is because the horse uses what is known as his proprioceptive sense to locate the position of his body parts.

As soon as the body schema changes, the horse's centre of gravity has to adapt to the new weight distribution. The smallest movement in one part of the body will result in an automatic adjustment of another part, in order that the whole body can stay in balance.

Balance reactions are, therefore, automatic movements which serve to maintain and restore balance during activities, especially when there is danger of falling. These adjustments of posture to changes in the centre of gravity are continuous while the horse is in motion.

Even the smallest change of balance has to be countered by changes in muscle tone. Whenever an animal's balance is disturbed, his muscles will immediately and automatically adjust to prevent him from falling over. (To give an example, a person who is pushed from behind will automatically adjust their balance by stepping forwards, and their hands and arms will make an automatic adjustment by shooting forwards in preparation for the fall.) A horse, or any other animal, will react in a fundamentally similar manner.

Exercise 1. Stand next to your horse. Push him, with your hands, behind his elbow, on the ribcage. His ribcage will move away from you while his head, neck and quarters will move towards you.

This reaction is the result of his weight being

Figure 1 Eliciting a balance reaction in the horse.

pushed sideways by the weight of his ribcage. In order not to fall over, he has either to move some other part of his body in the opposite direction, or step sideways. Because the weight displacement is minimal, he will automatically choose to adjust his balance by bringing other parts of his body (his head, neck and tail) to the opposite side. If you were to push harder, he would start moving sideways to balance himself. This is an automatic balance reaction which is important when going through corners – as will be discussed at a later stage. Most of the aids we use on our horses are based on invoking a balance reaction.

Righting reactions

These, in all animals, are automatic movements which serve to maintain and restore the normal position of the head in space and in its alignment with the spinal column.

Whenever part of a person or animal is turned in a given direction, the rest of the body will follow. If, for example, a person's head is turned to the left, the shoulders will eventually follow. If the head is turned even further to the left, the hips will eventually follow the shoulders. If the head is turned still more, the legs and feet will eventually turn in the direction which the whole body is now facing. In this way, it is possible to turn a person in little circles simply by cupping your hands over their cheeks or ears. This process works in reverse as well: when a person's hips are turned, their shoulders, neck and head will follow.

The righting reaction can also be demonstrated in other ways. When a person bends their neck forwards, their shoulders will follow, then the hips. If you push your head backwards, as far as it will go, your back will soon follow the movement and bend backwards.

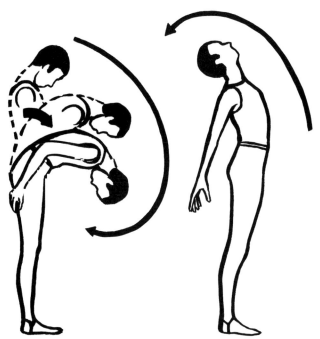

Figure 2 Demonstration of the righting reaction as a result of flexion of the neck. (a) The shoulders become rounded, which leads to the contraction of the abdominal muscles, which in turn leads to the contraction of the hip flexors. (b) In this righting reaction the neck extends, leading to the contraction of the back muscles and resultant hollowing of the back.

All animals will react in the same manner. This is not simply because the bones are joined to each other, but because of the action of little nerve bodies (proprioceptive organs) situated in the muscle endings and the joints. These tell the brain that parts of the body are turning and that the rest should follow, or increasing discomfort will result. When a horse's head is turned to one side, his neck, shoulders and hips will follow in sequence. When a horse flexes his head and neck downwards, his

abdominal muscles and hip flexors will contract in sequence. In the same way, when he lifts his head and neck, his back will become hollow (concave). The fact that all animals react in this way explains why we are able to turn horses so effectively with our reins and legs.

Exercise 2. Stand next to your horse and pull one rein only, sideways. He will turn his head towards you and then move his hindquarters away from you in an attempt to put his body in alignment with his head and neck.

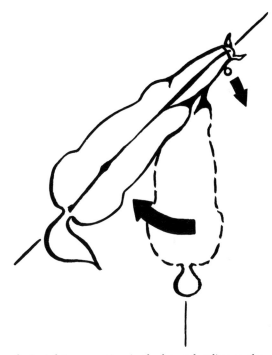

Figure 3 A righting reaction in the horse leading to the alignment of the head and spine.

Automatic changes of muscle tone as a protection against the forces of gravity

As soon as a muscle is brought into a position opposing the forces of gravity, it will contract. When a person bends forwards, their back muscles immediately contract to counteract the effect of gravity.

This reaction is discussed in terms of the movement of the horse's neck in Chapter 4.

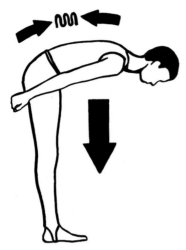

Figure 4 Gravity pulling on the upper body leads to the contraction of the back muscles.

Exercise 3. Place your hand under a partner's elbow. Lift their arm up to a horizontal position and support it there. They will relax and rest the arm in your hand. Now let the arm go, but tap it from underneath a few times. Your partner will soon get the message and keep their arm in this

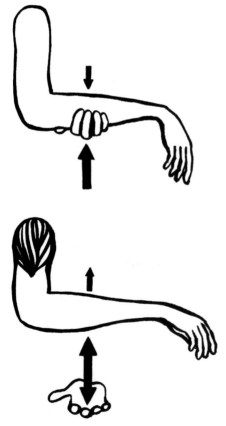

Figure 5 The shoulder muscle contracting against gravity.

horizontal position by contracting the deltoid muscle above the shoulder.

This is an example of the deltoid muscle coming into action against the force of gravity. The importance of this reaction will become clear when the neck and its muscles are discussed.

If we use these three basic principles of movement in the training of our horses, we will be able to teach them to do just about anything we want in a fairly short time. In order to understand these principles better, it will help you to do the following exercises with a friend. (Exercises 4 and 5 demonstrate righting reactions, and Exercises 6, 7 and 8 demonstrate balance reactions.)

Exercise 4. Stand behind your partner and place your hands on either side of their cheeks. Turn their head to the left until the shoulders follow, then turn it even further until first the hips and then the legs follow. Next, make your partner turn in a circle. Repeat the exercise to the opposite side in the same manner.

Figure 6 Demonstration of a righting reaction leading to the alignment of the person's head and spine (Exercise 4).

Exercise 5. Ask your partner to sit on a chair and hold them in the same way on both sides of the head. Next, try to make them stand up by turning their head to one side and at the same time lifting it. Or take their head forwards until they have to take their weight on their feet then, with a lifting action, make them stand.

Figure 7 Movement can be facilitated by influencing a person's righting reactions (Exercise 5).

Exercise 6. Ask your partner to stand in front of you, facing away from you, and place your hands on either side of their body, just above the waist.

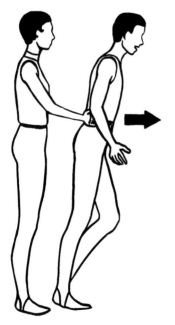

Figure 8 Facilitating a forward movement through the use of balance reactions (Exercise 6).

Then push them forwards with the heel of your hand. Because they lose balance, they have to take a step forwards. Next, push them with one hand only, in a sideways direction. Your partner will step sideways, as in half-pass, because balance has been lost. This is the basis of how the forward and lateral leg aids work on the girth.

Exercise 7. Holding your partner in the same manner on either side of the waist, push their weight onto their left leg with your right hand, and then move their right leg forwards by pushing with your right hand. Your partner should take a step forwards.

Figure 9 Facilitating the walk through the use of balance and righting reactions (Exercise 7).

Next, push sideways with your left hand so that your partner takes their weight on their right leg, and push their left leg forwards with your left hand. Your partner should take a step with their left foot. You have now taught your partner to 'walk'.

Exercise 8. Push your partner forwards as in Exercise 6, then prevent them from moving forwards by holding them (lock your elbows and press inwards). Your partner should halt. Remember this action when riding downward transitions with your horse.

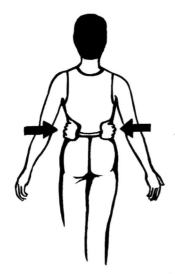

Figure 10 Facilitating the halt (Exercise 10).

Using these methods, and without saying a word to your partner, you can make them walk with their feet pointing in or pointing out; you can make them step forwards, backwards or sideways and you can make them stop, simply by holding them with your hands.

FACILITATION AND INHIBITION OF MOVEMENT

These two concepts were developed by Dr Carl Bobath and his physiotherapist wife, Berta. They used these concepts to describe the method of encouraging normal movement in spastic children. These concepts will be mentioned regularly throughout this book.

Facilitation of movement is the term used to describe the manner in which we encourage the horse to produce the correct movement – in other words, the aids. We explain to the horse, with our body, what to do with his body. Thus it is a body language which explains, very specifically, to the horse, which muscles to contract. We use the aids in a very specific way to influence the horse's natural balance and righting reactions and therefore facilitate the movement we want. (See Exercise 3, where the contraction of a very specific muscle was facilitated.) Exercises 1 to 8 are all examples of facilitating specific movements.

Inhibition of movement. In the same way as above we use aids to inhibit (prevent) unwanted movement by relaxing the muscular activity. This unwanted movement in horses is caused mainly by tension and anticipation. The movement we try to avoid most is hollowing of the horse's neck and back. Through inhibiting the action of the neck and back extensor muscles, we can prevent this hollowing. This process is described in detail in Chapter 4.

Exercise 9. Repeat Exercise 6 then do the following exercise: keep your hands in the same position and try to make your partner stand still again. You will find that you need to squeeze their waist and hold back in order for them to stand still (see Figure 10).

Exercise 10. Following on from Exercise 9, push your partner sideways and slightly forwards with your one hand still on their waist. Your partner will give a few sideways steps as a balance reaction.

Exercise 11. Push your partner with more force, so that they lose their balance and then, with your inside hand (the one your partner is moving towards) support them to help them find their balance. You are now doing a 'half-pass' with your partner. (A further balance reaction.)

The exercises described all indicate how we can communicate with our horse without the use of human language. This is done by influencing the horse's balance and righting reactions, as well as the body's automatic reaction against gravity, through facilitation and inhibition of movement. There are various ways in which we can influence the horse's balance mechanism: by putting more weight on one side we can make the horse move to that side; we can push him over with a leg; we can turn his head; we can turn our body, and so on. The following chapters will explain in detail how this is done.

KEY POINTS OF CONTROL

In order to facilitate movement in the horse, we only need to use certain areas of his body to influence the whole. These areas may be termed key points of control. When riding, we use the following key points of control:

The mouth (controlled by the hands). In the same manner as described in Exercise 2, we can use our hands to influence the horse's righting reactions.

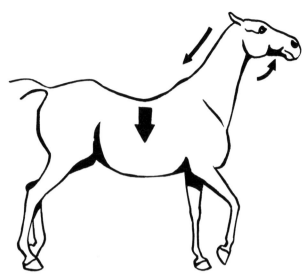

Figure 13 If the horse extends his neck, his back muscles will contract and lead to hollowness (righting reaction).

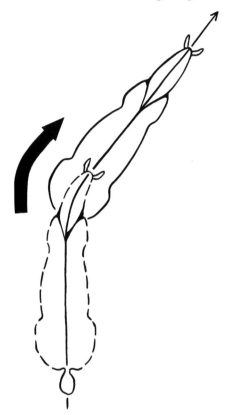

Figure 11 The body will follow the direction of the head (righting reaction).

If we turn the horse's head when he is moving forwards, his neck will normally follow the direction of his head and his body will then follow. (If the horse is trying to resist or evade the action, we will have to use other key points of control as well.)

With the same methodology we can flex or extend his head, and his neck and body will follow.

The ribcage (controlled by the legs on the girth). By moving the horse's ribcage with our legs we influence the whole horse's balance reactions by altering his weight distribution.

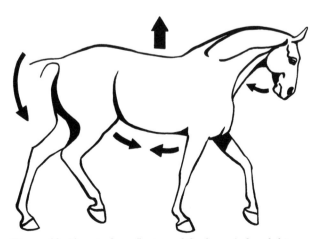

Figure 12 If we induce flexion of the horse's head, his abdominal muscles will contract and round the back (righting reaction).

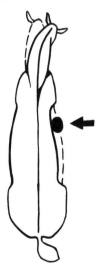

Figure 14 Influencing the horse's balance reactions by moving his ribcage.

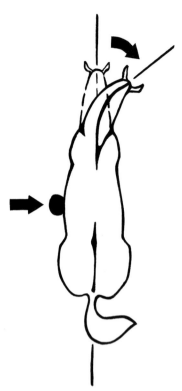

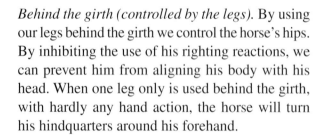

Figure 15(a) Preventing the alignment of the horse's spine and head (inhibiting a righting reaction).

Figure 15(b) Moving the horse's hindquarters with the leg behind the girth.

Behind the girth (controlled by the legs). By using our legs behind the girth we control the horse's hips. By inhibiting the use of his righting reactions, we can prevent him from aligning his body with his head. When one leg only is used behind the girth, with hardly any hand action, the horse will turn his hindquarters around his forehand.

The saddle area (controlled by our weight). By using our weight in the saddle we can control the whole horse by influencing his balance reactions: through weight pressure in the saddle we can encourage engagement of the hindquarters.

When riding or training the horse, we seldom use only one key point of control at a time. A combination of these points will normally be necessary to ensure effective communication with the horse.

The more we use the back end of the horse to control him, the less we need the forehand. Certainly, the more the forehand is used, the less the back end will be used. However, since the back end influences a larger part of the horse, and produces the more useful propulsion, we aim to gain increasingly greater control of this area.

CHAPTER 2

LATERAL BEND – FACT

OR FICTION

Much of the information in this chapter is derived
from the work of R.H. Smythe as described in his
book *The Horse Structure and Movement**.

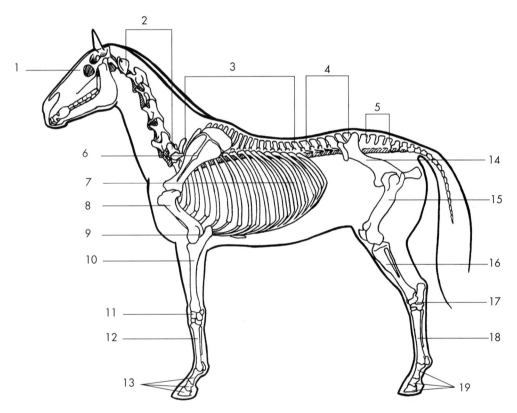

Figure 16 The skeleton of the horse.

 1) *Skull.*
 2) *Cervical vertebrae.*
 3) *Thoracic vertebrae.*
 4) *Lumbar vertebrae.*
 5) *Sacrum.*
 6) *Scapula (shoulder blade).*
 7) *Ribcage.*
 8) *Humerus.*
 9) *Elbow joint.*
10) *Ulna (forearm).*
11) *Carpal bones.*
12) *Metacarpal bone (fore-cannon).*
13) *Phalangial bones (pasterns
     and pedal bone).*
14) *Os coxae (pelvic bone).*
15) *Femur (thigh bone).*
16) *Tibia (shin bone).*
17) *Tarsal bones (hock).*
18) *Metatarsal bones (hind
     cannon).*
19) *Phalangial bones (pasterns
     and pedal bone).*

* Publishers note. This work, revised and updated by P.C. Goody and Peter Gray, is now published under the title *Horse Structure and Movement* by J.A. Allen and Co. Ltd., London.

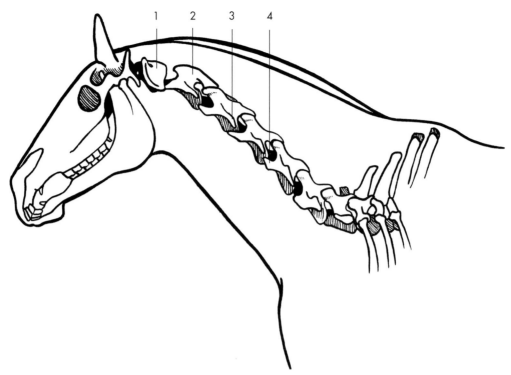

Figure 17 The seven cervical vertebrae. Note that there are no protrusions preventing movement.
      1) Atlas.   3) Transverse process (dorsal).
      2) Axis.   4) Transverse process (ventral).

THE ANATOMY AND MOVEMENT OF THE HORSE'S SPINE

THE CERVICAL VERTEBRAE

The horse possesses seven cervical (neck) vertebrae. The joint between the skull and the first cervical vertebra (the atlas) allows nodding of the head. This up and down movement provides the facility for putting the horse 'on the bit'. The next joint, between the atlas and the second cervical vertebra (the axis), allows some rotation of the head on the neck. (When the horse does this, his head will be tilted to one side, and his ears will be unlevel.)

The joints between the next five cervical vertebrae allow lateral (sideways) movement of the neck. These joints also permit flexion (rounding) of the neck as well as hollowing (concavity) of the neck.

The horse's neck thus has the ability to move in both the horizontal and vertical planes.

THE THORACIC VERTEBRAE

There are eighteen thoracic vertebrae in the horse's spine. The eighteen pairs of ribs are attached to these, and the cavity created by the ribs protects the horse's heart and lungs. Because of the transverse processes and the attachment of the ribs, there is very limited movement in any direction in this part of the spine.

The dorsal spines of the thoracic vertebrae are bound in a row by strong ligaments and each neighbouring pair of bones is firmly united the one with the other through the articular processes aided by a number of closely binding ligaments. It follows therefore that while the neck bones are freely movable the thoracic bones form an almost rigid column.

The Horse Structure and Movement R.H. Smythe.

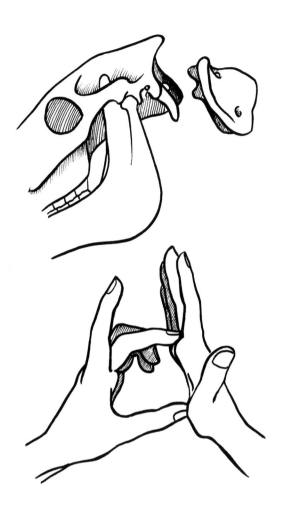

Figure 18 The joint between the skull and the first cervical vertebra (atlas) allows nodding. Imagine that you are looking at the joint from above. Place two fingers of your left hand against the palm of your right hand to represent the skull and atlas. If you keep your left wrist straight, your left arm will represent the horse's head. Note how your left arm can nod up and down, but not move from side to side.

The attachment of the ribs

The top part of each rib consists of two protuberances: a head and a tubercle. The heads of the ribs fit in between each pair of thoracic vertebrae. The tubercle of each rib is attached to the neighbouring vertebra. This attachment allows forward and outward rotation of the ribs, which expands the chest cavity to facilitate breathing.

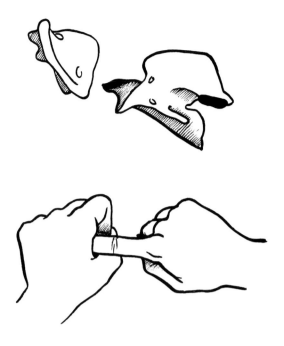

Figure 19(a) The joint between the first and second cervical vertebrae (atlas and axis) allows rotation. Your finger in the fist will demonstrate the process of rotation.

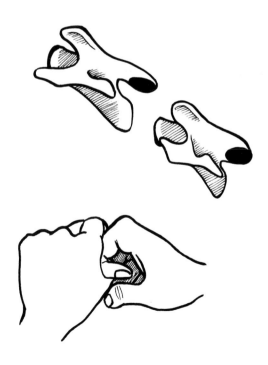

Figure 19(b) These cervical vertebrae allow movement in all directions as there are no ribs or bony protrusions to prevent this. They function as a unit because they are joined together by ligaments and muscles.

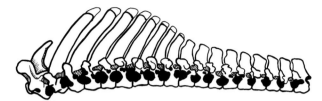

Figure 20(a) The thoracic vertebrae. The shaded areas denote the rib attachments.

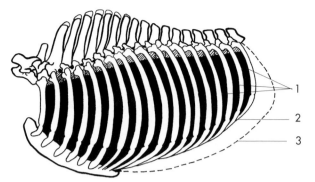

Figure 21 Contraction of the intercostal muscles.
1) Intercostal muscles.
2) The shape of the ribcage when the muscles contract.
3) The shape of the ribcage when the muscles are relaxed.

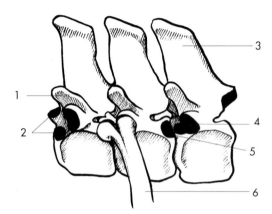

Figure 20(b) Three thoracic vertebrae. The rib attachments in the spaces between the vertebrae do not allow movement on a horizontal plane.
1) Transverse process.
2) Facets between the vertebrae (connections).
3) Spinous tuberosity.
4) Facet for attachment of rib head.
5) Facet for attachment of the other rib head.
6) Rib.

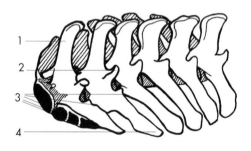

Figure 22 The lumbar vertebrae are connected by facets which prevent lateral flexion.
1) Spinous process.
2) Mamilloarticular process.
3) Alar articular surfaces.
4) Transverse process.

The contraction of the intercostal muscles pulls the ribs closer together, to assist expiration of the air from the lungs. If these muscles contract on one side only, the distance between the hindquarter and its corresponding forelimb is slightly shortened. The contribution of this action to the illusion of lateral bend will be dealt with shortly.

THE LUMBAR VERTEBRAE

While there are usually six lumbar vertebrae, occasionally only five are present. In such cases, there will be an extra thoracic vertebra. This arrangement is found especially in Eastern breeds such as Arabs.

The last three lumbar vertebrae are joined together by the mamilloarticular processes. These processes are linked on a vertical plane, which denotes strictly longitudinal flexibility. The joints of the lumbar vertebrae have a tendency towards arthritis, which may manifest itself as early as the horse's second year, and end with solid fusion of all these joints. This process often starts on one side only and, during this time, the horse may suffer discomfort and show a tendency to move unevenly. According to R.H. Smythe, most of these cases recover their efficiency when total fusion finally occurs.

Thus, in the lumbar region, there seems to be very limited lateral movement.

THE ILLUSION OF LATERAL BEND

The work of R.H. Smythe clearly indicates that there is very limited movement in the thoraco-lumbar and sacral areas of the horses's spine. The question then arises as to what causes the illusion of lateral bend in the horse. The answer lies in the movement of the ribcage and in the ability of the horse's legs to abduct (move away from the body) and adduct (move closer to the body).

Movement of the ribcage (thorax). The forelimbs are attached to the thorax of the horse by muscles, ligaments and tendons only. There is no bony or rigid connection between the forelimbs and the horse's spine. When the forelegs are in a weight-bearing position (both feet on the ground), the ribcage hangs loosely between them and can be pushed with ease from side to side (a fact that can be demonstrated by simple experiment). This arrangement allows a great deal of lateral movement of the ribcage. As previously mentioned, the intercostal muscles can contract to pull the ribs slightly closer together – an action which creates a slightly concave effect if occurring on one side only. Try the following exercise to illustrate this effect:

Exercise 12. Stand next to your horse and push the ribcage, with both your hands, to the other side. The ribcage will swing easily to the opposite side. Try from the other side and the same thing will happen.

Hind limb movement. The ball and socket joint of the hip allows movement in all directions (although the strong ligaments and muscles prevent this movement from being excessive.) The hind legs thus have the ability to both abduct and adduct.

The illusion of bend is thus created by the ribcage moving to one side while the legs on the same side abduct away from the thorax. The legs on the other side adduct and, simultaneously, the neck is bent to the inside. The contraction of the intercostal muscles to bring the ribs closer together completes the picture of lateral bend.

As you carry out the experiment of pushing the ribcage, observe carefully the horse's fore- and hind legs. You will see clearly that the hind leg and foreleg on the side you are pushing will move away from the horse. The foreleg on the opposite side, however, will move towards the ribcage. This,

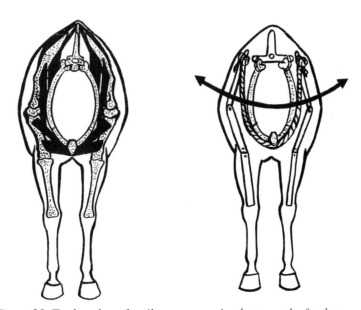

Figure 23 To show how the ribcage can swing between the forelegs.

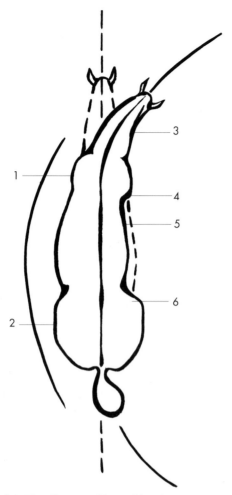

Figure 24 The illusion of lateral bend.
1) Outside foreleg adducts (moves closer to the body).
2) Outside hind leg adducts (moves closer to the body).
3) Neck bends to the inside.
4) Inside foreleg abducts (moves away from the body).
5) Ribcage 'swings' to the outside.
6) Inside hind leg abducts (moves away from the body).

together with the ribcage moving to one side and the contraction of the intercostal muscles, gives the horse, on one side, an impression of concavity (hollowness) and on the other side, an impression of convexity (roundedness). In other words there is an illusion of lateral bend, although the thoracic

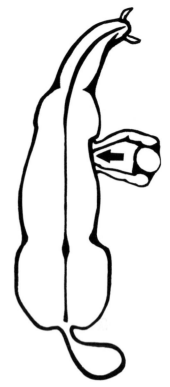

Figure 25 When the ribcage is pushed sideways the abducting effect on the inside legs can be noticed clearly.

and lumbar regions of the spinal column are not actually bending laterally. This process is only possible because the limbs are not skeletally attached to the spine.

The neck, showing considerable and actual lateral bend, completes the picture of 'lateral bend' through the body. (Note that the neck will move towards your side when you push the ribcage. This is a balance reaction to the horse's weight being pushed in the other direction.)

This ability to adduct and abduct the limbs also assists the horse in his ability to move forwards and sideways simultaneously. Other variable factors of conformation cause individual horses to differ in their ability to carry out such movements whilst maintaining perfect balance.

CHAPTER 3

MUSCULAR ACTIVITY –
THE BASIS OF SCHOOLING

If we wish our training to have the effect of turning the horse into a well muscled athlete, it follows that we must understand the key functions of his musculature.

THE HORSE'S NECK – HIS GREAT BALANCING MECHANISM

Look at the horse in Figure 26. If we should take away his neck, he would be left with a body perfectly balanced on four legs (almost like a table). His centre of gravity will be more or less in the centre of this table. The horse was, however, made with a rather long and heavy neck, which brings his centre of gravity significantly forward. The function of this long neck is twofold:

It enables him to graze – although slow-moving grazers (such as cattle) get by with much shorter necks because they do not need quick balance reactions.

It assists him with his balance. For the purpose of riding, this is the most important function of the horse's neck.

When a horse runs free he is continually and automatically using his neck to balance himself. He lifts his neck when he goes from trot to halt and stretches it forward when galloping.

To stay in balance, the horse needs to keep his centre of gravity over his base of support (his four legs). We can compare his head and neck to a weight on a fairly long lever: lifting his neck will move his centre of gravity backwards, and stretch-

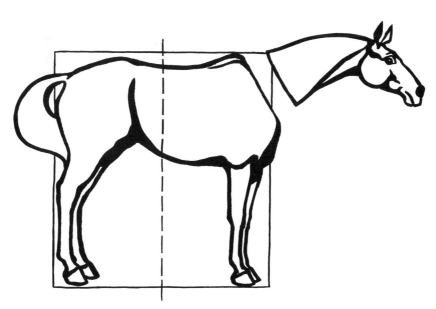

Figure 26 The horse's body in balance without head and neck.

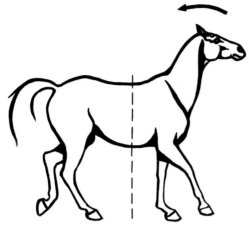

Figure 27(a) The horse lifts his head to bring his centre of gravity back to help him in the downward transition.

Figure 27(b) The horse stretches his neck forward to bring his centre of gravity forwards in the gallop.

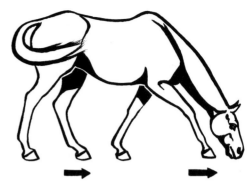

Figure 28(a) The horse broadening his base of support to maintain balance.

Figure 28(b) The horse flexes his hocks to move his centre of gravity backwards.

Figure 28(c) The gymnast flexing her knees and pushing her seat backwards to maintain balance.

ing his neck forward and down will move his centre of gravity forwards. To counteract the latter, he will have to bring his base of support underneath his centre of gravity. There are three basic methods he can use to regain balance:

1) He can move a front foot forwards, as he does when stretching down to graze. By doing this, he broadens his base of support so that his body is, once again, over his centre of gravity. This same action is the cause of 'running' in trot, when the horse is driven forwards while his centre of gravity is still too far forward. (Imagine that your hands were tied behind your back and you were pushed forwards, thus losing your balance. Since your hands would not be able to protect you from the fall, your only protection would be to move your legs underneath you as fast as possible – run.)

2) He can bring his hindquarters more underneath him, to help push his centre of gravity backwards. This can also be observed when horses are grazing.

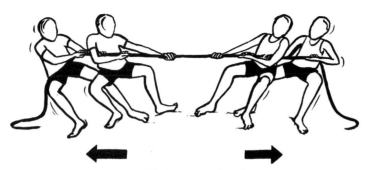

Figure 29 Two opposing forces.

3) He can flex his hocks while his legs are firmly on the ground. This action, which brings his centre of gravity backwards, can be compared to a gymnast landing after a vault – the gymnast's legs are bent, and the seat pushed back.

These, then, are the automatic balance reactions of the body which enable a horse to change his centre of gravity and prevent him from falling over. While the horse's neck is a tool which helps him to control his balance, it is also the rider's tool to encourage the horse to use his hindquarters. It is, therefore, necessary for any rider who wishes to become proficient at training horses to understand the mechanics of this neck action, and its effect on the horse's automatic balance reactions. These matters will be discussed in detail in due course.

RIDING ON THE OUTSIDE REIN

There should be a slightly stronger feel or contact on the outside rein than the inside rein. When there is a stronger feel on the outside rein it means that there is an opposing force against this rein. Imagine two teams of people pulling the opposite ends of a rope in a tug of war (see Figure 29). In the case of the horse, this opposing force to the outside rein is provided by the muscles on the inside of the neck (see Figure 30). The horse must have some slight contraction of these muscles in order to prepare himself to turn in a specific direction without loss of balance. Normally, when we ride around the arena, we will be preparing to perform turns, lateral work and canter departs towards the

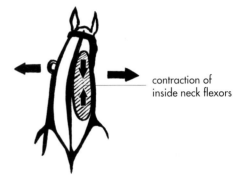

contraction of inside neck flexors

Figure 30 Two opposing forces. The outside rein and the inside neck flexors.

inside of the arena, so the horse must be prepared to move in that direction. Once you decide to change direction, you change to your new outside rein.

Figure 31 Slight inside bend. The horse is on the outside rein.

WHY WE NEED TO RIDE ON THE OUTSIDE REIN

The horse does not automatically know where the rider would like him to go at any particular moment. In this respect, riding is almost like leading a blind person. If you should suddenly pull a blind person in the direction you want them to go, or pull them when you want to change direction, they would surely stop dead in their tracks or, at least, resist your efforts. So it is with the horse; he needs ample warning before he is asked to perform a movement. Having him on the outside rein is already encouraging the correct use of muscles for any movement he would need to do to the inside, be it shoulder-in, half-pass, turns, pirouettes, serpentines or canter departs.

HOW WE ENSURE THAT THE HORSE IS ON THE OUTSIDE REIN

To be on the outside rein, the horse needs to use the muscles on the inside of his neck. We ask him to do this by direct flexions – through a 'squeeze and release' on the inside rein. We take the inside rein to say 'flex your neck' and, as soon as he responds, we soften the rein again. The light feeling we get from this action is created by the horse contracting his muscles to that side. This can be done by 'sponging' the rein with the fingers (if the horse is quick to react), or by flexion of the wrist (see Figure 32). If the horse is particularly resistant, the desired response can be obtained by moving the whole arm. The inside leg simul-taneously pushes the ribcage over to facilitate con-traction of the intercostal muscles on the inside.

When the horse reacts correctly by contracting the muscles on the inside of his neck it is extremely important that he is rewarded immediately. Yielding the rein to him and giving him a little tickle on the neck with the *inside* hand indicates to him that he has responded correctly. Remember that we are communicating in his 'language' and he must be told immediately when he has understood correctly. This is essential if confusion is to be avoided.

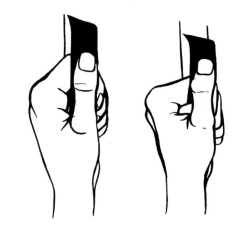

Figure 32(a) Squeezing the rein.

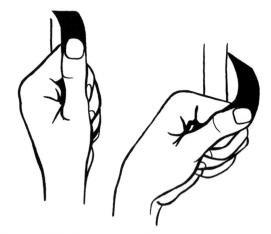

Figure 32(b) Flexing the wrist.

Figure 32(c) Moving the whole arm back.

Figure 32(d) Releasing the rein when the horse responds.

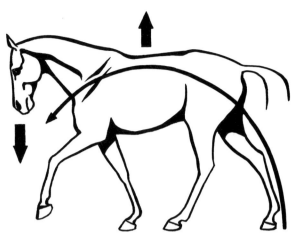

Figure 33(a) A rounded or arched back is stronger and can carry more weight.

Figure 32(e) Rewarding with a tickle.

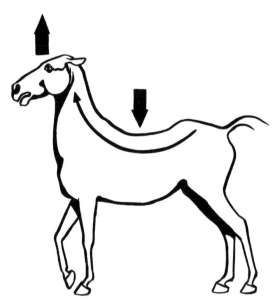

STRENGTHENING THE BACK

Figure 33(b) A hollowed back is weak, and may sustain injuries when carrying weight.

As soon as a rider is seated on a horse, the horse has to take more strain on his body. To enable the horse to cope with this strain without injuring his muscles, he must round his back – a rounded back is a strong back. The muscles responsible for this action should be strengthened to give the horse more weight-bearing ability and to prevent injury to his back. To demonstrate this action, try the following exercise:

Exercise 13. Stand on your hands and knees and ask a child to climb on your back. Hollow your

Figure 34 Abdominal muscles contracting to produce a rounded back.

back and feel the strain that it takes. Now round your back and feel the difference in your weight-bearing ability. Take note of which muscles you were contracting to produce a rounded back.

The flexor muscles of the body have higher muscle tone than the extensor muscles, and are the power muscles. They are generally stronger than the extensor muscles, and are used in positions of weight-bearing. The higher muscle tone is demonstrated quite clearly in the position of our hands and fingers at rest: the fingers, hands and wrists are always slightly flexed.

HOW THE HORSE ROUNDS AND STRENGTHENS HIS BACK

A horse's back becomes rounded as soon as he starts using his abdominal muscles and his spinal flexor muscles. Physiotherapists around the world advise back sufferers to strengthen their abdominal muscles as a protection against back problems. The abdominal muscles have to counteract the back muscles, which are constantly contracting isometrically against the forces of gravity. The action of these two muscle groups encases the spinal column in a strong brace, but the abdominal muscle contraction is more important for strengthening the back. The rider can activate the abdominal muscles through the horse's righting reactions. When he rounds his neck by contracting the muscles on the underside of his neck, his back will follow this movement through the contraction of his abdominal muscles. The contraction of the abdominal muscles will tilt the horse's pelvis and he will bring his hindquarters more underneath him. With this contraction of the abdominal muscles the horse becomes rounder in outline and more engaged; his steps become springier; his back will be stronger and more able to carry weight and he wil be more comfortable to sit on.

The feeling of the horse 'lifting' or arching his back to meet the saddle is the result of the contraction of the abdominal muscles. When the horse uses his back muscles, his back will become hollow and 'drop down'.

Try the following righting reaction for yourself:

Exercise 14. Bend your head forwards as far as you can. Your shoulders will follow this action and, as you curl yourself further, your back will become rounded and then your hips will follow this movement. Next, bend your neck backwards and note how your back will become hollow. This is one of the principles involved in encouraging the horse to use his abdominal muscles.

The progressive action described above defines riding 'long and deep' and shows the necessity of doing this exercise until the horse has a strong back. Riding 'long and deep' is dependent upon acceptance of the bit, submission and relaxation. These concepts will be described in the following section.

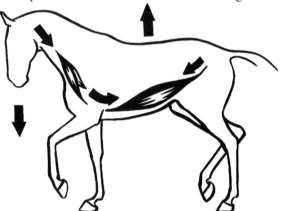

Figure 35(a) Contraction of the neck flexors leads to contraction of the abdominal muscles, with the resultant rounded or arched back.

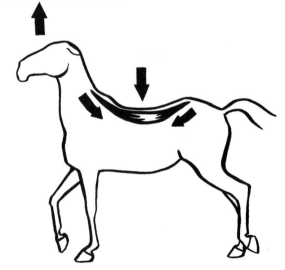

Figure 35(b) Contraction of the neck extensors leads to contraction of the back muscles, with the resultant hollowing of the back.

ISOTONIC AND ISOMETRIC MUSCULAR CONTRACTION

The word isotonic is derived from Greek and means equal tension (*isos* = equal: *tonos* = tone). During isotonic contraction the muscle shortens, but the tension in the muscle stays more or less the same. An example of this is when you flex your elbow without carrying weight: the biceps muscle shortens while it lifts the forearm. An example of this action in the horse is the contraction of the brachiocephalic muscle which shortens to lift the horse's shoulder.

Figure 36(a) Isotonic contraction of the biceps muscle leading to the lifting of the forearm.

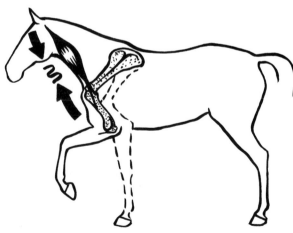

Figure 36(b) Isotonic contraction of the brachiocephalic muscle leading to lifting of the shoulder.

The word isometric is also derived from Greek and means equal length (*isos* = equal; *metros* = measure). During isometric contraction, the tension in the muscle is increased without an appreciable change of length. This contraction is evident when muscles are activated by the force of gravity, which plays a significant role in muscular activity. For example, if you lean forward you will feel all your back muscles come into action. The horse's neck extensors contract in this way when he is ridden 'long and deep'.

Figure 37 Isometric contraction of the neck extensor muscles against the forces of gravity. The muscles do not shorten.

Exercise 15. Lift your arm sideways to the horizontal position. Keep it there and note how tired it becomes. During the first part of the contraction the muscle shortened in isotonic contraction, but the second part of the contraction is against the force of gravity and is isometric contraction (see Figure 38).

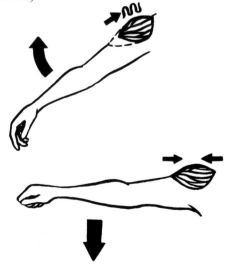

Figure 38 In the first part of the contraction the muscle shortens and lifts the arm. In the second part the muscle length stays the same.

THE EFFECT OF GRAVITY ON THE HORSE'S NECK AND BACK MUSCLES

Let us examine the muscular activities behind the main positions of the horse's head and neck.

Head in neutral position

When the horse has his head in a neutral position, as he would when standing alert in the paddock, he is using no muscular effort in his neck. The position of his head and neck is maintained by the strong nuchal funicular ligament. This is attached to the occipital tuberosity of the skull and to the dorsal spine of the fourth thoracic vertebra. On the lateral sides it connects, with the nuchal lamina (an oblique fascia), to the lower two-thirds of the cervical vertebrae. When the animal is at rest, it supports the head without fatiguing the muscles. When the head is lowered, muscular effort is needed but as soon as the muscles are relaxed, this elastic apparatus contracts and helps to bring the head back to its original position. This is why a novice horse often has to be reminded to stay in a rounded frame and needs rest periods from the 'on the bit' position.

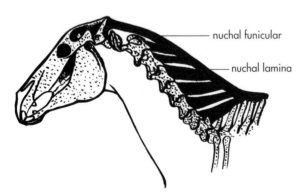

Figure 39 The nuchal funicular and the nuchal lamina.

Head and neck 'on the bit'

When a horse is ridden 'on the bit', the muscles (neck flexors) below his cervical vertebrae must shorten to flex his head at the poll and (in conjunction with the engagement of the hindquarters) give the roundness and lightness we so desperately require. This muscle action is the isotonic form of muscular contraction, which shortens the muscle without much appreciable difference in muscle tone. It is not a particularly strong form of muscle action and therefore the muscles on the underside of the neck do not build up very quickly.

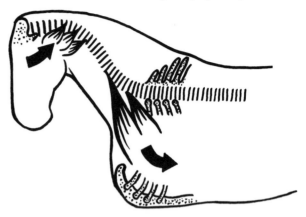

Figure 40 The neck flexors contracting isotonically, bringing the nose closer to the chest and putting the horse 'on the bit'.

Head and neck 'long and deep'

When ridden 'on the bit' and 'long and deep', the horse's neck is stretched forward and down. The gravitational pull starts to take effect when the horse begins to stretch down and, the closer his neck is to the horizontal, the more the gravitational force will act on it. The muscles (neck extensors) above the cervical vertebrae will immediately contract as a result of their automatic reaction to the effects of

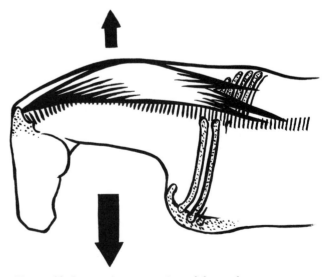

Figure 41 Isometric contraction of the neck extensors against the force of gravity.

gravity. This is isometric contraction, whereby the length of the muscle stays the same, but the muscle tone increases considerably. This type of contraction is very tiring and therefore builds a large and strong topline in a relatively short time.

Hollow outline of neck and back

When a horse pulls against the rider's hands or hollows his neck, he is using his neck extensors isotonically (shortening the muscle): his topline becomes hollow as he shortens these neck muscles. This type of contraction should not be confused with the isometric contraction of the same muscles when the horse is 'on the bit'.

When the horse's back muscles contract, his abdominal muscles will have to relax – a situation which causes weakness of the back and diminishes the horse's weight-bearing capacity. An additional consequence of hollowness is that it produces, through the righting reaction, a tendency to extend (straighten) the hip joints and thus counteract engagement of the hindquarters.

Figure 42 The neck extensors contracting isotonically against the rider's hands. The head is brought closer to the back, with resultant hollowing of the neck and back.

Hollowness can occur for the following reasons:

1) The horse tries to evade the effect of the bit. In this case, the rider should first ensure that rein contact and rein aids are appropriate; if so, the evasion can be overcome by riding the horse 'round' from head to tail; 'long and deep', to

stretch the back extensors whilst contracting the abdominal flexor muscles.

2) The rider, bumping and thumping on the horse's back, causes discomfort, which leads to contraction of the back muscles. In this case, the remedy is improved rider posture.

3) Loss of balance, which the horse seeks to maintain by lifting his neck. This can be corrected by 'sponging' the reins to encourage him to use his hindquarters for balance, rather than his neck.

Stretching the neck forward and down after activity

Once the horse has been ridden 'on the bit' for some time during a schooling session, his muscles will need a rest. Allow him to stretch down. You will find that most horses will stretch down for a few strides and then go back to the neutral position, because stretching down uses muscle power. All horses do not have the same neutral position; some seem to have a more rounded position than others. The shape of the neutral position appears to depend on the length and elasticity of the nuchal funicular ligament. The tighter this is, the straighter the neck will be.

Stretching down is a reaction caused by the stretch reflex of the muscles (see p. 57). The horse will need to stretch his neck extensors, which have been contracting isometrically, as well as his neck flexors, which have been contracting isotonically.

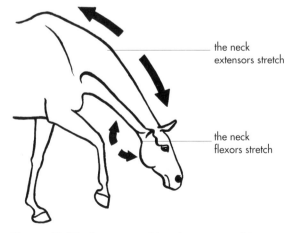

the neck extensors stretch

the neck flexors stretch

Figure 43 The horse stretching down to rest his muscles.

CO-CONTRACTION

For most actions, there is a group of muscles working together (the agonists) and an opposing muscle group (the antagonists). When the agonists contract, the antagonists must relax, or the action cannot take place. (For example, if you flex your elbow, the biceps muscle has to contract, but the triceps muscle must relax, or little contraction of the biceps can occur.) In co-contraction, however, opposing muscle groups contract simultaneously (when you make a fist, all the muscles in your forearm contract).

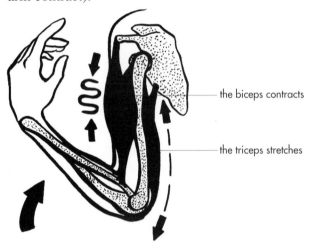

the biceps contracts

the triceps stretches

Figure 44 Normal muscular action; when the biceps contracts, the triceps will relax.

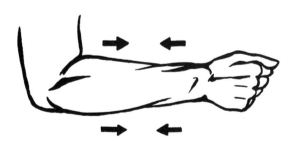

Figure 45 Co-contraction of the forearm muscles.

In the horse, co-contraction often occurs as a protection against loss of balance. The neck is the horse's main balancing mechanism and, as such, is often brought into action automatically. As soon as he is brought off balance by the rider not preparing him in advance for transitions or changes of bend, the horse will stiffen all his neck muscles in co-contraction to prevent himself from losing

balance and falling. He becomes hard in the hand and sets his neck. This is very often seen in horses who have been pulled 'on the bit' by the rider's hands and held there with too strong a contact. It can also be seen with riders who 'hold' their horses on the bit and feel they have to help the horse to balance. Such a horse will never achieve a free, floating action. 'Riding into a firm contact' is often misinterpreted, and results in the horse bracing his neck in co-contraction.

Co-contraction is an undesirable reaction in the horse, leading to stiffness throughout his body, loss of the free, floating action, and loss of immediate reaction to the rider's communicating aids. Rather than this, the horse's neck should be pliable and move in the direction required at the slightest suggestion of the rider's hands.

Figure 46(a) Co-contraction of all the neck muscles.

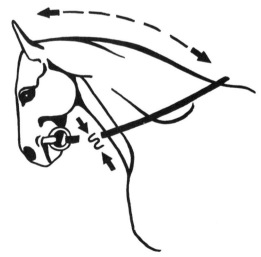

Figure 46(b) Neck flexors contracting while the neck extensors stretch.

CHAPTER 4

THE NERVOUS SYSTEM

AND RELAXATION

All good riding seems to be dependent upon a relaxed horse. In dressage, we find that a tense or anxious horse will make many mistakes. In jumping, the same situation is found: if the horse is not relaxed, he will have difficulty in seeing his stride before a fence.

You can only really start riding a horse once he allows you to put your legs on him and push him. An excited horse cannot concentrate and will continually lose rhythm and balance as he strives to run off. A tense horse cannot become supple because his neck will be in co-contraction (braced). This will also have the effect of blocking the communication through the bit. Therefore, the first condition to achieve in the training of the horse is calmness.

THE PATHWAY TO RELAXATION

THE STARTLE REFLEX

This is an automatic, primitive reflex which is found in all animals. It is there to protect them from danger and to put their muscles in readiness for flight. Remnants of this reflex are still present in humans, but are only exhibited in young babies, and disappear rapidly after the age of three months. In adults it may be observed only when they are awakened suddenly. The head, neck and back go into extension and the hands and arms are thrown upwards. As man's cortex developed, his logic started overriding this reflex until it was no longer of use to him.

Figure 47 The startle reflex in a baby.

The startle reflex was important to horses in the days when they were still roaming free, and can be observed when horses grazing in the paddock are startled by an unusual occurrence. Immediately, all their neck and back muscles go into extension, in readiness for action. They lift their heads, extend their necks and backs, their tails stand up and they erupt into a stiff-legged trot. When a horse being ridden out shies, he often gives a little straight-legged jump on the spot. The head and neck always pop up, and the back hollows.

For the purpose of this book the muscle groups responsible for these actions will be called the 'alert' muscles of the horse. They consist of the neck, back and tail extensors.

THE RELAXATION MUSCLE GROUP

When a horse eats and his head and neck are stretched down, he can only see the grass around him and he is totally relaxed. He will only eat if he is relaxed but, as soon as there is any sign of 'danger', he will lift his head, look around and lose this complete relaxation. Thus a horse has a second group of muscles, opposite to the 'alert' group, which he uses when grazing. We can name

Figure 48(a) The startle reflex in the horse. Note the contraction of the neck and back extensor muscles.

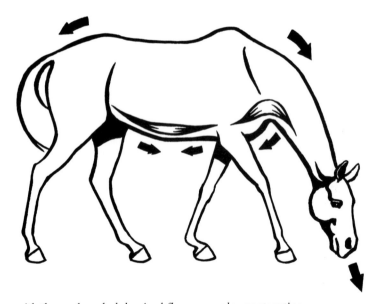

Figure 48(b) Relaxed horse with the neck and abdominal flexor muscles contracting.

this the 'relaxation' group. This group consists of the neck flexors and the abdominal and spinal flexors.

In order to inhibit the automatic startle reflex, we have to facilitate the action of the antagonistic muscle group: the neck, abdominal and back flexors – we do this by riding 'long and deep'. By stimulating the relaxation group of muscles, we also encourage more engagement of the hindquarters. We shall discuss the process of riding 'long and deep' – and the associated benefits – more fully in due course.

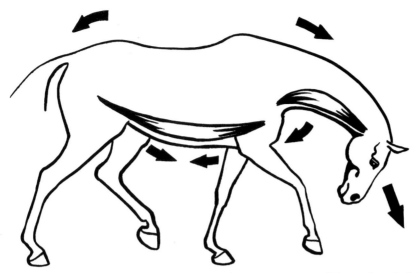

Figure 49 The horse in a 'long and deep' frame with the resultant contraction of the neck and abdominal flexors.

CEPHALO-CAUDAL DEVELOPMENT

Neuro-muscular development in all animals, man included, follows a cephalo-caudal (head-to-tail) direction. (Babies are born with little head control. They start to develop the head control first, then body control and finally, lower limb control.)

In the horse, tension starts in the brain and travels down the spine to the body, limbs and tail. The most important of the horse's sensory organs – those of hearing, sight, smell and taste – are positioned in his head. As soon as he sees, hears or smells something he is afraid of, a message is sent to the brain, and he then becomes tense. This tension automatically moves down the spine along the nerve pathways. His neck becomes tense, followed by his back and tail. Imagine your own tension: it starts either with a headache or a stiff neck and shoulder girdle, and a massage to the neck often helps you to relax. (Lines of communication also start at the head, and travel down the spine to the limbs. This is why we use the horse's mouth to initiate so many of the movements.)

It is logical, therefore, that we should start to relax the horse at the head area, where the core of the problem is seated. If you can relax the head and neck by inhibiting the action of the 'alert' group

of muscles, the relaxation will follow the head-to-tail pathway and you will soon have a relaxed horse.

The main 'alert' (extensor) and 'relaxation' (flexor) muscles of the horse's neck are listed below.

MAIN EXTENSOR MUSCLES OF THE NECK

Serratus ventralis. This muscle closes the angle between the cervical vertebrae and the scapula, thereby lifting the horse's neck and blocking the freedom of the shoulder.

Rhomboideus. When contracting, this hollows the neck and holds the scapula in position, thereby blocking the freedom of the shoulder.

Complexus. This muscle, in isotonic contraction, lifts the head and hollows the outline of the neck.

Splenius. This extends and hollows the horse's neck.

Trapezius. The cervical part hollows the outline of the neck and, together with the thoracic part, stablises the scapula. When in contraction, it blocks the freedom of the shoulder.

Figure 50 The main flexor and extensor muscles of the neck.

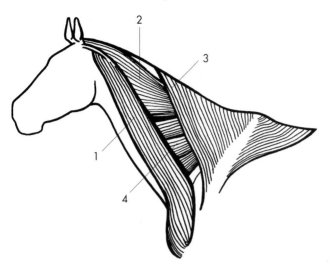

Figure 50(a) 1) Brachiocephalic muscle (flexor).
2) Splenius muscle (extensor).
3) Trapezius muscle (extensor).
4) Serratus ventralis muscle (extensor).

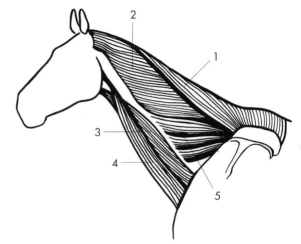

Figure 50(b) 1) Rhomboideus muscle (extensor).
2) Splenius muscle (extensor).
3) Sternahyoid and omohyoid muscles (flexors).
4) Sternocephalic muscle (lateral flexor).
5) Serratus ventralis muscle (extensor).

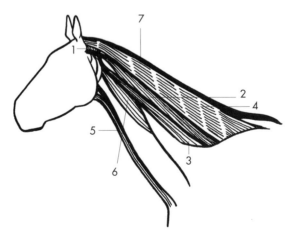

Figure 50(c) 1) Cranial oblique muscle (rotates the head).
2) Longissimus capitis muscle (lateral flexor).
3) Longissimus atlantis muscle (lateral flexor).
4) Complexus muscle, part of semispinalis capitis muscle (extensor).
5) Sternohyoid and sternothyrohyoid muscles (flexors).
6) Rectus capitis ventralis muscle (lateral flexor).
7) Nuchal funicular.

MAIN FLEXOR MUSCLES OF THE NECK

Sternohyoid and omohyoid. These two muscles close the angle between the horse's head and neck. When the contraction is stronger, the neck will have a deeper flexion.

Sternocephalic. When the left and right sterno–cephalic muscles are contracting simultaneously, the horse will bend his head and close the angle between head and neck. When the muscle on one side of the neck contracts by itself, the horse will turn his head. If the contraction becomes stronger, the whole neck will turn.

Brachiocephalic. This is the powerful muscle which moves the shoulder forwards. Through its attachment to the skull, it also acts to turn the head sideways.

Longissimus capitis. This muscle helps to bend the horse's head to the side.

Longissimus atlantis. This muscle is attached to the second cervical vertebra and turns the horse's neck to the side.

Rectus capitis ventralis. This produces lateral bend of the head and neck.

ACHIEVING RELAXATION

If your horse is fresh, lunge him first to get the edge off him. This done, you can commence the following exercises.

RELAXING THE RIDER

Gaining confidence and trust in his rider will help the horse to relax. A relaxed rider will instil trust and confidence.

1) Mount your horse and allow your legs to hang down like wet rags.

2) Make your seat feel like a bowl of jelly or think about 'enlarging' your seat. Let it 'spill' over the side of the saddle.

3) Relax your arms and push them forwards a little to relax the biceps muscles. When a rider becomes tense, these muscles usually begin to contract as a defence mechanism. Horses tend to resist such constraint but will relax to yielding of the reins.

4) Do a little role playing and 'act' relaxed.

Once you are relaxed you can begin the process of relaxing your horse.

SUBMISSION AND RELAXATION IN THE HORSE

1) Explain to your horse, with your hands, that he must drop his head and neck down and look at the ground. This is done very simply by 'spong-ing' the reins with the hands. Ask a little with the left hand and then with the right hand and, as soon as he has reacted, release the reins. This should be done with relaxed hands and arms

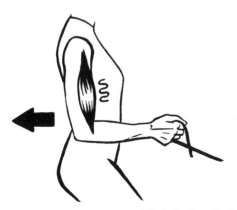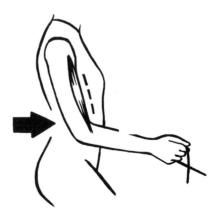

Figure 51 Relaxing the biceps muscle to soften the hands.

so as not to block the horse's response. It is extremely important to release the reins immediately, as soon as the horse yields with his neck and mouth. This release of the rein is his reward for the correct response, and if he is not rewarded he will not know whether he has understood correctly.

As soon as the hands yield, the horse will start stretching his head and neck down. 'Sponge' the reins again and he will stretch down further. Repeat this process until he stretches his neck all the way down to his knees. If necessary, you may lean forward a little initially, to help the horse understand the concept.

This position puts the horse in submission, because he cannot see around him to protect himself. He has, therefore, to submit to you and trust you to do all the protection for him. This action of bringing his head and neck down has the effect of facilitating the action of the neck and abdominal flexors and thus preventing the startle reflex.

2) Stroking the horse's neck with long actions of the inside hand, while the outside hand keeps contact, has a relaxing effect on the horse. When a horse is tense, his eyes are wide open and have a 'hard' expression. As soon as he is looking down and is relaxed in the mouth and neck, his expression changes to 'soft', blinking and relaxed eyes. When you watch horses from the ground be on the outlook for this expression-in addition it tells you that the horse is accepting the bit.

3) Once the horse is walking around with a relaxed head and neck posture ('long and deep') you can start to trot him. It is important that he is kept in this submissive outline throughout the transition. In order to do this he must stay balanced throughout the transition. Start by 'sponging' the reins alternately so that he knows that he should relax, then slowly ease him into trot by gently squeezing with both legs until he makes the transition. Remember that the horse has no idea of what he is going to be asked, so the question must be very clear or he will lose his balance, throw his head and neck up, 'run' and lose the relaxation so patiently achieved. 'Sponging' the reins throughout the transition will help the horse to understand that he should not hollow his neck in an attempt to maintain balance.

4) Trot him in a large (20 m) circle with his head down and with total lightness in your hands until you feel he is completely relaxed and balanced. He will now display a good rhythm and be balanced with slow, deliberate, floating steps.

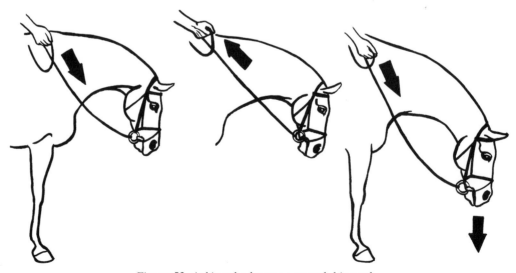

Figure 52 Asking the horse to stretch his neck.

Once the horse has stretched down in these preparatory exercises, you should maintain the lightest possible contact, so that the horse balances himself and becomes confident that your hands will not upset him. The horse should not pull on the reins when his head is down.

5) Once he has achieved this balance, change the rein and ride a circle on the other rein.

6) Only now is your horse ready to canter: put him into canter on a 20 m circle. You will find that he will go into a slow and rhythmic canter with his head down, his neck arched and his back well rounded.

You will now have a relaxed horse, who is ready to start his work. Should he become tense again, go back to trotting 'long and deep' on a 20 m circle.

RIDING 'LONG AND DEEP'

As we have seen, when ridden 'long and deep', the horse's outline is long and rounded, with his neck carried low and deep. The neuro-muscular dynamics of this position are as follows:

1) The horse's head is lowered through facilitating the action of the neck flexors (alternate 'sponging' of the reins).

2) This position brings the horse's centre of gravity forwards.

3) The 'long and deep' position prevents him from using his neck to restore balance. He thus has

no choice but to balance himself by bringing his hindquarters more underneath him by using his abdominal, hip and hock flexor muscles. This action will lead to the centre of gravity being moved back over his base of support.

4) In addition to this balance reaction, flexing the neck will also lead to the righting reaction of abdominal and hip flexion, further encouraging engagement.

5) As a result of these actions, the horse's back becomes rounded.

The precise position of head and neck may vary, depending on the needs of each particular horse. Some may not need a very deep position, while others have to be ridden extremely deep to achieve the desired effect. Furthermore, while one horse may need to be ridden quite deep at a particular stage of training and then never again, another may need continuous training in this way, or intermittent training only. Therefore, despite its basic importance, one should not be too rigid about this exercise.

When a horse is ridden in this manner, the angle between his head and neck should remain consistent. Although there may be an impression that the horse is 'behind the bit', it is actually the neck alone which is at a different angle to the body.

Once introduced to it, some young horses may prefer to stay in a long, rounded frame. They will, however, start to carry their heads and necks higher as soon as their hindquarters have developed enough strength.

Figure 53(a) 'Long and round' outline.

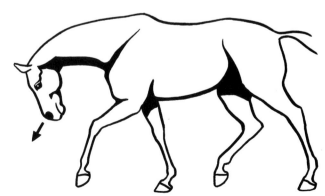

Figure 53(b) 'Long and deep' outline.

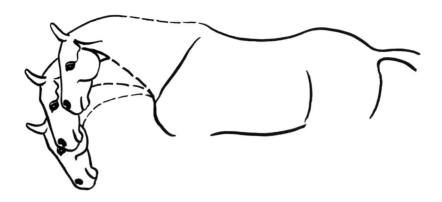

Figure 54 Although the whole neck is lowered, the angle between the head and neck stays constant. This is very different from being 'behind the bit'.

Figure 55 The effects of riding 'long and deep'.

Reasons for riding 'long and deep'

Riding 'long and deep' is essential for the development of the horse for the following reasons.

1) It helps to strengthen the horse's back by developing his abdominal and hip flexors.

2) It helps to build the horse's topline through isometric contraction of the neck extensors against the effect of gravity.

3) It is the main method of relaxing the horse. By stimulating the contraction of the neck, abdominal and hip flexors, the startle reflex (and therefore tension) can be prevented. In addition, this position helps to produce submission as the horse's field of vision becomes minimal and he therefore has to rely on his rider for protection.

4) It initiates engagement of the hindquarters through the horse's balance and righting reactions, as described in Chapter 3.

5) It helps the horse to find his balance by moving his centre of gravity backwards. In addition, this improved balance helps him with the process of accepting the bit (see page 39).

6) Through being ridden 'long and deep' the horse's shoulders gain more freedom and his stride becomes longer and more elevated.

7) It develops longitudinal suppleness by stretching the nuchal funicular which, in some horses, is contracted.

CONTACT AND COMMUNICATION

Contact is our direct line of communication with the horse. It is the gentle feel of the hands, via the reins, on the bit; the feeling of the legs resting 'like wet rags' on the horse's ribcage and the feeling of the seat on the horse's back. With such contact we have direct channels for communicating our desires to the horse. Through contact with the mouth we can facilitate any action of the forehand of the horse, and some movement of the hindquarters as well. Through contact with the legs and seat we can facilitate the movement of his ribcage and hindquarters. Also, and importantly, we can feel the reaction of the horse to our commands.

Contact with the hands to the mouth should feel like holding hands on a hot day. When holding hands with a friend, one never squeezes their hand, but holds it gently and with love. Only with a soft contact can the horse 'hear' what you explain through your hands, and only with a soft contact can you feel the nuances of balance or resistance.

Some horses may prefer too light a contact at first, but will accept a more positive contact as soon as they are balanced and have confidence in the rider's yielding hands. A strong contact encourages the horse to lean on the rider for balance. If we want to develop lightness, we should not give the horse anything to lean on. The horse will not develop the light, cadenced steps he is capable of if he has a strong contact with the hands.

Heavy contact may be caused by tension in the jaw or neck, or by lack of engagement. Once the horse has accepted the bit, is supple, in balance and rhythm, he will accept consistent contact.

(There seems to be a common misconception about the horse's ability to 'hold on to the bit'. A horse cannot hold on to the bit with his mouth to produce a firm contact, because the bit lies in the space between his front teeth and his molars. If he tries to bite on the bit, his teeth will get in the way. The only way that he can bite on the bit is by pulling it onto his molars with his tongue. This is a severe

Figure 56(a) The horse cannot hold onto the bit unless he pulls it between his teeth with his tongue.

Figure 56(b) When the horse opens his mouth he will lift his head slightly or tighten his neck extensors, and therefore harden the contact.

evasion, but is certainly not contact. When the horse opens his mouth he will automatically lift his head and hollow his neck a little. This will often produce a strong contact, but it is not the open mouth that does this – it is the head and neck extensor muscles.) The correct contact is brought about by the balanced use of the horse's neck muscles. Compare this to balancing a chair on its back legs only. Hold your finger on the backrest and maintain that balance. If the chair falls back, push it forward slightly and if it falls forwards, pull it back slightly.

Figure 57 Maintaining correct contact by balanced use of the horse's neck muscles is comparable to keeping a chair balanced on its back legs.

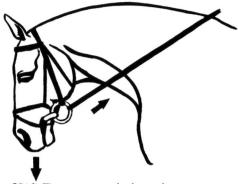

Figure 58(a) Light contact: the horse is accepting the bit in a round frame. In this illustration the horse is using his neck flexors and abdominal muscles correctly. His neck extensors contract isometrically against gravity and this builds up his topline muscles.

Figure 58(d) Firm contact: the horse has put too much weight on his forehand and is leaning on the rider's hands. He lacks engagement and his centre of gravity is too far forward.

Figure 58(e) Contact too light: the horse has become behind the vertical and is evading the contact by using too strong an action of the neck flexors.

Figure 58(b) Firm contact: the horse has come off the bit by using his head extensors and lifting his head slightly. Even if he does not actually lift his head, through contraction of the head extensor muscles, he will pull against the rider's hands.

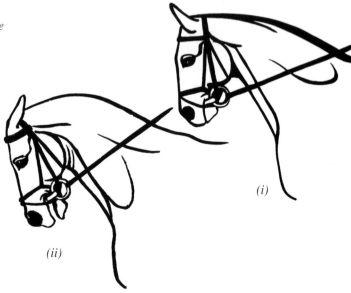

(i)

(ii)

Figure 58(c) Firm contact: the horse appears to be 'on the bit' but has contracted his neck extensors and has become slightly hollow in front of the wither.

Figure 58(f) False contact: the horse is light in the hand and appears to be on the bit (i) but if he is asked to shorten or lengthen his frame, he will give a rigid feeling in the hand (ii). His neck muscles are all braced and his mouth does not readily follow the rider's hand.

Contact with the legs should feel like wet rags on the horse's sides. The legs should be relaxed around the horse's sides in order to be ready for action and to feel the horse's reactions. The basic leg contact should be consistent so that it is ready for immediate use but will not cause the horse to get a fright every time the legs are used for an aid.

Contact with the seat should be free from tension. The rider's seat must be able to feel the horse's movement beneath it, and the muscles should be ready to act as and when necessary.

Contact should be as if you are ballroom dancing with your horse. In dancing, if your partner holds too tightly, all you want to do is escape but, if their hold is non-existent, you cannot feel what to do.

ACCEPTANCE OF THE BIT

Through the bit, the rider can have a constant 'conversation' with the horse, but this is only possible when the mouth is relaxed and the horse is accepting the bit. Only with a relaxed mouth will he be able to feel the lightest rein aids. When the horse is accepting the bit and 'on the bit', he will be using all the correct muscles to strengthen his back and engage his hindquarters.

If a horse does not accept the bit, he is either using his neck extensors, overbending, or else his neck and jaw muscles are in co-contraction and therefore hard. When the neck is stiff and hard, it is not easy to bend or flex. The horse will not be able to become supple, do circles, lateral movements or a correct strike-off at canter and he will become 'hollow' through all transitions. When a horse's neck is stiff or hollow, the shoulder action will be blocked and free forelimb action will be impossible. He will be difficult to steer, his movement will be stifled and uncomfortable and he will not move forward freely. He will not be able to maintain a constant rhythm and will also be difficult to stop.

The terms 'acceptance of the bit', 'on the bit',

'contact' and 'roundness' are often used to describe the same concept, which we shall now examine in detail. Acceptance of the bit comprises four elements:

Physical acceptance of the bit.

Acceptance of the rider's hands.

Submission and relaxation.

Balance.

PHYSICAL ACCEPTANCE OF THE BIT

It is extremely important that the horse has a happy and relaxed attitude towards the bit. The mouth is a key point of control; the horse's 'steering wheel.' Without this control we would not be able to train our horse, or have much success in competition. However, the control should resemble 'power steering'– the slightest touch having the desired effect. The horse will react to discomfort or pain from the bit by resisting it and becoming hollow and unsteady in the neck. He will thus lose rhythm and balance, and the flow of his movements will be impaired.

The bit should lie on top of the horse's tongue, with his mouth completely relaxed around it. The effect of this relaxation of the mouth around the bit is that the tongue will start to suck up softly against the palate. Try the following exercise.

Exercise 16. Close your lips, but let your jaw drop down in a totally relaxed fashion. Now become aware of where your tongue is. It should be sucking up against your palate. That is how your horse should react to the bit. When sucking a sweet, your tongue will hold the sweet against the roof of your mouth.

When you 'sponge' on one rein or the other, a horse who is accepting the bit should turn his head to whichever side it is led. If a horse is not accepting the bit, the jaw muscles and the complexus muscles which lift his head will be contracted and he will be opposing the action of your hand. This will lead to a 'hard' feeling in your hands. When your horse has accepted the bit he will feel 'soft' in your hand when you give a rein aid.

There are various reasons why a horse may be reluctant to accept the bit. These should all be investigated thoroughly:

1) The presence of wolf teeth – have them removed.

2) Teeth in need of care – have them filed.

3) Horse uncomfortable with the feeling of metal in his mouth – use a rubberised snaffle or cover the bit with latex.

4) Horse has a small mouth – use a thinner snaffle.

5) Horse has a highly sensitive mouth – try a thicker snaffle.

When it comes to the choice of bit, riders all seem to have their own preferences. The eggbutt snaffle, however, gives a direct feeling on the horse's mouth, which allows more direct communication.

ACCEPTANCE OF THE RIDER'S HANDS

By far the most important aspect of acceptance of the bit is the role of the rider's hands. A horse will only accept the rider's hands if he has confidence in them: he has to know that they will not hurt him. The mouth is highly sensitive and the horse will

feel discomfort there quite easily. Discomfort causes tension, which is the cause of stiffness, hollowness and loss of rhythm. The rider, therefore, should be certain that his hands are not causing discomfort through the bit. The rider's hands, elbows and shoulders should be relaxed but ready for action; ready to yield to the horse's mouth whenever neccesary.

When a horse is uncomfortable with the rider's hands, he will try to evade them by pulling against them or by going behind the effect of the bit – or even by running away from their effect. When he pulls against the rider's hands he will hollow his neck and use the neck extensors isotonically. When he tries to go behind the effect of the bit, he will overbend his neck and communication with him, through the bit, will be non-existent.

Soft and hard hands

Let us examine what is meant by these terms, and analyse their effects.

Soft hands are relaxed hands, wrists, elbows, and shoulders. They communicate with 'sponging' fingers or a 'take and give' effect with the hands, wrists or elbows. They move *with* the horse's mouth and yield when necessary.

Hard hands may be the result of unyielding hands or a false belief that the rider should 'hold' the horse on the bit.

Unyielding hands are caused either by tension in the elbows, hands or shoulders or by hands which

Figure 59(a) The horse is resisting the rider's unyielding hands by contracting his neck extensors.

Figure 59(b) The horse is evading the rider's unyielding hands by overbending.

cannot feel when the horse is yielding to the pressure of the bit.

Hands that 'hold' the horse on the bit do so through blocking of the elbows and shoulders. Often the reins are clamped in the hands while the wrists and elbows are tight. In such cases, the rider's arms are in co-contraction so, although the hands seem still, they in fact have the effect of pulling back on the reins, and stiff elbows have the effect of jerking the bit at every stride.

Hard hands can lead to serious problems, such as refusal to move forwards, rearing, bucking, kicking out, or the horse using evasive techniques such as coming 'behind the bit', bracing the neck muscles, tilting the head, swinging the quarters, or going crooked.

The concept of riding 'from the front'

Attempting to establish acceptance of the bit from the front to the back of the horse is undesirable and should not be confused with 'sponging' the reins. Riding 'from the front' means riding with hard, unyielding hands; hands that pull back. Riders who do this think they are doing nothing, but they are, in fact, pulling on the horse's mouth. This is at variance with the effect of hands that 'talk' to the horse with a 'sponging' action, helping to relax the jaw so that the horse is balanced when the energy flows through from behind.

SUBMISSION AND RELAXATION

Horses are naturally herd animals and always look for a leader. Therefore, they will usually be prepared to submit to a rider as a lead figure. There seem to be two ways of acquiring submission in horses: one is through domination and the other is through persuasion. It is extremely difficult for a young rider or lady rider to force a large animal with the strength of the horse into submission, since they would be opposing the force of the horse's neck muscles, which are many times the strength of their arm muscles. In any case, we should approach the horse as a public relations officer would approach a client. We have to per-suade the horse that what we want him to do is actually what he himself would like to do. A public relations officer who tried to dominate a client would soon be without that client! If we try to dominate a horse with brute force we are sure to lose, because he is stronger. Only the very meekest horses would allow such domination and, were it attempted, they might well break down into nervous wrecks.

How to guide a horse into submission

1) Remove distractions. When a horse is working 'long and deep', the position of his eyes makes it difficult for him to give much attention to his surroundings. He then has no option but to trust in the rider. Therefore we have first to remove any distractions by riding him in such an outline.

2) Inhibit the 'alert' group of muscles. By causing him to use his 'relaxation' group of muscles, we inhibit the automatic startle reflex and thus the 'alert' muscles. Once again, because he will not be able to react to 'danger' he will be compelled to submit to the rider and trust the rider to do the job of protecting him.

3) Make him feel comfortable. A horse reacts to discomfort by becoming anxious. When he is anxious he loses concentration and submission. While it is difficult to train a horse without *ever* causing some discomfort, care should be taken not to ask questions which are mentally or physically too difficult for him. Most horses will feel comfortable when the bit is lying in a relaxed mouth with no pull on the reins. If you ask for roundness of outline and then yield with the hands, the horse will feel comfortable and stay 'on the bit' with little difficulty.

4) Give him confidence in your hands. By riding with relaxed and yielding hands and not block-ing the horse's movement or causing discomfort in the mouth, the horse will be persuaded to relax his jaw and neck, will be less inclined to resist the rider, and will thus be more submissive.

Indications of submissiveness and relaxation

1) The horse's topline will appear slightly longer as a result of the action of his neck and jaw flexors.

2) The little hollow area in front of the withers disappears. (This area becomes hollow when the trapezius muscle is shortened in isotonic contraction.)

3) The eyes become relaxed, with a 'soft' expression, and the horse starts blinking.

4) The stride becomes longer and looser, with more 'bounce'; the horse appears to be almost 'floating'.

BALANCE

The final important part of acceptance of the bit has to do with the horse's balance reactions.

We have already seen that a horse uses his head and neck automatically for balance and in the early stages of training, when he has not achieved enough engagement of the hindquarters, he may lose some balance and lift his head and neck during transitions. This is usually evident in walk – trot transitions, but is often very clear in early canter – trot transitions, when the horse may need the assistance of quite a few half-halts to recover his balance. When this happens he will become hollow in outline and appear to be resisting the effect of the bit. This apparent resistance is, however, caused by loss of balance and is not a result of non-acceptance of the bit.

If, in such circumstances, the horse is prevented from lifting his head and neck to help him when he loses balance (is forced to remain 'on the bit'), he may tighten all the muscles in the neck instead (brace the neck). Again it may seem as though he is not accepting the bit, but the problem remains one of lost balance, and the horse is using an automatic balance reaction to restore it.

Another balance reaction takes place if the horse's centre of gravity has moved too far forwards and he has lost the engagement of his hind-quarters. In such circumstances, he will lean on the rider's hands to help him balance. This again should not be seen as a *refusal* to accept the bit.

TEACHING THE HORSE TO ACCEPT THE BIT: TWO METHODS

The young horse should first be introduced to the bit without a rider. If this introduction is done with tact and the rider subsequently uses yielding hands, the horse should have no difficulty in accepting the bit. There are two methods of teaching the horse to accept the bit and become light in the rider's hands. While some of the criteria for both methods have already been touched upon, let us examine both in detail, by way of comparison.

METHOD ONE

This method is by far the easier and more logical way of creating lightness, balance and roundness. It is within the grasp of all riders and horses.

Start at halt, or at walk. Imagine that you have extremely long arms, so that your index fingers and middle fingers are able to hook onto the rings of the bit. Next, imagine that you are pulling on these rings to ask the horse to look down. To have any effect you would have to pull a little on one side and then on the other, just as you would move a heavy piece of furniture a little on one side and then a little on the other. Therefore, 'sponge' the rein on one side then the other, then let the reins slip through your fingers a little so that the horse can stretch down. You are using a language that every horse can understand when you ask him first to use the flexor muscles on one side of his neck, then explain to him that his reaction was correct by rewarding him (yielding the rein), and then repeating to the other side.

If you do this with commitment, the horse will soon look down and relax his jaw, using only his neck flexors to round his neck. As soon as he yields

Figure 60(a) Moving a fridge a little at a time, one side and then the other.

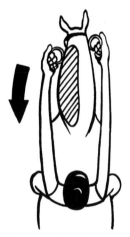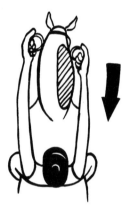

Figure 60(b) Imagine that you are riding with long arms and 'sponging' the bit with your fingers.

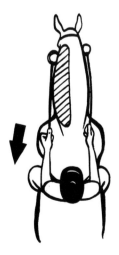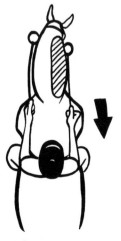

Figure 61 'Sponging' the reins alternately.

Figure 62 Releasing the rein to reward.

a little you should relax your hands, let the reins slip through your fingers and start again. Any correct action from the horse, however small, should be rewarded.

If a horse has already acquired the habit of resistance, you may need a slightly stronger method of facilitating the action of the neck flexors. Push the horse forwards with your legs and simultaneously play a little stronger with the reins; one hand, the other hand and then release. It is important that you play *through* the hard resistance to a soft feeling in the hand, and then yield. If the horse does not yield to this action, you will end up with him swinging his head from one side to the other. He will be swinging his head because he is resisting, not yielding to the hand and this will have a similar dulling effect as constant, nagging leg aids. It is therefore important that you are immediately successful, and reward the horse immediately for yielding to the bit. (It is also important that the 'sponging' should never deteriorate into a rhythmic, automatic, left-right, left-right action, since this will just encourage such a response from the horse. Rather, the feeling should maintain a 'conversation'

with the horse, explaining to him which muscles he should use.)

Provided that you keep your arms and hands relaxed, you may try to facilitate the action of the neck flexors by moving your whole arm back and relaxing it again as soon as you feel the rein softening. Any hard feeling on the rein is caused by the horse contracting the neck extensors, not the neck flexors, against the action of the bit.

If you are unsure of the feeling you are aiming for, take the hand of a friend, ask them to pull against you, and then ask them to release the pull suddenly. You will be left with a feeling of total relaxation in your hand – this is the feeling you should be after.

With a lazy horse, from the beginning of this exercise, you should push him forwards with your legs – especially the leg on the same side as the active rein. When you 'sponge' with the inside rein alone, the inside leg should be used on the girth to help the lateral flexors, as previously described in the section on balance reactions in Chapter 1. However, with an anxious and/or forward-going horse, the exercise should be ridden with half-halts.

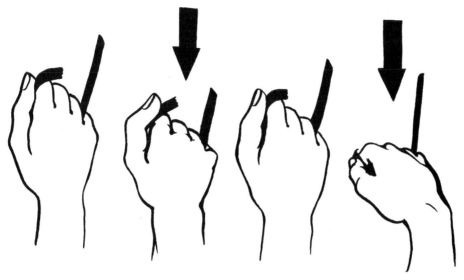

Figure 63(a) 'Play and release' the reins with the fingers or wrist.

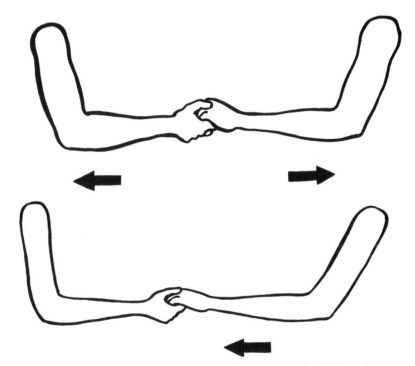

Figure 63(b) Hold and release hands with a friend to simulate the feeling of rein contact.

Once the horse is happily accepting the bit and is *balanced* you can start to use your legs, together with your hands, to ask for more engagement. However, if there is *too much* forward driving at an early stage, the horse may lose his balance, his centre of gravity will move forwards and his stride will shorten.

Once the horse has accepted the bit, your hands should automatically become quiet, having a very light contact with the horse's mouth so that he may find his own balance and gain confidence in your hands.

METHOD TWO

This method, if it is to be used at all, is for powerful, experienced riders only. While it can be effective with horses who are not very resistant, anxious or stubborn, it may lead to serious resistance in anxious, stubborn or sensitive horses, horses with a short and tight nuchal funicular, or horses who have already been damaged. The Portugese Master, Nuno Oliveira, had the following to say of this method: '*Few horses, because of temperament, constitution, or sometimes because of acquired faults, tolerate this system. I entirely agree that when trained, the horse must, on demand, go onto the bit, as it is commonly termed, but not by force*'. This method is therefore, described primarily for interest and, if it is to be practised, great care and discretion will be called for.

At trot, the rider takes up fairly short reins and a fairly firm contact. He then closes his lower legs on the horse and rides him forwards into this contact. The horse will either drop his nose and yield to the pressure of the bit, or he will resist the pull of the bit very strongly. In general, quiet, easy

and experienced horses will yield fairly easily to this method. Strong-willed, stubborn, excitable horses and horses with sensitive mouths will usually object to this kind of handling. If the horse yields, and as soon as he yields, the rider must immediately release the reins and reward the horse. This cannot be stressed enough. The horse must be told immediately that his reaction was correct by a complete release of the reins. If the horse resists very strongly, the rider carries on pushing with his legs and blocking with the reins until the horse yields in the mouth and neck. Such a horse must be rewarded as soon as he yields even a small amount by a yielding of the reins. The rider then immediately takes up the contact again and starts the same action. The second, and every consecutive time after that, the horse should yield to the aid more quickly. This concept will be easier to understand if you imagine the horse being pushed against a wall until his outline is rounded.

The most important part of this exercise is the extremely quick release of the reins – as soon as the horse yields and not a second later. If this is not done, the horse will become resistant to the hand and will not stop fighting with his mouth and

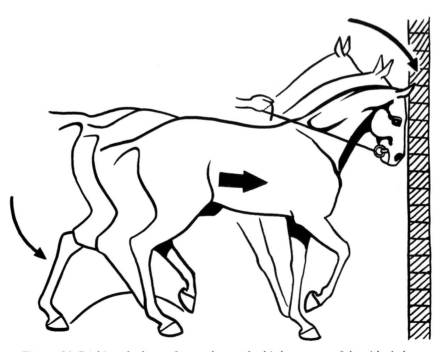

Figure 64 Pushing the horse forward onto the bit by means of the rider's legs.

Figure 65(a) The horse is being pushed onto the bit by the rider's legs, while the hands are holding the reins quietly.

Figure 65(b) This rider is trying to pull the horse onto the bit with no forward leg aids.

neck. This method should never deteriorate into a pull on the reins without the use of legs. This is what is meant by 'getting the horse on the bit from the front'.

It cannot be stressed enough that this is not a method to be used by inexperienced riders. It can cause strong resistances, from hollowing, over-bending and running away from the bit, to rearing.

Using both hands together will lead to resistance unless the rider uses very strong forward-driving leg aids. The horse will pull against the rider's hands with his neck extensors and hollow his outline.

Riders who use this method often talk about 'not using your hands,' or having 'quiet' hands. They are however, under a false impression, as they are blocking the horse with co-contracted elbow and shoulder muscles. This has a much harder effect on the mouth than soft 'sponging'.

These two methods actually have the same effect on the horse's muscles. Driving the horse from behind into so-called 'quiet' hands forces him to submit and use his neck flexors, while asking him gently with alternate hands quietly facilitates the desired action of the same neck flexors (see Figure 66).

The best way to teach your horse acceptance of the bit is by using a combination of these two methods. Play with the bit by squeezing the rein like a sponge while you are pushing the horse forwards with your legs. Yield with the hands as soon as you start to feel the horse yield. By this means you produce a horse who accepts the bit with confidence and calmness. Once the horse reacts to the alternate 'sponge and yield' method, you may push him into both hands for short periods (as in Method Two) should circumstances require it.

In some cases, the 'softness' created by acceptance of the bit may initially last for a few strides only, as muscle power is needed for this action and the horse will want to lift his head and relax the neck flexors. The nuchal funicular ligament has to stretch, while the neck flexors need to strengthen and the neck extensors, which work isometrically, have to become strong. (This can be observed in the development of the horse's topline). In such cases the 'sponging' should be done every few strides. As soon as the horse has developed enough strength in his neck muscles, he will stay readily in a rounded outline and little 'sponging' will be necessary.

Other horses may, initially, feel 'too light' and carry themselves too deep. This situation will right itself as soon as the horse has developed enough

Figure 66(a) The rider is asking the horse to contract his neck flexors by means of rein 'sponging'.

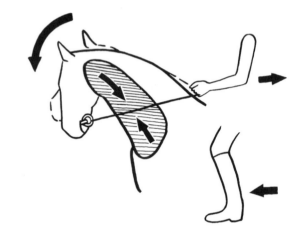

Figure 66(b) The same neck flexors are contracted by pushing the horse forwards with the legs and holding the reins.

balance through engagement of the hindquarters - provided that the rider does not hang on to the reins.

RIDING 'ON THE BIT'

Only when the horse has accepted the bit will he be ready to come 'on the bit'. Through working 'long and deep' his balance improves and his hindquarters become more engaged; they start becoming stronger and take more weight. All this enables the horse to lighten the forehand, carry his head and neck a little higher and remain steady 'on the bit'. When a horse is 'on the bit', he is in complete balance and self-carriage and will be ready to act on whichever aid he is given.

Once your horse has accepted the bit, is trotting consistently and rhythmically 'long and deep' and is moving forwards energetically with strong and engaged hindquarters, he is in balance and will automatically come 'on the bit'. All it will take is a little collection. Put both legs on the horse to ask for more engagement and shorten your reins a little and you will have him 'on the bit'. However, the horse's head should never be *pulled* in. This may give a superficial appearance of the horse being 'on the bit', but he will be using his neck extensors to pull against the bit in the opposite direction.

TROUBLESHOOTING – problems with acceptance of the bit

THE HORSE PREFERS TO STAY 'LONG AND DEEP'

It is probable that his hindquarters have not become strong enough to carry more weight. Do more strengthening work, such as trotting uphill. He *will* start to come up in front as soon as his strength and balance permit.

OVERBENDING OR 'BEHIND THE BIT'
Corrections
a) Yielding with the rein or riding with a loose rein until the horse has confidence in your hands and is balanced at a slower pace.
b) Driving him forwards with leg aids.
c) Performing a half-halt.

d) A quick up-and-down lift of the outside hand might be used to raise his head.

LEANING ON THE HANDS
This has everything to do with balance. If a horse feels a need to lean on his rider's hands, he has moved his centre of gravity too far forwards and is carrying too much weight on the forehand. He will be using the rider's hands to help him to balance. If his centre of gravity is too far forward he will not be able to do transitions, changes of bend or complicated movements without losing his balance. His weight must be carried by the stronger hindquarters to enable him to stay in balance during the different movements.

PULLING ON THE REINS
There is a difference between 'leaning' and pulling. A horse may lean on the bit simply because his centre of gravity is too far forward but, in pulling, he is using his neck extensors actively to resist the hand. In this case, he has not yet accepted the bit, and must be taught to do so as previously described.

JERKING THE REINS FROM THE RIDER'S HANDS
You are, more than likely, not responsive enough in the arms and hands. The solution is to relax the elbows and develop a yielding arm and hand but,

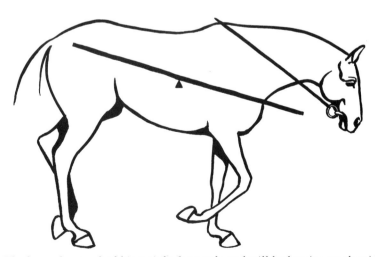

Figure 67 The horse has pushed his weight forwards and will be leaning on the rider's hands.

as soon as the horse attempts to jerk the reins you should immediately block with your elbows and then yield again.

TONGUE OVER THE BIT
This is usually caused by tension in the mouth. Try to prevent this by keeping the horse's mouth soft and relaxed.

GRINDING TEETH
This is another sign of tension and should be remedied by keeping the horse free from tension. If it becomes apparent in a horse who has not previously done it, it may be that he has developed a physical problem which is making his work difficult and uncomfortable.

REARING
This is the ultimate defiance of the rider's aids. Although it is not always associated with non-acceptance of the bit, this can be a major cause, so it is appropriate to discuss it at this juncture.

Horses have excellent balance and usually know how high they can rear. Other than in exceptional circumstances, they only fall over when the rider pulls on the reins in an attempt to retain balance. Because it is such a frightening experience, few riders will mount again after falling from a rearing horse. As a result, the horse knows he has a powerful weapon against his rider. Thus the only way to cure this vice *is* to get back on again and attempt to teach the horse not to rear.

Rearing can occur as a result of underworking, overfeeding and freshness, in which case the cure is to reduce the feed and lunge the horse to remove the freshness. Other causes are:

Stubborness and resistance to going forwards.

Horses with sensitive mouths may fear the bit or the actions of rider's hands, and try to escape from their effects.

Riding with unyielding hands and too much pushing with the legs. The horse has nowhere to escape, but up.

Corrections

a) Never lean back or hold onto the reins when the horse rears. Instead, lean forward, take the weight on the balls of the feet and yield with the reins. Either wait the rear out, or pull the horse sideways. As soon as his feet touch the ground, pull the rein to one side and ride the horse in a tight circle a few times.

b) A horse usually does a few marching steps before he rears. As soon as you feel this, open one rein only and pull the horse sideways. This will unbalance the horse and prevent any rearing.

c) Lunge the horse with a lungeing cavesson over the bridle, the lunge rein onto the side ring and the rider mounted. As soon as he attempts to rear, pull him sideways with the lunge rein. This will unbalance him. A horse can only rear if he is able to stand on his two hind feet.

Alternatively, allow him to stand and become relaxed for a few seconds after the rear and then send him forwards with the lunge whip.

d) A horse who fears the bit or the rider's hands should be taught to accept the bit. If the rearing continues, try riding with one rein only until the horse learns to go forwards again. Obviously, a rider whose unyielding hands provoke or contribute to rearing must start to develop 'soft' hands.

CHAPTER 5

DEVELOPING THE ATHLETE

All athletes, including the equine variety, need superb rhythm, balance, suppleness, straightness and energy. Without these attributes they can only be participants and will never achieve greatness.

RHYTHM AND BALANCE

Rhythm and balance are extremely important and are inextricably linked in riding. Consistent success in any equestrian discipline will not be attainable if the horse does not possess rhythm and balance.

Rhythm is one of the first requirements for any athlete, whether human or equine. It should be established initially at trot, followed by canter. Rhythm at walk should develop from riding across country. When first backed, young horses do not always possess an even rhythm: they tend to trot either too fast or too slow, depending on which part of the school they are working in at that moment. Usually, they trot faster towards home and slower away from home.

Initially, rhythm should be fairly slow, to help the horse establish his balance. Once this has been achieved, the horse may be asked to move in a more energetic, forward-going manner. This forward action should not, however, deteriorate into 'running'. When a horse 'runs', his centre of gravity has moved too far forward and he is throwing his forelegs forwards to keep his base of support under his centre of gravity, as described in Chapter 1. If this happens, half-halts should be performed until balance and rhythm are re-established.

It is often more difficult to establish rhythm in a 'hot', forward-going horse, and frequent half-halts may be necessary, both to re-balance the horse and to explain to him that rushing around is not what is required.

Good balance is essential for all riding. When a horse is not balanced he will lose fluidity of movement, become hollow in outline, lose rhythm and lean on the bit. Many horses are naturally well balanced, but 'hot' horses often lose balance by throwing their weight around. Some horses are very agile and, because of this agility, can throw themselves off balance without a moment's notice. Horses who anticipate often lose balance because they start a movement without preparation. Poor balance is most noticeable during transitions, when a horse will become hollow in outline or fall onto the forehand.

The rider should not try to balance the horse by taking a firm contact – this will lead to tension and stiffness. Instead, the horse should be in self-carriage. This means that he is in balance and has his centre of gravity over his base of support – in other words, that he can carry himself and his rider to optimum effect. With a light contact and self-carriage the horse will flex his hocks and lower his hindquarters, thus taking his centre of gravity back as far as possible.

Balance can be improved through:

Establishing acceptance of the bit.

Establishing rhythm.

Improving suppleness.

Preparing the horse for every change of direction and transition with half-halts and 'sponging' the reins to prevent him from using his neck for balance.

Encouraging engagement.

SUPPLENESS

In order to become truly athletic, a horse has to develop both lateral and longitudinal suppleness.

Lateral suppleness is the ability of the horse to bend, throughout his neck and body, equally to both sides. A horse is usually more supple to one side of his body than the other – a factor which will affect his straightness (see next section). Suppleness is a product of the elasticity of the muscles: if a horse's muscles lack elasticity, he will not be able to bend sufficiently. Elasticity can be developed through stretching exercises.

Lateral suppling exercises are thus exercises to stretch the horse's muscles, with the aim of making him equally supple to both sides. Not only do the neck muscles need stretching, but also the intercostal muscles (rib muscles), the oblique abdominal muscles and the leg adductors.

Longitudinal suppleness. Stiffness in a horse's back is usually caused by contraction of the muscles running over the top of his neck and back. When these muscles contract, the horse's outline becomes hollow. He then becomes uncomfortable to ride; his stride shortens; he cannot engage his hindquarters and he is difficult to keep 'on the bit'.

Longitudinal suppleness is evidenced when the horse's topline can stretch and he can be ridden 'long and deep' with ease. In order to become longitudinally supple, he will have to contract the neck, abdominal and hip flexors.

WHY THE HORSE HAS TO BE SUPPLE

1) A supple horse is not so likely to injure a muscle as a stiff horse.

2) Without supple muscles, the horse cannot become straight. Straightness is essential for correct work, especially advanced movements such as flying changes, extended gaits, lateral work, etc.

3) Suppleness improves the horse's ability to change direction without loss of balance and also improves balance, as a relaxed muscle can

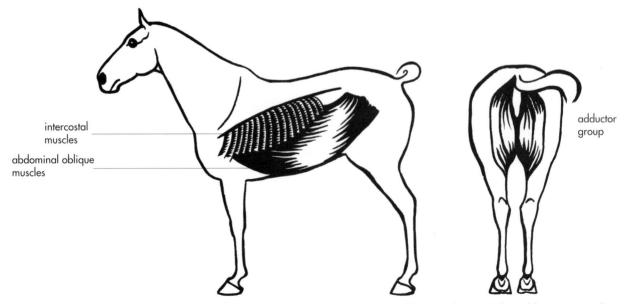

intercostal muscles

abdominal oblique muscles

adductor group

Figure 69 The intercostal, abdominal oblique and leg adductor muscles, which need to stretch and become supple.

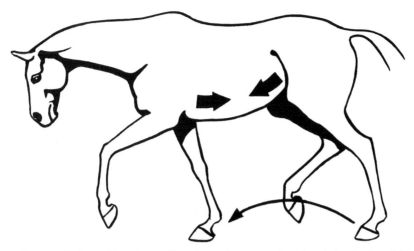

Figure 70 Stretching the topline through contracting the abdominal and hip flexors.

adapt quicker than a stiff muscle. It is essential for all movements where this ability is required, including circles and figures based on them, lateral work and pirouettes. If the horse is not supple, he will 'fall' into circles and 'push' against the rider's leg because he cannot stretch the outside muscles.

4) Longitudinal suppleness is essential for weight-bearing. It ensures that the abdominal muscles are strengthened and the back muscles supple and relaxed so that the horse can arch, round or 'lift' his back – which is essential for weight-bearing.

5) Longitudinal suppleness helps with the engagement of the hindquarters through the contraction of the abdominal and hip flexors.

MAKING THE HORSE SUPPLE

For lateral suppleness we make use of the two basic postural reactions; righting and balance reactions.

To stretch the muscles on the outside, it is necessary to do the following:

1) Push the ribcage to the outside with your inside leg on the girth. The horse will automatically bring his neck and tail slightly to the inside (balance reaction).

2) Squeeze or 'sponge' on the inside rein to encourage the horse to flex the inside neck muscles and follow the movement of your hand (righting reaction). The head should follow the hand with no resistance. Too much contact on the inside rein will mean that the horse is using the muscles on the other side of his neck, as described in Chapter 1.

3) The outside hand uses the 'long arm' technique of moving the head, neck and shoulder to the inside (righting reaction).

4) The outside leg, behind the girth, prevents the horse from straightening his body with his hindquarters through his righting reactions.

Suppling exercises
LATERAL SUPPLENESS

1) Start with a 20m figure-of-eight. This gives a horse the intermittent stretching when changing direction plus a full 20m circle to regain any lost balance.

2) Riding a serpentine is one of the most useful exercises to make a horse supple. When one group of muscles is stretched continuously, as happens when riding a circle repeatedly, it has the effect of putting those stretched muscles in spasm. To demonstrate how the muscle will

react to stretching, stretch your hamstrings behind the knees, by trying to touch your toes. If you hold this position for too long you will have to bend your knees suddenly to relieve the pull on the muscles. This is a consequence of the automatic stretch reflex. A serpentine, however, prevents this continuous stretch because the same position is not maintained for too long before the change of bend to the other side.

a) Start with three 20 m serpentines and increase the number of loops until the horse can do six without difficulty (60 × 20 m arena).

b) A small serpentine up the centre line

teaches the horse to change bend rapidly and is a very useful suppling exercise. Start with a few loops and then progress to as many as you can fit in.

c) Try to ride as many serpentines as you can through the whole arena by doubling back (see illustration).

d) A variation of the serpentine is the following: ride large round the outside of the arena. At V, ride a 15 m half circle and continue back to E. Change the bend at 5 m before E. Ride to S and do a 15m half circle back to E, changing the bend at 5 m from E. Repeat this exercise and slowly decrease the size of the half circle.

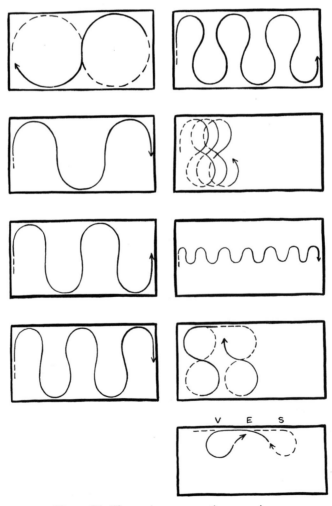

Figure 71 The various serpentine exercises.

3) Ride deep into the corners.

4) Ride 10 m circles and voltes.

5) Shoulder-in is an extremely good suppling exercise. Start by riding shoulder-in at walk. Ask for a few strides and then straighten the horse, then ask again. Practise this on both reins. Travers and renvers are also good suppling exercises.

6) Spiralled decreasing and increasing of circles at trot and canter are very valuable suppling exercises.

7) Counter-canter stretches the muscles on the outside of the body.

LONGITUDINAL SUPPLENESS

The remedy for longitudinal stiffness is to stretch all the topline muscles of the neck and back by riding 'long and deep'. The abdominal muscles have to become strong to pull the hind legs into engagement. The centre of gravity will then move back and give the horse more balance and 'jump' in the stride. The lower he has his head and neck, the more he will engage his hindquarters and thus strengthen them.

To stretch his topline, the horse must yield completely to the rein. This will mean that he is using his neck flexors and, through his righting reactions, also his abdominal flexors. Any strong feeling in the hand will indicate that he is using his neck extensors. You should be able to place his head wherever you want it, without any resistance.

It is important to start and end the riding session with this exercise as it will release any strain on the horse's back muscles and ensure a supple back.

STRAIGHTNESS – THE DEVELOPMENT OF AMBIDEXTERITY

Straightness, essentially, is an absence of crooked-ness. All horses naturally seem to be crooked in their body. One side of their body can flex more readily than the other, stiffer, side. (This does not

Figure 72 The crooked horse. The muscles are tighter on one side of the body.

mean, however, that the horse is necessarily crooked through the spine.)

In Figure 72, the muscles on the horse's right side will flex more readily than those on the left side. In this case, the right side would be commonly referred to as the horse's 'soft' side, while the left side would be referred to as the 'stiff' side. Physiologically, however, the opposite is the case: the muscles on the right side of this horse are easier to contract (so he will yield quicker to the effect of the rein aid) because the opposite (left) side muscles will stretch more readily. When asking the left side to contract and the right side to stretch accordingly, you would find that the right side muscles have difficulty in stretching. Try touching your toes: the reason you have a problem is because your hamstrings are tight – not because your hip flexors will not flex. Next, try the following experiment:

Figure 73 Tight hamstrings lead to difficulty in hip flexion.

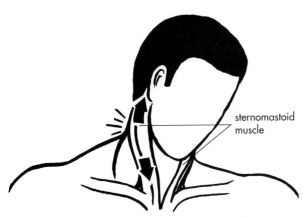

Figure 74 Human 'one-sidedness': the muscle on one side of your neck will be slightly tighter than the other.

push your chin in and move one ear closer to your shoulder. The sternomastoid muscle on the opposite side will feel tight. Do the same on the other side and take note of which muscle is stiffer. Similarly, a horse will also feel the tightness of the brachiocephalic muscle more on one side than the other. (The sternomastoid muscle in humans corresponds to the brachio-cephalic muscle in horses).

Be mindful, therefore, that when riders refer to a horse being 'stiff' on one side, they are traditionally talking about the side to which it is harder to make him flex – but this is because the muscles on his *other* side are 'stiff' and cannot stretch readily.

DOMINANCE

As with humans, horses seem to have a dominant and a non-dominant side of the body. This is caused by one side of the brain taking a dominant role. Right-side dominance is more common in humans than left dominance, but there are many variations in the pattern of dominance in humans. A person may be right-handed, but left-footed, or right-handed with the left eye dominant. This is called crossed dominance. Furthermore, a human may use the right foot for accuracy, but the left foot for balance.

In horses, a statistical study of dominance has not yet been made and it would thus be difficult to ascertain whether the pattern of crossed dominace

occurs, or which side might be considered dominant. However, some indications of dominance in humans, which might also be applied to the horse, are as follows. In general, dominant muscles are more co-ordinated and relatively stronger, but also less elastic than non-dominant muscles. (Stronger muscles have a tendency to be thicker and less elastic than weaker muscles, which is why athletes continuously do hamstring stretching exercises before competing.) The dominant side also has a better balancing ability than the non-dominant side. (When humans are asked to balance on one leg, they will usually choose the dominant leg to stand on.)

At walk and trot, most horses are more flexible to one side, because the stronger muscles on that side are more used to contracting, while the weaker muscles on the other side will more readily stretch. A horse will usually accept the bit more readily on the side to which he will more easily flex. If, then, we apply the criteria above to these observations, it would be reasonable to suggest that the concave side of the horse is the dominant side.

At canter, three reasons why a young horse may show a preference for cantering on one side only tend to support this view. These are:

1) Because of his natural crookedness, he is already bent to one side (his hollow side) and looking in that direction. His muscles are thus already prepared to canter to that side.

2) When a young horse is pushed forward into a stronger trot, this will cause discomfort to the short muscles on the concave side and trigger the stretch reflex (discussed shortly). In consequence, rather than stretching into a longer trot stride, the horse will prefer to take a short canter stride to that side.

3) Sometimes, however, the opposite happens, because the horse may prefer to strike off with his stronger hind leg and thus canter to his convex side – even though this canter may be less balanced and comfortable than that to his concave side. This reaction serves to suggest that while we might, generally speaking,

Figure 75(a) The horse is slightly bent in one direction and will strike off into canter in that direction.

Figure 75(b) Discomfort caused by the stretch reflex will lead to cantering to the right.

Figure 75(c) The horse strikes off to the left with his dominant right hind leg.

consider the concave side to be dominant there is no scientific proof of it yet.

In any case, while such considerations are of great interest to students of equine bio-mechanics, ascertaining the horse's dominant side is not the primary concern – making him truly ambidextrous ('straight') is the really important issue.

WHY STRAIGHTNESS IS NECESSARY

If a horse is to be used for the purposes of sport, it is essential that both sides of his body are equally developed, equally supple and equally balanced, first to ensure that he does not injure his muscles and second, to maximise his level of performance.

Straightness allows the horse's hind feet to step into the same path as the forefeet, and improves the ease of his movements. Advanced dressage movements such as flying changes and piaffe cannot be performed correctly if the horse is not straight. Furthermore, the overall test score will be improved if the good quality of movements on one rein is matched by the movements on the other. In jumping competitions, equal suppleness and balance on both sides of the horse will reduce the chance of dropping a pole, and will make him quicker going round corners in the jump-off.

HOW TO ACHIEVE STRAIGHTNESS

Suppleness and straightness are closely related and improving the former will have the effect of improving the latter. To straighten a horse we need to develop his ambidexterity. In other words, both sides have to be equally strong, co-ordinated, supple and balanced. (It is probably not possible to achieve *perfect* ambidexterity because the one side of the brain will always remain dominant – but this should certainly be the goal to aim for.)

The stretch reflex
Before we begin stretching exercises to straighten the horse, it is important to understand the stretch reflex. Each muscle fibre has a little nerve attached

to it. As soon as the fibre stretches beyond its comfort limit, the nerve will be stimulated to 'ask' the muscle to contract immediately in order to prevent injury. This is an automatic reaction and exists to protect the muscle fibres from injury. Overstretching will cause spasm in the muscle. This is why counter-flexion can be so useful. The stretch reflex is clearly demonstrated when we have to stand in a queue. We stand on one leg, but after a short time the tendons behind the knee start to 'pull'. We then change to the other leg and allow the knee flexors of the first leg to contract, and thus relieve the stretch on them.

When we are working towards suppleness and straightness this stretch reflex should be considered; stretching exercises should be done intermittently. A good example of such intermittent work is riding serpentines.

Since the most effective way of straightening a horse is to make him supple on both sides, the suppling exercises previously mentioned (page 54) should be practised. Additional points to bear in mind are:

1) Make sure that you work slightly more on the difficult rein than on the easy one. Working equally will only improve both sides at an equal rate. Overworking the difficult side will, however, create more contraction as a result of the stretch reflex.

2) The best way of strengthening the non-dominant hind leg is by cantering to its opposite side.

3) Counter-canter improves the horse's strength, balance and co-ordination on the non-dominant side. It can be used as a stretching exercise when asking the horse to bend away from the leading leg.

4) Counter-bend exercises make use of the stretch reflex to encourage contraction on the stiff side. Trot a 20 m circle on the side to which the horse does not easily bend. Bend him towards the outside and ride him this way for a little while. You will find that he starts to pull against the outside rein. As soon as he starts to do this, change the bend to the inside. The stretch reflex has stimulated the inside neck muscles to contract and, so doing, has put the horse on the outside rein.

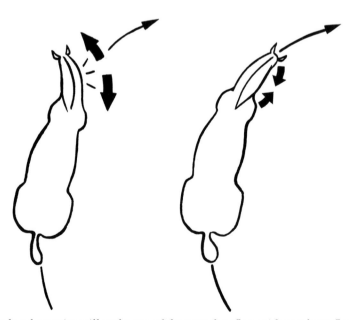

Figure 76 The counter-bend exercise will make use of the stretch reflex, with resultant flexion to the other side.

ENERGY – RIDING FORWARD WITH IMPULSION

This fundamental requirement of equitation is sometimes described as forwardness. The essence of forwardness is that the horse pushes off from the hind legs with long, powerful strides. He moves forward actively, rhythmically, with impulsion and without constraint or a continuous reminder to move on. There should be a feeling of energy flowing through the horse; he should surge forwards with long, ground-covering strides, but not with faster action. He will respond as soon as the rider gives him an aid, but he is not hurried.

This quality is essential if the horse is to produce the energy needed to carry himself and perform the more advanced movements: engagement and strength can only develop through propulsion from the hindquarters. This forward propulsion helps to develop straightness and balance and should lead to a longer and more elevated stride. It also maintains the purity of the gaits: the four-beat walk and three-beat canter. Riding forward helps to put the horse 'on the bit'.

HOW TO PRODUCE ENERGY

There are various ways to encourage the production of energy, but a rider should demand only as much impulsion as he can maintain without the horse losing balance or becoming tense. We can only start *asking* for forward action when the horse allows us to push or drive him. An excited or 'hot' horse will most likely be pulling the ground with his forefeet instead of pushing with his hind legs. Therefore, a horse with an excess of energy will have to be slowed down with repeated half-halts until the rider is able to push the horse forwards from his own leg aids. If the horse is allowed to rush forward he will lose balance and therefore lose rhythm.

As horse and rider progress, the rider should be able to ask for increasingly more impulsion. Eventually, once the horse has fully understood the forward aid, maximum impulsion can be achieved without effort or strain, in conjunction with perfect, balance and lightness.

1) To teach the horse to respond energetically to the forward aid, give the forward command by squeezing him on with both legs. If his response is not adequate, he should be tapped ever so lightly with the whip immediately behind your leg. If he responds appropriately he should be rewarded immediately with a tickle on the wither and a 'Good boy'. Repeat this procedure three or four times, but not more than four. When next you use your legs on the horse, he should surge forwards. This, of course, must be followed by reward. Should the horse becomes lazy to the leg again, this procedure must be repeated: there should be no 'nagging' by the legs. If you use your legs continuously, the horse will soon become dull to the aid.

2) If you have a lazy horse, you can start your warm-up at canter (after walking your horse and doing a little trot work to stretch the muscles). Ride the horse at working canter, ensuring that his frame is long, round and deep. Canter a few circuits to the left, followed by a few to the right. You should then find that he has become quite forward-going at trot.

3) One of the best ways of engaging the horse's hindquarters is through transitions. Once a rhythmic trot is established, ask for a downward transition to walk, walk one step and ask for trot again. This should be repeated until the horse starts moving freely forwards. If you feel he is not engaging his hindquarters enough, tap him gently as you ask for the downward transition and you will find that he will be more engaged for his next trot step. Transitions from working trot to lengthened trot and back again will activate the hindquarters.

4) A good warm-up exercise is to ride a 20 m circle from A. Continue up the long side and lengthen from F to P then collect and ride a 20 m circle

at P. Lengthen again to the next marker, collect and ride a 20 m circle again (see Figure 77). Repeat this exercise at each marker.

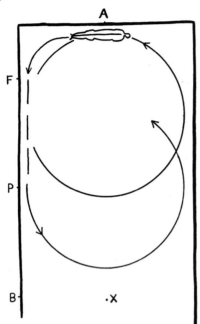

Figure 77 A good warm-up exercise in trot.

5) Canter – trot transitions can be used in the same way. Canter a few strides, prepare the horse for trot and then ask for a balanced trot transition ensuring that he does not become unbalanced and hollow his outline during the transition. Repeat as necessary. A further development of this exercise is the canter–walk transition, but this can only be done with a fairly advanced horse. A few strides of collected canter are followed by a few walk strides and then a few canter strides, etc. This improves the collection, and thus the engagement, at canter as well as trot.

6) Shoulder-in can also be used as an engaging exercise to produce more forward movement, since it has the effect of activating the inside hind leg. A few shoulder-in exercises on both reins should have the effect of producing more forward activity in the horse. For this purpose the exercise should be performed at a lengthened gait. An advanced exercise that may be used for engagement and forward activity is to ride a canter shoulder-in followed by a walk shoulder-in followed again by canter shoulder-in, etc.

7) Medium trot to walk transitions are very difficult, but quite effective for engagement and obedience (advanced horses only.)

8) If the horse is entirely too lazy and working in the school upsets him or makes him buck, he should be ridden cross-country and egged on with a noisy crop. (In cases of sustained or abnormal lethargy the horse's physical well-being should be investigated.)

ENGAGEMENT OF THE HINDQUARTERS

A horse is said to become engaged when he takes increasingly more weight on his hindquarters by stepping underneath himself more and flexing all three joints of the hind leg. This moves his centre of gravity backwards. The horse is enabled to become engaged through strengthening of his abdominal, hip and hock flexors. When his centre of gravity moves back, he becomes fully balanced, and forward aids will produce a lengthened stride rather than a hurried one.

In addition to arching and strengthening the back, engagement lightens the forehand and frees the shoulder for better extensions, lateral movements and flying changes. Without engagement, a horse will not be able to perform advanced movements correctly.

DEVELOPING AND IMPROVING ENGAGEMENT

Early development of engagement is promoted by riding 'long and deep'. This stimulates the neck, abdominal and hip flexors into action as previously described. Once the horse is working in this outline, the next step is to push the hindquarters more underneath the horse with your leg and seat aids, but control the energy with your rein aids; inhibit any 'running' through the use of half-halts.

All the exercises described for promoting forward action and collection will help the horse to become more engaged; in particular, transitions stimulate the forward propulsion and improve balance and engagement.

You can check whether your horse is really engaged by riding a few lengthened strides. When he is engaged, he will perform these with ease.

COLLECTION

A horse is fully collected when he has moved his centre of gravity so far back that he is taking as much weight as he can on his hindquarters. His hind legs step underneath him to create maximum upward thrust and elevation: his hocks are substantially flexed to help him carry the weight on his strong hock flexors. He produces great energy and impulsion, with the result that his strides become more expressive and vigorous. His head and neck are carried higher (though fully arched) and he becomes completely light in the hands. When properly collected, the horse is ready to produce any action at the lightest signal.

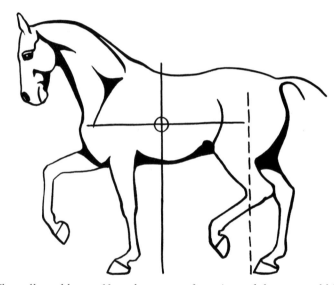

Figure 78(a) The collected horse. Note the centre of gravity and the engaged hindquarters.

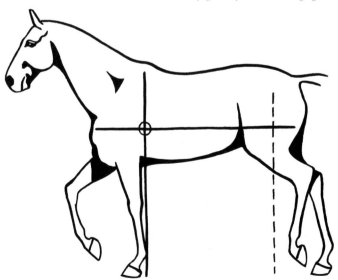

Figure 78(b) The horse without collection. The centre of gravity is too far forward and the hindquarters are not engaged.

WHY COLLECTION IS NECESSARY

Collection improves balance, strength and impulsion in the horse. Without it, the horse would not be strong or balanced enough to perform advanced movements such as flying changes, canter pirouettes, piaffe, passage, and counter-changes. A collected horse is more comfortable to ride, easier to maintain a deep seat on and takes less effort for the rider to balance. He is more forward-thinking and responds to lighter aids. In short, the collected horse has more power for instant use and is in total readiness for any movement.

Figure 79(a) In his natural state, the horse moves his centre of gravity back by lifting his head.

Figure 79(b) The centre of gravity is moved back through lowering of the hindquarters.

TEACHING THE HORSE COLLECTION

To become collected, the horse has to move his centre of gravity backwards. He would do this naturally by lifting his head and neck and then bringing his quarters more underneath him to balance. However, to lift his head and neck he has to use his neck extensors isotonically and this would create hollowness of his neck and back.

In order to keep the roundness which is important for the protection of his back, we need to find a method which impels him to use his abdominal muscles. If we keep his head and neck flexed ('on the bit') and bring his hindquarters more underneath him, he has to work his abdominal muscles and his hip and hock flexors. His head and neck will then automatically assume a higher position. From this it becomes clear why we can only create true collection from the hindquarters not from pulling the horse in from the front.

Preparing for collection

Before we can produce collection, we need a supple and straight horse with lots of energy and impulsion. It is also of utmost importance that the horse has developed enough strength to maintain collection without injuring any muscles. So, from the onset of training, we will have been doing strengthening exercises. These will include:

1) Hill work at trot and canter, which has the dual purpose of strengthening the horse and getting him fit.

2) Frequent transitions walk-trot-walk. During these transitions, the walk should be only a few steps. This impels the horse to quicken his reactions and use more power to produce the transition. Gentle tapping with the whip in the downward or upward transition will motivate him to step underneath more and give a stronger 'push'.

3) Frequent transitions trot-canter-trot. This exercise not only strengthens the horse, but also pushes his centre of gravity back, improving his balance and producing more engagement of the hindquarters.

4) Shoulder-in. Because this requires the horse to step under with the inside hind leg, more engagement and strengthening will develop. Travers and renvers have similar functions.

5) Decreasing and increasing the diameter of the circle at canter causes the hind legs to become more engaged and thus become stronger.

6) Quarter, half and full pirouettes strengthen and engage the hindquarters. Novice horses will do quarter pirouettes, Elementary horses will do half pirouettes and Medium horses will do complete small circles with quarters in.

Once the horse has mastered trot – canter – trot transitions, the walk – canter – walk transitions can be incorporated to work towards collection. If you proceed in this manner you will find, once your horse has become strong enough to ask for proper collection, that he has already become more engaged behind and lighter in front.

The aids for collection

We have to explain to the horse that he should generate energy in his hindquarters and move on, but then from the front we explain to him that we do not wish him to use this energy to go faster or become longer in outline. The energy is thus transferred upwards. The procedure for producing collection is:

1) Use your leg aids to ask for more engagement of the hindquarters and more energy.

2) The energy produced must be caught in your hands so that it does not become dissipated. The wrists, elbows and shoulders should be held in co-contraction (the flexors and extensors act simultaneously).

3) The fingers 'sponge' the reins so that the horse does not become tense in the mouth or neck, which would result in hollowness.

The hands and arms should do no active backward pulling. This will result in stiff, straight steps.

As soon as the horse responds, the aids are relaxed. The process is repeated as soon as more collection is required.

The result of these actions is that the forehand will raise and the head and neck carriage will become higher and more compacted, with a lighter contact. The back will 'swing' and become more comfortable (the rider seems to become part of the horse). The period of suspension will become longer and there will be more impulsion, engagement and elasticity.

TROUBLESHOOTING –
problems with collection

INSUFFICIENT ELEVATION AND LIGHTNESS OF THE FOREHAND

If you find that your horse does not start lifting his forehand, he has not yet developed enough strength in his hindquarters. Do more strengthening work. He will become more engaged and develop a higher head carriage as soon as he has developed sufficient strength.

INSUFFICIENT ENGAGEMENT AND ACTIVITY

A common error with novice riders is that they do not ask for enough impulsion and engagement because they do not yet know what collection should feel like. When you think you have enough, ask for more. Collection is a distinct feeling which is so good that you will know when you have it.

True collection gives a sensation and picture of forward power under control – a slow gait with little engagement is not enough. The horse should be moving forwards vigorously in measured fashion.

PART TWO

COMMUNICATING WITH

THE HORSE

CHAPTER 6

HOW THE HORSE LEARNS

The horse can only learn through a language that he understands. Each rider must try to learn this horse language as well as teaching the horse some of the rider's own (verbal) language. Through the centuries the aids that we still use today have been based on this particular horse language. This horse language is based on eliciting automatic postural reactions through the facilitation and inhibition of movement as described in Chapter 1.

When the rider asks for a movement through the *correct* use of this horse language, every horse will understand and will not become confused. The same question will elicit essentially the same answer from every horse.

THE THEORY OF LEARNING

Any learning process is dependent upon the following elements:

Willingness to learn (motivation). Although horses, by their submissive nature, show a certain willingness to learn, they cannot possess an inner motivation to perform an action correctly. Such motivation is present only in the human being with his highly developed cortical brain. The horse will only want to do that which is comfortable for him. He does not possess concepts such as 'no pain, no gain' and cannot perceive that an uncomfortable position (such as a stretching exercise) is for his own good. Discomfort will lead to confusion and anxiety. Therefore the rider should, as far as possible, work through what is comfortable for the horse, and only ask a little at a time. In other words, we should

find the easiest and most comfortable way to make the horse do what we want him to do.

Perception of a stimulus and reaction to it. All animals learn by three processes: *assimilation*, *association* and *memory*. Assimilation is the process of gathering information. Memory is the process of storing the information, and all new material is then associated with this stored up information. The better the memory of the animal, the more information can be stored. As horses seem to have fairly good memories, we should use this facility when we train them. Repetition helps with the process of assimilation and memory.

Reward (or punishment). Since the horse learns by repetition of the correct work it is of the utmost importance that he knows when the work has been correct. The only way he will know that his reaction was correct is through reward. The horse associates the reward with the correct action (or the punishment with the incorrect action). The more the correct action is repeated, rewarded and understood, the quicker the horse will learn and remember the aids, and the rider can stop going through the whole process of facilitation of movement.

Once learning has taken place, the stimulus (aid) and the reaction become completely bound up, so that the stimulus alone will bring about the correct reaction and no reward will be necessary. (The stimulus has become associated with the reaction).

Figure 80 Horses showing affection.

LEARNING BY SIGNS

A horse does not necessarily have to learn the aids through facilitation of movement. He can learn many movements through entirely meaningless signs or signals. An example of learning through signs is when a horse is taught to trot in response to the rider's knuckles pressing on the wither. Similarly, a circus horse may be taught to 'count' by stamping his foot when a certain sign is given. These methods however, cannot teach *quality* of movement, such as a half-halt or *degrees* of collection; only specific movements such as walk, trot and canter. The horse learns the sign more or less 'accidentally' and is rewarded for his reaction.

We use this method of teaching on the lunge. The horse is pushed forwards with the whip, together with a verbal command. Because he is scared of.the whip, he will break into trot and is then rewarded for the correct action. He then associates the verbal command with the whip and the trot action. When next the verbal command is given, he will break into trot.

When training a young horse, it is initially easier to teach walk, trot and canter by this method rather than mounted, because a horse is rather too big to use the method of facilitation of movement before he has learnt that he was placed on earth to be ridden. Advanced movements, however, are usually more correct when taught through facilitation of the movement rather than by signs.

REWARD AND PUNISHMENT

In horse language the phrases 'yes, that's right' and 'no, that's wrong' are represented by reward and punishment.

Reward
When a horse is being trained it is essential that the language employed is extremely clear, as we do not want to confuse him. Imagine attempting a conversation with a foreigner who did not understand your own language. You would explain a concept to him and wait for him to show that he has understood. If his reaction was incorrect you would shake your head, say 'no' and repeat the instruction. When he has finally understood, you

would smile and say 'yes, yes, yes', and he would know immediately that he had understood correctly. So it is with horses. They must be told immediately that their reaction to the question was correct: the reward must be patently clear.

Every little effort as well as every correct reaction of the horse should be rewarded. This is the only way the horse will know that his action was correct. The correct action will be linked to the aid and he will have learnt a new 'word' in his horse language vocabulary.

There are three basic rewards appropriate in riding:

Physical contact. Since horses enjoy affection, we should use it as a reward. Since horses cannot pat each other, patting on the neck is actually an inappropriate action for a reward. If we observe horses showing affection towards each other, we will notice that they stand facing each other with their heads slightly over each other's withers. They then tickle each other with circular movements of their muzzles on the wither. We should therefore reward our horses in the same manner. Each time the horse shows the correct action, he should be tickled in a circular motion on the neck with the fingers of the inside hand. With this method there is little displacement of the hands, and the horse knows immediately that he is acting correctly. This

Figure 82 Stroking, leading to relaxation.

method also seems to have a relaxing effect on the horse and is a clear reward.

Stroking as a reward is highly successful when teaching the horse to listen to the action of the rider's hand. When the horse is asked to contract the muscles on one side of his neck and he reacts correctly, a long stroke down his neck on the side to which his reaction was correct will reward and relax him. This will also help to reinforce the action of the hand on the bit as he will become even lighter in the hand.

The voice. The horse can be rewarded verbally. If the rider says 'good boy', or 'braaf', or any gentle sounding word, together with a little tickle, the horse will soon associate the word with the reward action. Very soon a 'good boy' alone will be sufficient reward for him.

A rest period. As soon as the horse has performed a movement successfully, he will have deserved a rest period. Tickle him, say 'good boy' and walk him on a long rein for a short time. If his performance was particularly successful, you may want to end the whole training session and put him away for the day.

Punishment

Punishment is a difficult concept for any animal to understand. Whereas reward produces a feeling of

Figure 81 The circular tickle.

goodwill, punishment can produce either sub-mission, resistance or anxiety. A horse can as-sociate pain with an action that was not required, and pleasure with one that was, but he cannot plan to do wrong, as humans do.

Punishment should be meted out in very small doses. A horse is seldom naughty on purpose, but riders often assume that a horse is naughty when he is actually confused. If a horse is punished for confusion, he will become anxious and tense and his performance will deteriorate. Therefore, the rider must be absolutely certain that the horse has understood the instruction before considering punishment. Even then, great care must be exercised – even justified punishment can do more harm than good if it produces tension and anxiety, which are a rider's main enemies. Punishment is also a communication blocker.

There are three main methods of punishment:

The voice. A harsh 'no' should be adequate for the horse to understand that his action was incorrect.

The legs. A slap with both legs can be used for more serious misdemeanours, or when the horse ignores the rider's legs.

The whip. This should be used as a last resort, but never harshly. It should be used lightly behind the leg as soon as the aid has been given and only if the horse has ignored the aid. This reinforces the instruction, via the leg aid, to the horse. (Often a nappy horse will veer towards the direction of the stable while the rider is attempting to circle or turn a corner. The whip held against the shoulder, or a little tap on the shoulder on the side the horse is hanging to, will rapidly solve such a problem.)

The horse should never be afraid of the whip, as this will cause tension and thus become a commu-nication blocker. If you find that your horse is afraid of the whip you can make him comfortable with it by first stroking him gently with it all over his neck and body. Once he is happy with this stroking you can start to move the whip past his face and eventually swing it past his face on both sides until he does not react to it at all.

The whip (and spurs) should be used mainly for encouraging forward action and engagement of the hindquarters when the leg aid is not sufficient, and as little as possible for punishment. In addition, the spurs are used as a back-up to the leg for lateral movements or when the horse does not understand the lateral aid clearly enough.

MEMORY

One of the greatest assets in the training of the horse is his excellent memory: he seldom forgets a lesson learnt. This, however, also applies to incor-rect lessons, so all riders should be very careful what they teach their horses. A horse who learns that he can lose his rider by rearing or bucking will remember to use this same method again.

All animals have various kinds of memory:

Visual memory. This type of memory is not particularly useful in training. It is a major cause of shying, because the horse remembers all the objects in the pathway and when any of these change position he will become suspicious.

Auditory memory. We make use of this memory in initial learning when we use voice aids.

Tactile memory. The horse uses this to remember the aids. Reward, punishment, the pressure of the leg aids and the feeling on the sides of the mouth from the pressure of the bit are all registered through skin sensations, and remembered.

Kinesthetic and proprioceptive memory. This is the memory of actual movement of the muscles, tendons and joints through the proprioceptive organs and is the form of memory we, as riders, should be most concerned about. The horse learns mainly through this sense of movement and re-members all the movements he has learnt through this particular sense. He also uses this memory, in conjunction with his sense of smell (olfactory sense), to find his way home.

(The horse also has memory for taste and

smell, but these forms of memory are not used in training.)

Repetition of work

A horse learns through reacting correctly to an aid and being rewarded immediately for his correct reaction. Only by repetition of correct work will the horse consolidate and remember the effects of the aids. To achieve perfection, the work should be repeated, with reward, until he can react correctly to the lightest of aids.

Through repetition, a pattern of movement is permanently stored in the brain, ready to be reproduced as soon as the correct mechanism (aid) triggers it off. This pattern of movement is stored by the kinesthetic memory.

THE PROCESS OF LEARNING AN AID

There are four major steps in this process:

1) The first step in learning is that the horse must understand what is asked of him; he must understand what to do. Through facilitation of the correct movement, using natural postural mechanisms as described in Chapter 1, he will understand completely what is expected of him.

2) As soon as he gives the correct reaction, he is rewarded. He associates the correct action with a reward. It is thus important that the rider is very effective in eliciting the correct action; half a correct action will only lead to a much longer learning process.

3) Through repetition of the aid, correct reaction to the aid and reward for this action, the horse indelibly links the aid to the correct reaction and will act correctly every time, even without the reward.

4) Once the horse understands the movement, the aids can become lighter. Eventually the horse will understand this language so clearly that he will start to 'pick up' nuances, and the lightest muscular action from the rider will elicit the desired effect.

THE ROLE OF THE NERVE PATHWAYS

A description of the learning process would not be complete without a brief look at the neurological process involved in conveying a stimulus (aid) and a reaction to it.

All animals possess two sets of nerve pathways. The first group run from the sensory organs of the body to the brain and are called sensory nerves. The second group run from the brain to the muscles and are called the motor nerves. The sensory group take the messages, passed on via the aids, through the sensory organs to the brain. The brain interprets these messages and sends appropriate instructions to the muscles, via the motor group of nerves. *From this description it should be clear that the hindquarters cannot send any messages, over the horse's back and through his poll, to his mouth. No pathways exist to allow this.* (There seems to be some misconception in riding circles concerning this concept.)

CHAPTER 7

COMMUNICATING

THROUGH THE AIDS

The most important facet of riding is the communication between the horse and rider. The language used should be so clear that there will be no misunderstanding. For the rider to use hands, legs, seat and weight effectively for the purposes of communication, it is necessary to become independent in the seat, and to learn to use the arms and legs separately.

Effectiveness should be a key factor in the use of the aids. Every aid should be immediately effective and the rider should feel a difference in the horse. For example, an aid for forward movement should produce a surge forwards. Continuous kicking, with no clear response, will only dull a horse. Every time an extra aid is used, the next time the same response is desired, it will take twice as long. To turn riding into a true pleasure, the horse should be attentive to every aid. To insure an immediate response, the rider should either carry a whip or wear spurs as a back-up for when the horse does not listen. The rider should constantly aim for lightness of the aids. Remember, a very clear body language *does* exist and is available to all riders for use in the training of the horse. If our horses do not respond in the correct manner immediately, then we are not using this correct language.

THE VOICE

The horse has acute hearing. This can be noticed by the way he turns his ears backwards when the rider talks. In fact, the horse also moves his ears when the leg aids are given. He 'listens' to both voice and body aids with his ears. Once he has learned them, the horse never forgets the 'words'. The voice can, therefore, be used extremely effectively as an early learning aid and as an aid for conditioned learning. A wonderful example of the latter use is the Gray's Scouts of the Rhodesian bush war and their horses. These hardy little horses were trained entirely by voice aids because the riders needed free hands to use their guns when necessary. Words such as 'left', 'right' and 'lie down' were used (the horses had to lie down when the enemy was near, or at night when sleeping next to their riders.)

Although a horse can learn quite a large verbal vocabulary during his lifetime, the verbal commands are too limited to explain the finer nuances in riding, such as 'half-halt', 'slight inside bend', etc. For classical training the voice is used mainly at the beginning of training, to reinforce the other aids, as a reward or punishment and to calm the horse.

When lungeing a horse, the words 'walk', 'trot', etc. should be used together with the whip. The horse will soon associate the word with the action and will then need only the word to elicit the action.

When beginning the mounted work, these words should be used together with the aids to produce the specific movement. The horse will then associate the rider's aids with the word as well as the action, and soon only the aid will be needed to elicit the correct movement.

Other voice aids such as tongue clicking, to encourage forward action, and a soft whistle to bring the horse to a slower gait, may also be incorporated in the horse's vocabulary. 'Whoa' is an important aid in the initial training and has helped many a rider to bring the horse to a halt in difficult situations. Lower the voice on the second syllable to create a calming sound.

THE HANDS

The rider's hands are the most important agents in the communication between the horse and rider. Because of the sensitivity of the horse's mouth, they can make or break the training of the horse. Any tension in the arms or hands will show up in the horse, and lead to resistance. The most serious faults in the training of the horse usually arise from incorrect use of the hands.

The arms and hands should work completely independently from the rest of the rider's body. To achieve this independence, the rider should be in complete balance and the arms and hands should be completely relaxed. Without this re-laxation the rider cannot feel what is happening in the horse's neck and mouth and – even more important – the horse cannot relax his mouth and neck if the rider has stiff hands and arms. Thus the feeling in the rider's hands should be soft, light and elastic, like holding hands on a hot summer day – all you want to do is touch, or your hands become sweaty! Through soft hands, the rider is able to communicate and feel every nuance of movement.

The reins are only the extension of the rider's arms. The reason we have reins is because our arms are too short to reach the bit! Imagine having long arms which can attach to the bit: you would never dream of hanging onto the bit if your connection was this close to the horse. Instead, you would hold the bit gently. (The 'feel' in the hands may become slightly heavier for short periods during downward transitions, half-halts, etc., but it should never be *hard*, as this would mean that the horse is not balancing himself, or is resisting the rider's hands. Since pulling on the bit will create resistance, the horse should be *coaxed* into acceptance and relaxation.)

The hands can be used in the following ways:

'Sponging' (take and give). 'Sponging' has the effect of relaxing the jaw and neck extensors and facilitating contraction of the neck flexors. By 'sponging' the reins alternately we ask the horse to use his neck flexors, to come into a rounded outline or 'on the bit'.

Inside bend is requested by a 'sponging' of the inside rein, together with use of the inside leg aid. This technique is used for circles, shoulder-in, half-pass, canter, etc.

Co-contraction of the elbows. Co-contraction is when all the muscles of the hands and elbows contract simultaneously. When riding downward transitions, this contraction should be held for a few seconds only and, as soon as the horse reacts, the arms and hands should go back to relaxed neutrality. For half-halts, block the elbows in the above manner for a few seconds, then yield again.

When using co-contraction (bracing) of the arms, the hands should 'sponge' simultaneously to keep the flexion of the head and neck. Pulling back with both hands will cause resistance, hollowness of outline and throwing up of the head.

The 'long arm' technique. As previously mentioned, the rein is an extension of the rider's arm. If our arms were long enough, we would be guiding the horse with our fingers on the bit.

The 'long arm' technique is our main controller

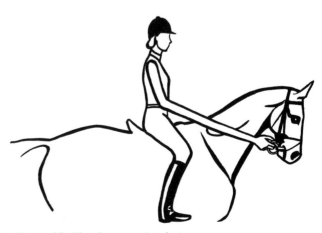

Figure 83 The 'long arm' technique.

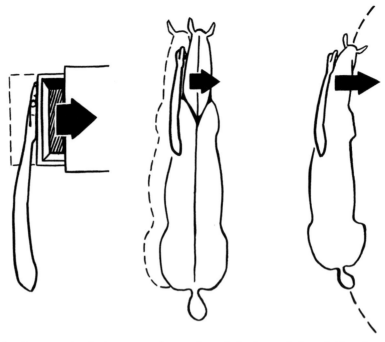

Figure 84 Using the 'long arm' technique to push a cupboard, the horse in leg-yield and on a circle, sideways.

of the horse's shoulder and is used for lateral movements, turns, serpentines, leg-yielding and pirouettes. Imagine that the whole rein up to the bit is your arm, with two fingers holding the bit. To facilitate lateral movement you would move your whole arm, hand and fingers inwards. This will move the horse's shoulder, as well as his neck and head, sideways. This is done in the same way as pushing a small cupboard sideways with your whole arm.

For leg-yielding you should use this 'long arm' aid on the outside rein, together with opening and closing of the inside rein. For half-pass and circles you use the 'long arm' technique on the outside whilst 'sponging' the rein on the inside, to ensure inside bend.

Contact on the outside rein. Quiet, light contact is kept on the outside rein, and may support the horse's balance mechanisms for short periods only.

Reward. The hands can be used to denote reward by relaxing in between the aids. As soon as the horse has responded to an aid, the hands should yield to the neutral position. This will become an automatic reward for the horse.

THE LEGS

The leg aids are our main aids for the facilitation of movement through their effect on the horse's righting and balance (postural) reactions. They have a direct effect on the horse's hind legs ('engine') and body (balance). The legs are used in the following ways:

1) A light tap or touch with the lower leg, for forward action.

2) A light 'push' with the lower leg for creating inside bend.

3) The 'push-through and let go' with the whole leg and hip, for lateral weight displacement of the ribcage or hindquarters.

4) The 'hold' with the knees or the whole leg, depending on the level of training, for downward transitions and half-halts.

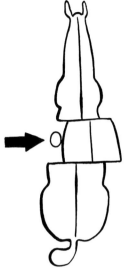

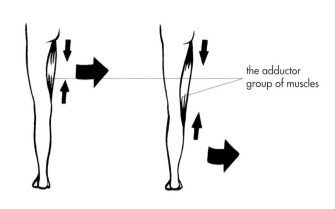

the adductor
group of muscles

*Figure 85 The 'push through'
technique.*

*Figure 86 The thigh, as well as the lower leg, is moved sideways by the same
group of muscles – the leg adductors.*

The rider mainly uses one group of muscles for all these aids; the adductor group on the inside of the thigh. These muscles are responsible for moving the thighs, as well as the lower legs, inwards. The calf muscles merely control the position of the rider's feet and toes.

ROLES OF THE INSIDE AND OUTSIDE LEGS

The inside leg, on the girth, is often referred to as a pivot around which the horse should bend. This is not entirely logical, as a pivot should be a fixed object and the leg is a movable object. What is in fact happening is that the leg pushes the ribcage over, thus eliciting a balance reaction in the horse, as described in Chapter 1.

The inside leg is used mainly on the girth to create the inside bend, forward action and downward transitions. The outside leg is used either on the girth for forward action and downward transitions or behind the girth for lateral displacement of the hindquarters and the aid to canter. The outside leg behind the girth has a second function of preventing the hindquarters from swinging out as a result of the righting reaction, which attempts to keep the body in alignment. As soon as the aid is given, the legs should go back to the neutral position and hang relaxed against the horse's sides.

THE SEAT AND BACK

THE SEAT

The seat is used mainly for engaging the hindquarters and, together with the whole leg, to produce lateral movements.

To develop a deep seat, the seat muscles and adductor muscles should be relaxed and all the weight of the rider should relax into the seat. The pelvis should move with the horse and tilt with every stride.

Engaging the hindquarters
When we talk about using the seat, we are in fact, referring to the gluteal muscles of the seat. The normal function of these muscles is to straighten a person's hips: they are the main muscles of support when standing. They can, however, be used isometrically. As an aid, we contract them isometrically (contract them without straightening the hip) to encourage movement of the hindquarters. Contract the gluteals bilaterally (together) for trotting or downward transitions and contract unilaterally (alternately) for walk.

A novice rider will have difficulty contracting these muscles individually. To practise this, stand initially on both feet. Then straighten one knee and

Figure 87 Use the seat by contracting the gluteal muscles.

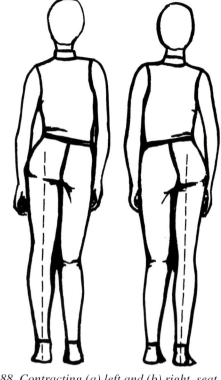

Figure 88 Contracting (a) left and (b) right, seat muscles.

Figure 89 Contract the abdominal and seat muscles to tilt the pelvis backwards.

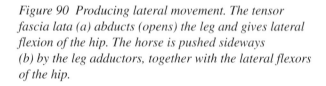

Figure 90 Producing lateral movement. The tensor fascia lata (a) abducts (opens) the leg and gives lateral flexion of the hip. The horse is pushed sideways (b) by the leg adductors, together with the lateral flexors of the hip.

(a)

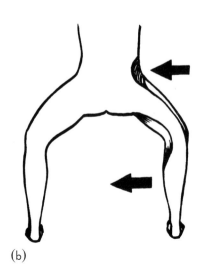

(b)

hip by contracting the gluteals, whilst allowing the other knee to bend slightly. Next, straighten the other hip and knee with the same method. Practise this until you have no difficulty in doing it. Once you have mastered this muscle action, you may utilise it on your horse.

When more forward pressure is required, the gluteals and tops of the hamstrings contract, together with the abdominal muscles, to give a feeling of pushing the horse forwards with the seat. This has the effect of tilting the pelvis backwards and straightening the lumbar curve of the spine.

Producing lateral movement

When moving the horse sideways, the whole leg as well as the hip should be used to push the horse over. The muscle responsible for this lateral push of the hip is called the tensor fascia lata.

THE BACK

The back is used in a bracing effect when riding half-halts and halts or downward transitions. When we brace our backs we co-contract all the back and abdominal muscles to form a strong tube. In downward transitions, the back is used mainly for redistribution of weight, with the rider leaning back slightly.

WEIGHT EFFECTS

Using the weight can be a difficult concept for a novice rider, but all it means is a repositioning of the body. For example, leaning back puts more weight on the hindquarters. A horse can feel every little movement of the rider and automatically adjusts his weight accordingly. He soon learns, through the rider's reward, which movements are meaningful and which are merely balance adjustments on the rider's part. We call this foreground background perception. The horse keeps the meaningful weight changes in the foreground, whilst moving odd weight changes to the background of his perception. Some anxious horses tend to confuse this perception and will react to all weight changes of the rider. Such horses may have

difficulty in learning flying changes, as the weight change makes them anxious.

To understand this concept, put a young child on your back and feel what the weight change does to your body.

Weight changes are one of our main communicating aids with the horse. They affect the horse's balance mechanism, thus impelling him to react by adjusting his balance (balance reaction). Weight changes are achieved either by the contraction of specific muscle groups (such as the gluteals, as described) or by moving the position of the body (for example, leaning back).

Specific weight effects can be produced as follows:

Halt. Moving the upper body back slightly will bring more weight over the hindquarters.

Rein-back. Lighten the seat by leaning forward slightly, flexing the hips and contracting the lower back muscles. This frees the hindquarters.

Moving forwards. Contract the gluteals. This puts more weight in the seat.

To collect. Contract the gluteals, putting more weight in the seat.

For lateral movements and canter. Weight to the inside: lift the outside hip slightly, which will cause the inside hip to 'drop' and put more weight on the inside leg.

The more the legs, seat and weight aids are used, the less work the hands will have to do.

FEEL – THE PROPRIOCEPTIVE AND KINESTHETIC SENSE

The proprioceptive and kinesthetic senses allow both horse and rider to know where their own limbs are at any moment: it is their main sense of balance. The nerve bodies responsible for these senses are situated in the inner ear and in all the joints and muscle endings. Whenever any joint or limb moves or is moved, these bodies are stimulated, and perceive exactly where that particular body part is in relation to the rest of the body. This can be observed in the horse when walking over an obstacle: the horse cannot see his hind legs, but knows exactly when to pick them up to avoid bumping into the object. (This same sense will tell a person where their arms are, even when their eyes are closed.) The bodies in the inner ear tell the horse where his head is at any moment, and in which direction his head is moving. These little bodies are also important for communicating to the horse when he is off balance.

These senses are especially highly developed in the horse, who will perceive all vibrations – thunder, earthquakes, hoofbeats, etc. before humans can perceive them.

Let us examine how proprioceptive and kinesthetic senses in both horse and rider can be used beneficially in riding and training.

IMPROVING THE RIDER'S 'FEEL'

'Feel' is one of the most important attributes a rider can possess: only with good 'feel' can a rider become a great rider. It gives the rider the ability to evaluate what the horse is doing and anticipate what he is about to do. The rider can feel the slightest possibility of incipient stiffness, loss of balance, etc. and make a pre-emptive correction. Furthermore, it is only a rider who has learnt to feel the reaction of the horse who can consistently ask for the same reaction and expect the same result. This quality is not dependent on magic, but arises from the rider's proprioceptive sense. It is the duty of all riders to develop this sense.

The following are examples of how our proprioceptive sense will help us to communicate with the horse:

1) When a rider decides to canter in a given direction and looks in that direction, their body will make an automatic adjustment as a result of the proprioceptive sense. Their shoulders will follow the movement, their hips will turn slightly (righting reaction) and this will influence the leg position slightly. All this will change the rider's weight distribution which, in turn, the horse will pick up with his own proprioceptive sense and thus prepare himself to canter in the direction required.

2) When schooling without a mirror, the rider learns to feel the correct position and angle of the horse in half-pass, and also learns to feel when the horse's quarters are leading.

Figure 91 The effect (righting reaction) of turning the head to the left.

3) The rider's proprioceptive sense can help in anticipating the horse's frame of mind. Relaxation or anxiety can easily be felt and then dealt with as appropriate. 'Contact' is entirely dependent on the rider's proprioceptive sense. The rider can feel, through hands, legs and seat, the exact state of the horse's muscles. The 'magic' communication that a horse and rider develop after many years of training is a result of this

proprioceptive sense. When the rider thinks 'canter left' the horse knows immediately what to do because the rider's thoughts lead to automatic muscular adjustments, which the horse learns to recognise.

The following suggestions may help in cultivating this 'feel':

1) Close your eyes or look up and away from your horse. Try to feel, through your hands and arms, what the horse is doing with his head and neck; try to feel before he lifts them, and correct it before it happens. (This exercise is especially effective if the trainer leads the horse, to give the rider a longer time to ride with closed eyes.)

2) Be constantly aware of the effect of an aid or any change in the horse.

3) Try to feel on which diagonal you are rising; which leg the horse is leading on in canter; which of the horse's legs is moving forward at a particular time. For example, while the horse is walking, lift your knees up and sit on your seatbones. Feel the hind legs move, one by one, with the horse's walk, and feel which leg is forward.

4) When halting square, feel how high the horse's back lifts underneath the saddle If it is too high, then he has one hind foot too far forward and is not square.

5) In canter your leg and hip will move slightly forwards on the side of the horse's leading leg – try to feel this.

6) Practise discerning the 'feel' of softness the horse gives through the hands.

IMPROVING THE HORSE'S MOVEMENT

We can make use of the horse's own proprioceptive senses to improve his movement. An example would be teaching him to halt square. Rewarding him for a square halt will soon make him associate the squareness with the reward, for he will know when he is square through proprioception. Similarly, when schooling over trotting poles, cavalletti or fences we can teach the horse to lift his legs higher. When learning lateral work, such as half-pass, the horse will eventually know exactly what angle and position are required. He will rely more on his proprioceptive sense and less on the precise guidance of the aids.

THE OTHER SENSES

The horse's skin
The tactile sense of the horse is situated in the skin. We use the tactile sense mainly for reward and for the effect of the bit and the leg aids. As we have seen, stroking and tickling are perceived as pleasant sensations by the horse and are therefore important aids in training.

Squeezing on the reins causes sensations on the corners of the horse's mouth, which are perceived through the tactile sense. The horse soon learns to differentiate between the different sensations of the rein aids.

The leg aids create pressure on the skin and thus stimulate the horse's tactile sense. The different kinds of sensations on his skin (light touch or deep pressure) are remembered and are used, together with his other senses, to remember the aids.

Smell and taste
The horse has a fairly primitive brain which is more dependent on sensory information than is the case with the highly developed human brain (cortex). The most important senses, for the purposes of training, have already been discussed. For the rider, the horse's sense of taste is only important in establishing which titbits are most effective as a reward for hard work!

The horse's sense of smell is, however, very highly developed. This can be observed when a new object is put in his way. He will approach it gingerly and will not be satisfied as to its safety until he has smelt it. He will also want to smell strange water before crossing. He can smell home from miles away. A horse will not voluntarily eat anything that may be bad for him. He doesn't taste it first however, but sniffs it before eating. In our training, we should remember to allow the horse to use his sense of smell to put him at ease in new situations – this can be an important factor, and is one which is often overlooked.

A sense of humour

All trainers should cultivate a sense of humour! This gives us more patience and perspective when training the horse. It counteracts the frustration we often feel when things aren't going as planned.

PART THREE

THEORY INTO PRACTICE

CHAPTER 8

ACQUIRING THE CORRECT
SEAT AND POSTURE

The classical posture is the most effective for the rider as it puts the body and legs in the best position to have an effect on the balance and righting reactions of the horse and thus facilitate movement. The precise position of the rider changes continually as the legs and seat have a 'conversation' with the horse: the rider has to change position when eliciting different righting and balance reactions and the seat canot be entirely static as it is continually adjusting to stay balanced upon a moving object.

Slight variations of posture may occur as a result of a rider's natural physique. We do not all possess the perfect body or posture for riding. This should not, however, prevent us from becoming good riders. Although riders' postures are not always attractive, the horse has excellent balance mechanisms and can adjust with ease to slight deviations of a rider from perfect posture. Generally speaking, a rider's weight will be approximately 10 per cent of the horse's weight. The demands upon a horse carrying this weight can be compared to a human (in a crawling position) carrying a baby of approximately 5-7 kg – a simple enough task.

THE HIPS AND LEGS

The correct position of the legs is important for eliciting the desired reaction from the horse, for example legs on the ribcage for pushing it sideways to create inside bend, or further back to move the hindquarters sideways. Novice riders are inclined to use their legs a little too far back when first attempting lateral work. This is the result of inadequately developed co-ordination or muscle strength, which renders them ineffective. Time and experience will, however, improve their position. (Novice horses who have not yet associated the aid with the action may need the lateral aids slightly further back until their reactions become quicker.) The easiest way of acquiring the correct position of the hips and legs is by taking one or both legs off the saddle, in a sideways direction, rotating the hips inwards and then putting the legs back against the horse. This creates a perfect seat with three-point pressure on the saddle from the pubic bone and the two seatbones (ischial tuberosities).

The inward rotation of the hips automatically turns the toes more or less parallel to the horse's sides. The legs then hang down in the classical shoulder-hip-heel alignment and should rest like wet rags around the horse's body. The knees should not grip, but relax and 'breathe' with the horse.

In the early stages of training the toes should not be lifted as this causes flexion in the knee and hip, with the result that the leg is pulled up. This is because the body works in patterns of movement, with groups of muscles working together, and it takes practice, co-ordination and time to break a pattern of movement. (An example of a pattern of movement is the walk action. The toe lifts, the heel flexes, the knee bends and the hip flexes when picking up the leg to take a step.) Therefore, the foot should be relaxed and the weight of the relaxed leg on the stirrup should create the flexion required in the ankle. Once the pattern of movement is broken through practice and relaxation of the rider, it is possible to lift the toe without disturbing the relaxed leg.

Figure 92   Lift the leg sideways and rotate the whole leg inwards to achieve the correct leg position.

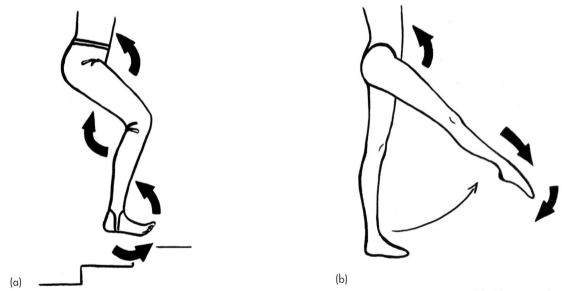

(a)

(b)

Figure 93 Two patterns of movement.   (a) The walk pattern of knee, hip and ankle flexion.   (b) The toe-pointing pattern of knee and ankle extension.

THE SEAT AND WAIST

The most important function of the rider's posture is to allow the rider to remain in balance and feel all the reactions of the horse. Good balance is the backbone of an independent seat and independent aids. Any tension created in the process of re-

maining in balance can cause loss of balance in the horse, and tension in his neck and mouth. This will adversely effect communication between horse and rider. An independent seat is one which allows the rider's hands and legs to be used without causing associated movements in other parts of the body. For example, when using one leg only, the other leg should not react at all, or should be able to do a completely different movement: or, when trying to maintain balance, the arms should not go into co-contraction and pull on the reins. The independent seat allows the arms and legs to be free to get on with the job of 'feeling' (listening) and communicating (replying).

Relaxation of the rider is essential, as balance is not possible without it. The contraction of muscles causes a change in weight distribution, which the horse has to counteract by changing his centre of gravity. Although, as mentioned above, the horse's balance mechanisms allow him to accommodate a less-than-perfect rider posture, he can still feel the slightest unwarranted weight change and may understand it as an aid, which can lead to confusion.

The rider, while totally relaxed, should be ready to react immediately when necessary, and then relax again.

The rider's seat should be completely relaxed so that it virtually becomes part of the horse. A deep seat is a relaxed seat. Try to make your seat feel like a 'bowl of jelly', flowing over the sides of the saddle. When your seat is completely relaxed you can feel your seatbones press into the saddle. It should feel as though your seat is stuck to the saddle. The pelvis should move with the horse at all times, tilting forward and backwards, and the lumbar vertebrae should become very mobile. This is only possible if your waist is totally relaxed to absorb all the movement. The best way to develop a deep seat is to start at walk. Move your legs sideways away from the saddle so that you are balancing on your seat alone. Take note of the feel of your seat in the saddle – this will give you a good indication of the feeling of a deep seat, with your full weight in the saddle and not on your legs.

The waist should be completely relaxed to allow the movement of the horse to be absorbed. This means that the waist will move forwards and back with every stride.

THE UPPER BODY

The upper body should be upright and the

shoulders straight. (If you have naturally rounded shoulders, an orthopaedic shoulder brace is of great value.)

The chin and neck should be pushed back onto the spine. The back of the neck will then become elongated by the stretching of the back muscles and the spine will be stretched up.

THE ARMS AND HANDS

These are the most important parts of the body for the purpose of training. Correctly used, they can produce total relaxation in the horse but, used incorrectly, they create most of the rider's problems.

The most important point concerning the rider's arms and hands is that they should be completely relaxed. Imagine what it would feel like to have a bit in your mouth with a tense arm attached to the other end: you would be in agony! The worst instruction a rider can be given is 'keep your hands still'. This creates co-contraction of all the muscles of the arm and a 'lead pipe' limb which causes discomfort in the horse's mouth. This, in turn, creates tension and evasive action in the horse.

The best phrase the trainer can use is 'relax your elbows'. Very often the rider's elbows are actively flexed and this, once again, creates tension. The arms should hang down naturally from the shoulders, the joints of which should be relaxed to allow the arms to move forwards and back with the movement of the horse's head and neck. The biceps should be relaxed so that the elbow can open and close with the movement of the horse's head and neck. The easiest way to feel this opening and closing of the elbow is by pressing your knuckles into the horse's wither whilst rising to the trot.

Each forearm should be rotated outward to mid position, which will bring the thumb uppermost. This position allows the wrist more freedom to flex when communicating with the horse's mouth. This movement will stimulate the contraction of the lateral flexors of the horse's neck. Flexion of the wrist in an inward rotated position will pull the reins down and lead to the elbows moving away from the rider's sides.

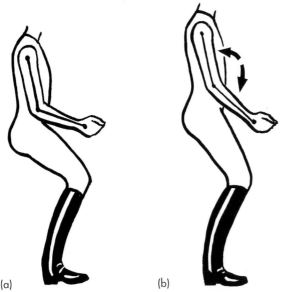

Figure 96 The hands hold the reins gently as if holding two small hamsters. You avoid hurting the creatures, but do not allow them to wriggle away either.

Figure 94 During the rising trot the hands maintain the same relative position to the horse's neck, while the elbows open and close. Sitting phase (a) and rising phase (b).

Figure 95 When the rider's hands are turned inward and the reins are 'sponged', the elbows will move away from the body.

The grip on the reins should be a relaxed one, like holding a small creature in each hand. All the muscles for finger flexion and extension are situated in the forearm. Contraction of these muscles will therefore lead to stiff elbows. The thumbs should not press into the reins but lie,

relaxed, on the reins. Any tension in the hands will cause tension in the horse's mouth.

The range of movements of the arms and hands should be from stretching the whole arm forwards when the horse's neck is extended, through some 'sponging' with the fingers or wrists, to slight backward movement of the upper arm when necessary.

In conclusion, the lower body, seat and legs virtually become part of the horse's body. The hands and arms become part of the horse's mouth. The back is used as a support base for the arms and legs in downward transitions and lateral movements. The upper body 'belongs to the rider'.

EQUIPMENT TO ASSIST THE RIDER

Dressage, whether for training purposes or competition, is probably one of the most difficult and skilful of sports. Not only does one have to contend with one's own co-ordination and balance, one also has to keep the horse co-ordinated and balanced at all times, whilst considering his own temperament and attitudes. Attention to correct equipment may make life a little easier for the rider.

THE SADDLE

The saddle has a definite effect on the rider's position. It can put the legs too far forward, too far back, or in the correct place. The stirrup leathers should be in a position that will allow the rider's legs to hang down to give the vertical seat – heel alignment required effortlessly. If a rider has to use effort to retain a correct leg position, then the saddle is probably incorrect for the horse/rider combination, or for the purpose of the moment. Also, the saddle should sit on the horse in such a way that is does not tilt the rider's body backwards or forwards. The rider's seat should fit snugly to ensure that as little energy as possible is required to maintain balance in the saddle.

Full leather-seat breeches

Because the body's muscles continuously and automatically adjust to maintain balance, energy is used to maintain balance in the saddle. Novice riders do not immediately possess much muscular energy and therefore tire quite rapidly, especially when sitting to the trot. Full leather-seat breeches have a slight grip on a leather saddle, and this helps the rider to stay in the saddle without wasting too much energy. The rider thus has one less problem to contend with.

THE REINS

The reins should be firm – preferably pimple rubber reins. Soft reins do not create a direct line of communication with the horse. As the reins are an extension of the rider's arms, they should resemble the arms as far as possible. This will lead to more effective rein aids.

Sundry equipment to assist rein aids

Leather gloves not only prevent blisters, they also give the hands a better grip on the reins. This will prevent the tight grip with the fingers and hands which causes tension in the horse's mouth.

The whip should have a knob to prevent it from slipping out of the rider's hand, thus leaving the hands free for the purpose of communication.

Moleskin plaster. From time to time a rider may experience blisters, especially after a break from riding. This form of plaster is very effective against skin chafes or blisters. It will stay on for a few days until the area is healed.

ORTHOPAEDIC BRACES

Shoulder brace

An orthopaedic shoulder brace is of enormous benefit to those unfortunate riders burdened with rounded shoulders. It will straighten the shoulders and leave the rider more energy and one less task to concentrate on – free to get on with the training of the horse. The shoulder brace will stretch the contracted pectoral muscles which are the cause of rounded shoulders, until the rider can eventually sit on a horse or walk with straight shoulders without the use of the brace.

Back brace

Riding can often lead to back problems. An orthopaedic back brace, made from rubber material, helps to support the abdominal muscles and, in so doing, protects the lower back. The effect can be compared to a balloon; blown up it is firm, but without air it becomes limp.

RUNNING REINS – CAUTION AND ADVICE

These are being discussed here for the specific reason that, used incorrectly, they can destroy a horse, yet they are used all over the world at an increasing rate. Because of the damage they can do, very few books discuss the use of running reins. Riders are usually advised not to use them unless they know how to do so correctly, but they cannot learn the correct use unless taught how.

Running reins should never be used to get the horse 'on the bit'. This can be done very easily without their help, as explained in Chapter 4. Legitimate uses are:

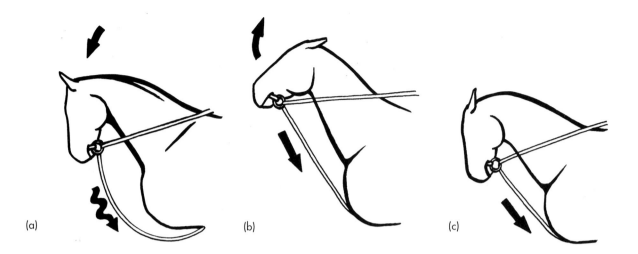

Figure 97(a) Correct method of using running reins. They should fit loosely. (b) The horse throws his head up and feels the pressure of the running reins. (c) Incorrect: the running reins should never be tight when the horse is on the bit.

Teaching the horse not to throw his head up and down. When the horse is in the required rounded frame, the running reins should hang loose and have no pressure on the horse whatsoever. As soon as the horse throws his head up, the running reins will become tight; he will feel pressure on the bit and will then drop his head to a position where the reins have no effect (see Figure 97 (a) and (b)).
The horse should never be ridden in tight running reins (Figure 97 (c)). Except for the few seconds when he is throwing his head up there should be no contact on the running reins.

Teaching the horse to yield to the hands. With completely loose running reins fitted, ask the horse, with the ordinary rein only, to yield to the hand by flexing his neck. If all the methods to encourage the horse to do this (as described in Chapter 4) should fail, the running reins may be used for a short period (a few minutes). 'Sponge' one rein and,

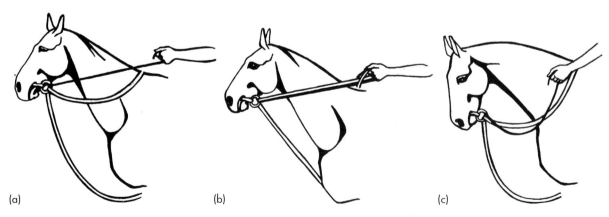

Figure 98(a) The horse resisting the rein aid. (b) Use the running reins together with the normal reins, to ask the horse to yield to the hand and not resist. (c) The horse yields to the reins, is rewarded, and the running reins are released.

if the horse does not yield, pick up the running rein on one side and use it, together with the normal rein, to explain to the horse that he should flex his neck. As soon as he yields, the running rein should be dropped and the horse rewarded with a tickle. Repeat this process of asking for the flexion with the normal rein and, if it alone is not effective, add the running rein. If you are not successful within ten minutes, you are probably not performing the exercise correctly and will have to ask for assistance from a trainer with experience in the correct use of running reins.

As soon as the horse understands the idea of yielding to the hands, the running rein should be removed permanently. *This concept should not take more than one schooling session to teach the horse.*

As a safety measure if riding out on a strong, keen horse who tends to put his head in the air and run off. The running rein should lie on the horse's neck for the duration of the ride, unless he becomes too difficult to stop when cantering. If this should happen, pick up the running reins and use them, together with the normal reins, to stop the horse. Once the horse has slowed down, the running reins should once again be placed on the horse's neck to render them ineffective.

CHAPTER 9

THE WALK AND ITS

EXERCISES

The walk is a distinct, four-beat movement. It produces little mechanical impulsion and is the most difficult gait in which to keep strong forward movement. For this reason, collected walk should only be taught to an Advanced horse once this strong forward urge has been developed.

The sequence of steps is as follows:

1) Right hind foot.

2) Right forefoot.

3) Left hind foot.

4) Left forefoot.

(Or, in the same sequence, beginning with the left hind.)

When this four-beat rhythm is lost, the walk turns into 'pacing' – which is a grave error. When a horse paces, his hind and forelegs on the same side are put down simultaneously.

THE GAIT VARIANTS

Four forms of walk are recognised in dressage:

Medium walk. This is the walk mainly used for teaching new movements to both horse and rider. (It is important for novice riders to practise the co-ordination of their leg aids for turns, serpentines and lateral work at medium walk before they attempt such movements at faster gaits.) Medium walk is a free, regular and unconstrained walk with moderate extension. The hind feet touch the ground in front of the footprints of the forefeet.

Extended walk. The horse covers as much ground as possible, without haste. The hind feet touch the ground clearly in front of the footprints of the forefeet. In the extended walk, the horse is 'on the bit', but is asked to stretch out his head and neck. This allows the shoulders more freedom.

Collected walk. This form of walk is only used in Advanced dressage. Each step covers less ground and is higher than at the medium walk, because all the joints bend more markedly. The hind legs should be engaged, with good hock action. The hind feet touch the ground behind, or at most, in the footprints of the forefeet (although short backed, long limbed horses will still overtrack). This walk should show more activity than the medium walk. The head and neck are raised and arched, and the head approaches the vertical position. The contact with the mouth remains light.

Free walk. The horse is allowed to stretch out 'long and deep'; the movement is slow but forward; the steps are long. This form of walk is used with young horses on hacks and with all horses at the beginning, middle and end of the schooling session.

With young horses, the free walk is used to develop a long, slow, deep and forward stride. At the beginning of the schooling session, just after a horse has come out of the stable, he is often slightly stiff. The free walk will help to loosen him up before the start of more strenuous work. In the middle of the schooling session, it is used to relax and rest both horse and rider. At the end of a schooling session the horse will want to stretch the flexor muscles below his neck, as well as the extensors above his neck, which have been contracting isometrically against the effect of gravity. Stretching downward eases the effect of gravity on these muscles (see Figure 41, page 26).

THE AIDS FOR WALK

The walk aid is the first aid we teach the horse. It is usually reasonably well established by the time the mounted work begins, as it has been practised on the lunge. Here the horse is taught the verbal command for walk and this is thus available for use under saddle.

1) To initiate the walk, both legs are used on the girth to produce forward action.

2) As soon as the horse starts to walk, the rider's legs are used alternately. This activates the hind legs to move individually and energetically. The rider usually has an instinctive feeling for the timing of these aids.

3) The rider's seat muscles (gluteals) are contracted individually to engage the hindquarters and to encourage a longer, slower stride.

4) 'Sponging' with the hands as necessary keeps the horse 'on the bit'.

TEACHING THE YOUNG HORSE

1) The hands and arms should be neutral and relaxed, with a loose rein.

2) The lower legs, with open knees, give the forward signal.

3) Simultaneously, the verbal command that has been taught on the lunge, is given; 'walk'.

4) As soon as even one step is given, reward the horse.

5) Once the horse is walking forward freely, the rider's legs may be used alternately to create more energy, but not to the extent of 'chasing' the horse along.

6) As soon as the young horse understands these aids (approximately three schooling sessions for novice riders, less for experienced riders), the seat aids can be used simultaneously with the leg aids.

7) Eventually, only the seat aids may be necessary – although the legs will be needed from time to time to produce more energy.

TROUBLESHOOTING – problems in walk

PACING
This is the result of the forelegs moving faster than the hind legs. The horse moves his forefoot forward too soon and puts it down more or less at the same time as the hind foot on the same side. This is usually caused by tension, anticipation of the movement to come, or by the horse being pushed forwards too much ('chased') in the walk.

Corrections

a) The fundamental correction is to relax the horse as described in Chapter 1.
b) Slow down, but do not block, the movement of the forehand. Push the horse forward with alternate hip aids rather than the legs, and set a slower rhythm. This will lengthen the stride.
c) Practise walk mainly in shoulder-in and travers positions. This prevents pacing.
d) Disturb the horse's balance by putting more weight over one of his hips (lean over slightly). This makes him reorganise himself.

SHUFFLING AND TENSE, HURRIED STRIDES
The horse gives short, shuffling strides, usually as a result of anxiety or blocking of his shoulders.

Corrections

a) Push him forwards with alternate hip aids instead of alternate leg aids.
b) Ensure that he is relaxed in the mouth and neck and is allowed to stretch forward to encourage

freedom of the shoulders.

c) Ride a few half-halts followed by 'sponging' of the reins to ensure a light contact during the collected walk.

d) Relax your seat.

HEAD AND NECK NOT STRETCHING ENOUGH IN THE FREE AND EXTENDED WALKS

This could be caused by tension or by the anatomical structure of the horse (tight nuchal funicular).

Corrections

a) Relax the horse.

b) Stretch the nuchal funicular through the use of the horse's neck flexors: ask him for flexion and a 'long and deep' frame.

THE HALT

For safety's sake, the halt is taught after the walk – it is very comforting to know that you can stop your young horse before you disappear into the sunset!

The halt should be square and balanced. Some horses always try to keep their centre of balance over their four feet, and will halt square from an early age. Many others, however, will only manage a square halt once they are truly engaged, in balance and collected. These horses have to be ridden into a square halt every time a halt is requested.

THE AIDS FOR HALT

1) Keep the horse's jaw and neck relaxed by 'sponging' the reins.

2) Close your knees to block the shoulder action.

3) Contract your seat muscles (gluteals) to engage the hindquarters.

4) Close your lower legs to engage the hindquarters.

5) Co-contract the elbows to 'catch' the forward action while maintaining the alternate 'sponging' of the reins to keep the rounded outline.

6) Brace your back slightly to help the arms give the blocking feeling. The horse will feel that he should slow down.

7) Relax the aids to complete the halt, as a reward and to relax the horse.

The blocking action of the knees

To understand the blocking action of the knees, refer to Exercise 8 in Chapter 1. Essentially, this uses a righting reaction (you blocked the waist and therefore the upper body and legs followed suit) to signal the halt. This exercise indicates precisely why the closure of your knees will block the horse's shoulders.

The whole leg may also be used for this movement if you need more forward action in the downward transition, but nervous horses – Thoroughbreds and many others – may become confused with the use of the lower leg for forward as well as halt movements. Using the knees for the initial aid to the downward transition is completely clear to all horses since it has the effect of blocking the shoulder action. It is one reason why the old-fashioned method of riding – holding on with the knees – has been abandoned.

TEACHING THE YOUNG HORSE

At walk, close your knees on the girth with a reasonable amount of pressure (as you would have done in the experiment above), but apply no pressure with your lower legs. At the same time, block your elbows in co-contraction and brace your back slightly. You may need to increase the rein contact a little the first few times.

When the horse halts, reward immediately by releasing the aids and tickling his neck. Repeat the process: you will find that the horse understands this very quickly and, after three or four attempts, will halt on the action of your knees alone.

PROGRESSION

Once the horse is schooled to the extent that he has become balanced, rhythmical, forward and supple and can walk, trot and canter on light aids, the square halt may be practised with the use of the aids as previously described. However, until the horse is collected, you may have to be satisfied with squareness in front and not complete squareness behind. At this stage this is acceptable so long as the halt is balanced. Better collection, balance and engagement will eventually lead to a square halt.

Note that it can be detrimental to tap the horse with a leg if the halt is not square. This may lead to shuffling at the halt. It is much safer to bring the horse into a square halt with the above aids and reward him for squareness.

TROUBLESHOOTING – problems with halting

THE HORSE HOLLOWING HIS OUTLINE INTO THE HALT

The most likely cause of this problem is that the rider has pulled back on the reins with both hands together. Pulling the horse in this way will always lead to a tug of war: the horse will always resist two hands pulling simultaneously.

Correction

Soften the jaw and neck with alternate 'sponging' of the reins and use more knee action to halt the horse.

HALT NOT SQUARE

The horse is either not in balance or not collected enough.

Correction

With the rein aids, ask for increasingly shorter steps into the halt while slowly pushing the hindquarters forward with your legs. Repeat the halt until the horse is balanced. Do not tap him whilst halting as this could lead to a habit of moving a leg after halting.

HORSE NOT IMMOBILE

The horse has probably been 'tapped up' to halt square. Alternatively, he could be a nervous horse who wants to go home.

Corrections

a) Repeat the halt process many times until the horse accepts immobility. Reward copiously when correct.

b) Halt facing away from home and insist that the horse waits. Once he will maintain the halt facing away from home, repeat the exercise facing towards home.

HALT NOT STRAIGHT

This could be caused by lack of engagement, or it could be a habit to halt with the hindquarters to one side.

Corrections

a) Strengthen the hindquarters with many transitions.

b) Ascertain to which side the horse prefers to move his hindquarters, and keep your leg on that side firmly behind the girth.

THE HALF-HALT

Having dealt with the full halt, now seems an appropriate moment at which to discuss the half-halt. Before proceeding, it should be emphasised that both the full halt and the half-halt have functions which transcend the gaits. The full halt, introduced from walk, will eventually be ridden directly from trot and canter and, in a similar way, the half-halt will be employed in different ways and to different degrees to improve the quality of all the gaits. While a rider with good 'feel' may employ the half-halt almost subconsciously in a variety of situations, the basic concept is most readily taught to a young horse in trot.

A half-halt is a momentary reduction in forward movement, together with an increase of energy. It is also a tool of communication, a balancing aid and warning system. It says to the horse 'listen, we are going to do another movement'. Through the centuries, different trainers have had various interpretations of the half-halt, all of which are of value to the rider. Together with shoulder-in, it forms the 'backbone' of training.

PURPOSE AND FUNCTIONS OF THE HALF-HALT

There are three main variations of the half-halt, which have slightly different functions:

The balancing half-halt is used to reduce speed when the horse is rushing, to balance the horse when going downhill or changing direction and to warn the horse that some change is about to take place.

The impulsion-increasing half-halt helps to establish rhythm and speed. It activates the horse and increases impulsion and balance before a specialised movement such as extended trot, half-pass, canter pirouette, piaffe, passage, etc. It does this by improving the engagement and elevation of the hindquarters and thus lightening the forehand and encouraging self-carriage.

The half-halt to raise the head and neck. The term half-halt is often used for the upward movement of the hand and forearm to lift the horse's head and neck when he carries it too low as an evasion, or when he is behind the vertical and evading the contact.

HOW TO RIDE A HALF-HALT

THE BALANCING HALF-HALT

1) Relax the head and neck by 'sponging' the reins.

2) Close your knees on the horse to block the shoulder action.

3) Release immediately when the horse reacts with a hesitation.

4) Apply the lower leg to give a forward aid to prevent the horse from coming to a halt.

5) 'Catch' the energy produced in slightly restraining hands.

THE IMPULSION-INCREASING HALF-HALT

This half-halt can only be effective if the horse has learnt to surge forwards from a light touch of the lower leg. The horse should already be moving forward freely with impulsion.

1) Relax the jaw and neck by 'sponging' the reins.

2) 'Pick the horse up' with the whole leg and seat (like picking up a barrel between your legs – see Figure 99).

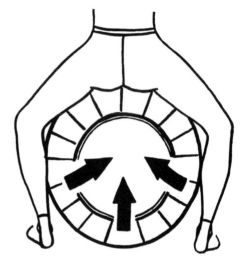

Figure 99 The feeling of picking up a barrel with your leg and seat muscles.

3) Block the elbows slightly and hold the reins without allowing the horse's neck muscles to go into co-contraction. Do not pull back, or the horse will resist. The forward surge from the leg aid will then be 'caught' in the hands and will produce more elevation and more engagement.

4) As soon as the horse responds, the hands should yield again.

THE HALF-HALT TO RAISE THE HEAD AND NECK

An upward movement of the outside hand and arm will lift the horse's head and neck immediately. As soon as the required response is achieved, the hand should go into the neutral position again. This is usually a quick (but not jabbing) movement and it is unnecessary to hold the head in this position.

The same effect can be achieved with a little slap, with both legs, on the girth.

Teaching the young horse

1) Teach the halt first.

2) At trot, bring the horse nearly to a halt with the halt aids and then push him forwards into an energetic trot again.

3) Yield the hand as soon as the horse hesitates, or he will resist the hand.

This is the basis of the half-halt: it is a 'check and drive' action. Eventually, it can be refined to a momentary action and there will be no noticeable change in rhythm.

THE REIN-BACK

The rein-back is a slow movement backwards. The horse's feet are raised and set down almost simultaneously by diagonal pairs. (Each forefoot is raised and set down almost imperceptibly before the diagonally opposite hind foot.)

THE PURPOSE OF REIN-BACK

The rein-back is a supplying and co-ordinating exercise for advanced horses. It is also an exercise which produces submission. If a horse is rushing forwards and out of your control, he can be halted and reined back to explain to him that you are requiring less forward action. It is often used as a punishment, but this can bring negative connotations and anxiety to the movement. A school movement should never be used as a punishment.

THE AIDS FOR REIN-BACK

1) 'Sponge' the reins alternately to maintain a light contact and relaxed jaw and neck.

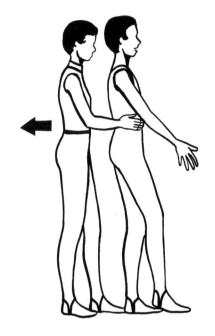

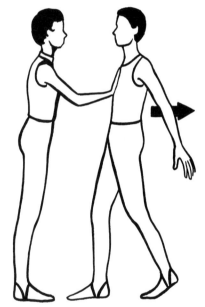

Figure 100(a) and (b) Disturbing a person's balance to facilitate a step backwards.

2) Lighten the seat to free the hindquarters and to allow the horse to move backwards.

3) Give the forward leg aids by pressing with both legs at the girth.

4) Brace the elbows in co-contraction to prevent forward movement.

5) Reward with a tickle.

TEACHING THE HORSE TO REIN-BACK

The rein-back should only be performed once the horse has developed sufficient strength in his hindquarters, when he has become supple and when he has become fairly straight and forward-going.

Introduction from the ground

Forward movement is natural to all animal species, man included. Therefore, teaching a horse to move backwards is fairly foreign to him. The balancing reaction used for the rein-back can be understood through the following experiments:

1) Stand in front of, and facing, your helper. Place both hands on their chest and push them backwards. You will disturb their balance and, to regain it, they will have to step backwards.

2) Stand behind your helper. Place your hands on either side of their waist and pull them back. Once again you have managed to disturb their balance in a backward direction with the resultant step backwards. Next, push them forwards and note that when you push them forwards you use the heel of your hand, but when you pull them back you use your fingers.

As these two experiments show, it will be extremely difficult to put this concept to a horse when mounted. Therefore, the easiest way to teach backward movement is from the ground, through the following exercises:

1) This exercise can be performed daily while you are handling your horse in the stable. Stand in front of him, place your hands on his chest and push him backwards. Simultaneously give the verbal command 'back'. You will be eliciting a balance reaction by disturbing his balance in a backward direction. He will immediately understand your action and associate the word with the action. Do this for a few days until he moves back from a light aid and the voice only.

2) For the second dismounted exercise, stand in front of the horse. Touch his fetlocks or chest with a schooling whip and simultaneously give the verbal command 'back'. (Standing at his side may lead to undesirable sideways movement.) Repeat this a few times a day until he is able to walk back a few steps on the command only.

Once these two exercises are understood by the horse, the mounted rein-back is quite easy. The procedure is as follows.

The rein-back ridden

1) Relax the horse's head and neck with 'sponging' rein aids, to ensure that he stays 'on the bit'.

2) Give the leg aids with both lower legs on the girth, but remember that the horse understands this as a forward aid.

3) Block the forward movement with co-contraction of the elbows. Do not pull back on the reins. If alternate rein aids are used, the horse may become confused during a halt exercise when the rider is only 'sponging' the reins to relax the head and neck.

4) Lighten the seat a little with a forward tilt of the body. Compare this to squeezing toothpaste from a tube. When you want it to come out of the front, as normal, you push with the heel

Figure 101 The hand position changes when pushing toothpaste out of the front or back of the tube.

of your hand but, if you wanted it to come out of the opposite end, you would squeeze it with the front of your hand. Compare this to the pulling and pushing with your hands on your helper's waist in the experiments previously described.) The lightened seat thus releases the energy to the back.

Simultaneously, give the horse the verbal command he has learned from you: 'back'.

5) As soon as he attempts even one short stride, reward him with a tickle on the neck.

6) Walk forwards, then halt again.

7) Give the forward aids and sit up very straight to walk forwards again, and then ask for a halt again.

8) Repeat the pattern of rein-back – walk; halt – walk; halt – rein-back a few times. Make sure that the seat aids for the rein-back, walk and halt are very clear. The forward tilting of the upper body for rein-back will eventually become an imperceptible lightening of the seat when the horse understands completely.

TROUBLESHOOTING – problems in rein-back

STEPPING WIDE BEHIND
The horse does not yet have enough strength in his hindquarters.

Figure 103 Incorrect rein-back. The horse is stepping wide behind.

Figure 102(a) In the halt, the rider's back and abdominal muscles co-contract, the seat muscles contract and the rider leans back slightly.

Figure 102(b) In the rein-back, the seat is lightened slightly by contracting (hollowing) the back muscles.

Figure 102(c) To walk, the rider sits up straight again and contracts the seat and abdominal muscles.

Correction

Build him up with hill work, engaging and collecting activities.

RUSHING BACKWARDS

This is usually caused by anxiety.

Correction

Do one rein-back step then halt. Walk forwards again. As soon as the horse accepts one step, ask for two and walk forwards again. Increase the number of steps as soon as the horse relaxes and accepts the previous number.

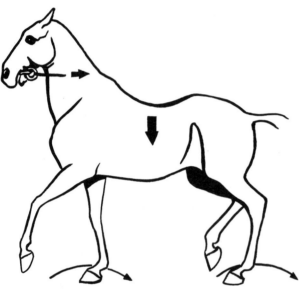

Figure 104 Incorrect rein-back. The horse is hollow in outline and giving short, stiff steps.

HOLLOWING THE BACK AND NECK AND GIVING SHORT STEPS

This is usually the result of pulling backwards on the mouth. If a horse is pulled back with both hands simultaneously, he will always resist because this causes discomfort or pain in his mouth.

Correction

To remedy this, 'sponge' the reins alternately to relax the neck and jaw and then ask for the rein-back with the legs, seat and blocking elbows.

STEPPING SIDEWAYS

This is the result of stiffness in the horse.

Correction

Do more suppling exercises and then return to the rein-back. Ride the rein-back with the horse's concave side to the wall. This prevents the horse's tendency to step towards that side.

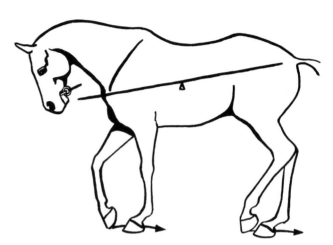

Figure 105 Incorrect rein-back. The horse is dragging his feet, and is on the forehand.

DRAGGING FEET

This is also the result of pulling the horse back with the reins. This time the horse is evading the discomfort by overbending, and therefore drags his feet. When he overbends, his centre of gravity moves forward (he becomes on the forehand). His body automatically adapts to this by bringing the hindquarters underneath him more. As a result, he cannot move them freely backwards.

Correction

The remedy, once again, is to use the correct leg and seat aids, together with the verbal command.

THE TURN ON THE FOREHAND

This is the first and easiest lateral movement that we should teach our young horse. It is ridden from walk through halt. The hind legs move sideways in a half circle, so that the horse pivots around his inside foreleg which should stay, as nearly as possible, on the same spot. The horse's head and neck remain more or less straight. The exercise has limited value in advanced training but is useful in helping the horse to understand the concept of moving away from the pushing leg aid. (It is also invaluable to the rider who needs to open and close gates whilst mounted.)

REASONS FOR RIDING THE TURN ON THE FOREHAND

1) It employs the first of the communicating aids to make use of the horse's reaction to the displacement of his weight to one side. He learns to move away when he is pushed from the side. This aid will be used in many of the lateral movements.

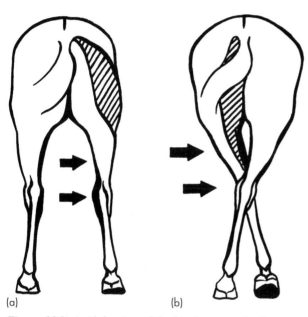

Figure 106(a) Abduction of the hindquarters in the turn on the forehand. (b) Adduction of the hindquarters in the turn on the forehand.

2) It is an early suppling exercise. The hindquarters are required to abduct (open) and adduct (close). This will stretch and supple the relevant muscles. (Remember that it is necessary to stretch and supple all of the horse's muscles.)

3) It has an activating effect upon the hindquarters. The horse has more impulsion after the exercise.

THE AIDS FOR THE TURN ON THE FOREHAND

1) The movement should be ridden fairly promptly from a good, balanced halt.

2) The hands 'sponge' the reins alternately to relax the jaw and neck. No attempt should be made to turn the horse round with the rein.

3) The elbows block (co-contract) to prevent too much forward movement.

4) The outside leg, behind the girth, pushes the hindquarters over, one step at a time.

5) The inside leg should remain passive, unless it is necessary to use it on the girth to prevent any backward movement.

6) The hands block the horse from escaping forwards in an attempt to evade.

As soon as the horse takes one step, relax the aid and reward him. Then ask for another step in the same manner until a half circle is completed. Novice riders may find it difficult to separate the action of their own two legs. To remedy this and practise the co-ordination of the individual legs, the rider may initially remove the inside leg from the horse. This may also help the young horse to understand more easily the facilitation of lateral movement.

TROUBLESHOOTING – problems with turns on the forehand

THE HORSE TAKES TOO MANY FORWARD STEPS
He is probably not listening to the restraining aids.
Correction
Apply the restraining aids more firmly, but still correctly.
THE HORSE WALKS BACKWARDS.
Correction
He should immediately be ridden forward into a brisk walk. Then start the exercise again. Make sure that your hands are not blocking the forward movement.

LEG-YIELDING

This is the second lateral movement we teach a young horse. It is taught at walk, but may also be ridden in trot. It is a movement in which the horse's body and neck stay more or less straight. The lateral bend of the neck is of little importance, as this is simply an exercise to consolidate response to the lateral aid and is never asked for in a dressage test. All four legs move forwards and sideways. The movement can be ridden down a long side of the arena with the horse's nose to the wall, or from a half circle to the centre line, leg-yielding back to the wall. As its use is limited, the exercise is only performed until the horse and rider can master it. Thereafter, more functional lateral exercises are used.

REASONS FOR LEG-YIELDING

1) Leg-yielding consolidates the lateral aid for the young horse.

2) The novice rider will find the co-ordination of all the limbs in shoulder-in and half-pass extremely difficult. This exercise is easier and will help the rider to develop the co-ordination necessary for using the legs individually for the more complex lateral aids.

3) Although shoulder-in is a better suppling exercise than leg-yielding, a young horse will not usually have mastered it. Leg-yielding does have some stretching and suppling effect on the leg abductors and adductors.

4) It has an activating effect upon the hindquarters.

THE AIDS FOR LEG-YIELDING

1) The hands 'sponge' the reins alternately to ensure relaxation and roundness of outline as necessary.

2) If the leg-yield is to the left, the left hand keeps

the contact and only becomes active and opens if the horse has moved his quarters over too far.

3) The right leg, behind the girth, pushes the hindquarters over to the left.

4) The right hand keeps the head and neck straight and helps the horse in the righting reaction of bringing his body into alignment after it has been moved to the side.

5) The left leg maintains the forward impulsion.

The aids are reversed for leg-yielding to the right.

TEACHING THE YOUNG HORSE TO LEG-YIELD

The easiest way of teaching this concept is along the outside track with the horse's nose to the wall. This is sometimes referred to as a full pass. The young horse and novice rider will find this easier as the rail prevents the horse from moving forwards and thereby facilitates lateral movement.

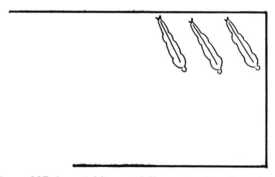

Figure 107 Leg-yielding or full pass against the side of the arena.

The leg-yield exercise may also be done from a half circle down the centre line and leg-yield back to the track, or from the track to the centre line and back to the track. For the former exercise:

1) Start to ride through the corner.

2) As soon as the horse has reached the appropriate angle in the corner, start to push the hind quarters to the inside of the track. Remember to push the quarters right over. If you are not successful, you are not pushing hard enough.

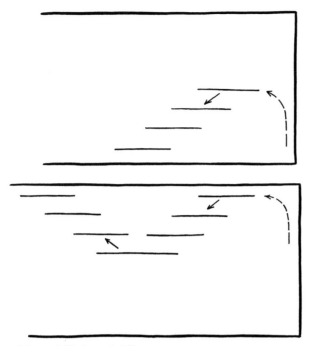

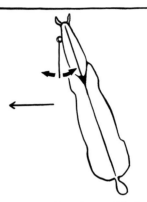

Figure 111 To control the angle in leg-yield, the inside rein opens and closes in relation to the neck as necessary.

3) The hand on the same side as the pushing leg helps the leg by *slightly* turning the head and neck and thus encouraging the horse to right his body by bringing the hindquarters in alignment with the head and neck.

4) The other hand prevents the horse from turning round completely, by opening and closing the rein from the neck.

5) The other leg stays fairly passive, but may act to ensure forward movement. Novice riders may take this leg right off the horse if their co-ordination is not developed enough.

Figure 108 Leg-yielding patterns.

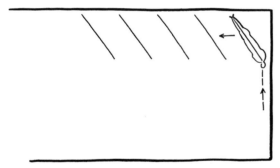

Figure 109 Start the leg-yielding as soon as the horse has reached the correct angle in the corner.

TROUBLESHOOTING – problems with leg-yielding

HINDQUARTERS NOT MOVING OVER ENOUGH
Correction
Use more leg or stop and ask for one step of the turn on the forehand and walk on again.

HINDQUARTERS MOVING OVER TOO FAST
Correction
Bring the forehand to that side with an opening inside rein, momentarily release the pushing aid and then start to push again.

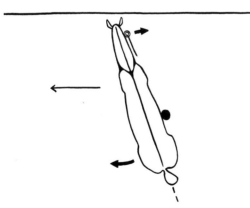

Figure 110 Righting reaction in leg-yield. The outside rein turns the head and neck slightly, compelling the hind legs to move to the inside and bring the spine in alignment with the head.

THE HORSE WALKS FORWARD INTO THE RAIL
Correction
Start the exercise on the quarter line and block your elbows when necessary.

THE HALF PIROUETTE IN WALK

This movement is performed at collected walk. The forehand describes a small circle around the 'marching' hind legs – the inside hind leg remaining as nearly as possible on the same spot. The horse should maintain the four- beat walk sequence throughout. The movement is required from Elementary up to Grand Prix Level, the perfected form being expected only at the higher Levels. At the lower Levels, a slightly larger circle should be acceptable. Although it is a relatively advanced movement, preparation can be started fairly early in training.

The half pirouette in walk is the preparation for the canter pirouette.

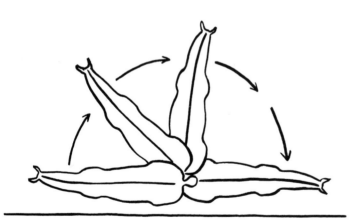

Figure 112 The half pirouette.

THE AIDS FOR HALF PIROUETTE IN WALK

1) Prepare with shoulder-fore (a slight shoulder-in). (For the aids for shoulder-in see Chapter 11 The Trot And Its Exercises.)

2) Ask for a slight inside bend by 'sponging' the inside rein and *opening* it a little to facilitate the movement. There should be no *pulling* on this rein.

3) The outside rein should keep a firm contact and move the horse's shoulder over with the 'long arm' technique.

4) The outside leg, behind the girth, pushes the horse's hindquarters into the small circle and prevents them from swinging out. It should be used alternately with the inside leg to maintain the rhythmic movement of the hindquarters.

5) The inside leg, on the girth, pushes the ribcage to elicit the inside bend and is used at each stride to maintain the impulsion.

TEACHING THE YOUNG HORSE

Many pirouettes have been destroyed by riders who want to make the circle too small too soon. This practice should be resisted at all cost.

1) Start with quarter pirouettes on a square or 'Greek' pattern.

2) Collect for a few strides before you ask for the movement.

3) Establish the inside bend with 'sponging' of the rein. If you are a novice rider you may have difficulty in maintaining the inside bend in the beginning. Do not be concerned, as your co-ordination will improve with practice. In addition, the inside rein should be opened to encourage the horse to step sideways, and closed when the sideways stepping leads to stepping out with the hind legs (righting reaction).

4) Lean back slightly; imagine you are swinging a little child by the arms in a circle or perform ing what we call, in South Africa, a 'tiekiedraai' (picnic dance – literally a turn on a small coin) – see Figure 114.

5) With a fairly firm contact on the outside rein, move the horse's shoulder over with the 'long arm' technique.

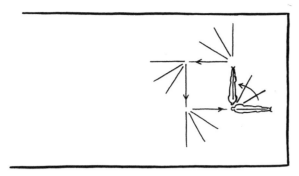

Figure 113(a) The square pattern.

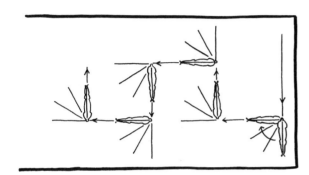

Figure 113(b) The Greek pattern.

Figure 114 'Tiekiedraai' (picnic dancing).

6) With your outside leg behind the girth, push the quarters over. (Your outside leg and arm should feel like a wall pushing the horse sideways.)

7) Reward and walk straight on. Then repeat the process or change the rein.

PROGRESSION

Practise the quarters-in on a large circle. Once your horse is more collected, your own co-ordination has been adequately developed and you can perform a quarter pirouette perfectly, increase the number of steps. It is preferable to ride a larger half circle with the quarters in, keeping the hind legs moving, than to ride a small half circle where the hind legs become 'stuck'.

Once the horse can do this with ease, a half pirouette may be attempted. When practising, stay with a larger pirouette and only attempt a proper pirouette every now and then to assess progress.

TROUBLESHOOTING –
problems with pirouette in walk

HIND LEGS 'STUCK'
Corrections

a) Increase the size of the circle and ride quarters-in.
b) The horse may 'stick' behind because he can not keep moving when his forehand has not turned enough. His forehand should be slightly ahead of his hindquarters. As soon as he starts to 'stick', lead his forehand over with an opening of the inside rein, then proceed with the normal aids.
c) Make sure that you are using your forward leg aids alternately at each stride.

LOSS OF RHYTHM
Rhythm is lost when a horse rushes the movement, when he is not engaged enough and when he gets 'stuck' behind.
Corrections

a) If the horse rushes, stop the movement with the inside leg and walk forwards. Repeat the exercise on a larger circle.
b) If the horse loses impulsion, go back to a larger circle.

INCORRECT BEND
This is usually caused by loss of balance. The horse

is tilting his head in an attempt to regain his balance. Alternatively, he may be purely showing resistance to the outside leg.

Correction

Play with the inside rein and re-establish contact on the outside rein. Open and close the inside rein a few times if necessary, then push the whole horse over with the outside leg and rein. Use a strong inside leg on the girth.

STEPPING BACK

The horse does not have enough forward impulsion, or has misunderstood the aids.

Correction

This is a serious fault and the horse should be pushed forwards into walk immediately. Thereafter the pirouette should be ridden on a slightly larger circle.

HINDQUARTERS STEPPING WIDE

The horse is resisting the rider's outside leg.

Corrections

a) Use a stronger pushing aid with the outside leg.
b) Practise turns on the forehand to re-establish the concept of moving away from the outside leg.
c) Practise quarters-in on a small circle.

CHAPTER 10

BASIC TRANSITIONS

AND FIGURES

Once we begin to consider riding in the various gaits, it becomes necessary to give some thought to the following questions:

1) How do we move from one gait to another?

2) What figures do we ride within the gaits, and to what purpose?

TRANSITIONS

The ability to perform all the movements in riding is not complete without the ability to connect them with fluidity and rhythm. The connections between the movements are called transitions. Ridden correctly, transitions have the training functions of improving impulsion, balance and engagement of the hindquarters. They are therefore one of the best tests of a horse's level of training, and will indicate where his problems lie. One of the most difficult parts of riding is to perform the transitions correctly.

HOW TO RIDE A SMOOTH TRANSITION

1) Before you perform a transition, ensure that the horse is in balance. A balancing half-halt (for downward transitions), or an impulsion producing half-halt (for upward transitions) should be performed before the transition.

2) 'Sponge' the reins throughout the transition. This keeps the horse in balance and ensures that he will use his hindquarters and not his neck

for the purpose of moving his centre of gravity backwards. If both reins are applied simultaneously, the horse tends to resist and become hollow in outline.

3) When riding an upward transition do not use abrupt leg aids, but *ease the horse into the upward movement* with slowly increasing leg aids. This will ensure a smooth transition. (Once the horse's schooling becomes more advanced, this easing into the movement will not be necessary.)

4) In a downward transition, the seat and leg aids should be applied a fraction before the restraining but 'sponging' hand aids. As soon as the horse has performed the downward transition, you should apply forward aids, unless the horse is halting. (Should the horse lose balance after a downward transition, he should be rebalanced with a series of half-halts.)

BASIC FIGURES

CIRCLES

Circles are used for suppling, calming, slowing down excitable horses, developing ambidexterity and for preparing the horse for various different movements.

How to ride a circle

1) Ride on the outside rein as described in Chapter 1.

2) Push the horse's ribcage over to the outside, with the inside leg on the girth. This elicits a balance reaction which turns the neck to the inside, abducts the inside fore- and hind legs and adducts the outside fore- and hind legs, giving the impression of inside bend.

3) Lead the horse into the correct size of circle by 'sponging' with the inside rein, to encourage the use of the inside neck flexors. Do this until you have the appropriate bend for the size of the circle.

4) The outside rein controls the degree of neck bend and puts the shoulder at the appropriate angle for the size of the circle.

Exercises

1) Circles may be ridden anywhere they will fit in the arena. Start with 20 m circles and attempt increasingly smaller circles once your horse has mastered these.

2) Spiral the circle from 20 m down to 8 m and then increase the size again, slowly.

3) Ride a circle of appropriate size at each marker.

TROUBLESHOOTING – problems with circles

FALLING INTO THE CIRCLE
The horse is not using his inner side flexors, but his outer side flexors. He is thus incorrectly bent to the outside and this pushes the shoulder into the circle.
Correction
Ride on the outside rein; push harder with the inside leg on the girth.

THE HIND LEGS DO NOT STEP IN THE TRACKS OF THE FORELEGS
The horse has not become straight or supple enough.
Correction
Ride various suppling exercises as described in Chapter 5.

Figure 115 The horse 'falls' into a circle because he is using his outside lateral muscles and therefore has the incorrect bend.

TURNS

Turns are ridden through the corners of the arena and when changing rein through the arena. Ridden properly, they can help in the suppling and straightening of the horse.

Turns and corners should be ridden according to the stride and development of the horse. A long-striding horse may have difficulty in going too deep into the corners. A novice horse will need a shallower corner than an experienced horse: a collected horse should go deep into the corner.

How to ride a turn

1) Prepare the horse with a balancing half-halt.

2) Ride on the outside rein.

3) The inside leg should put more pressure on the ribcage through the corner.

4) The outside rein pushes the shoulder to the inside with the 'long arm' technique.

5) The outside leg puts fairly strong pressure behind the girth to push the quarters into a half pirouette.

TROUBLESHOOTING –
problems with turns

LOSING THE QUARTERS TO THE OUTSIDE
IN THE CORNER
The horse has not developed enough suppleness or
straightness. The muscles on his outside cannot stretch
enough, and thus trigger off a righting reaction.

Corrections

a) Suppling and straightening exercises.

b) Use more outside leg behind the girth as well
   as more inside leg on the girth, together with
   intermittent 'sponging' of the inside rein.

SERPENTINES

Serpentines or loops are basically a series of half
circles strung together. They are the best suppling,
balancing and warming-up exercise for horses
of all standards. They impel the horse to concentrate and relax his neck completely.

How to ride serpentines

When riding a serpentine and changing the bend,
the horse has no idea where the rider is going to
lead him. We can compare this to leading a blind
person, who must be told along the way where there
are changes of directions, steps or downhill incli-
nations. If the person leading should suddenly pull
them in a new direction, the blind person will surely
resist, or lose balance. So it is with the horse, if we do
not communicate with him through all the movements.

Practise the following changes of bend, at walk
initially, to develop co-ordination:

1) Ride a 20 m half circle.

2) When you reach the quarter line, ride a balancing half-halt.

3) Relax the horse's jaw and neck by 'sponging'
   the reins.

4) Change the bend in the neck and body, but ride
   the horse on the straight line for a few strides.
   (This is the suppling and stretching part of

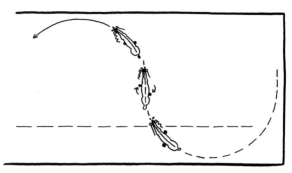

Figure 116 The aids for change of bend in a serpentine.

the exercise). The change of bend without the
change of direction indicates to the horse what
is about to happen (see Figure 116).

5) To change the bend, the new inside leg, on the
   girth, pushes the ribcage towards the new outside.

6) The new inside hand 'sponges' the rein to
   create inside bend.

7) The new outside rein takes contact, allows the
   inside bend and moves the shoulder to the inside when performing the turn (the 'long arm'
   method).

8) The new outside leg behind the girth pushes the
   hindquarters over during the last part of the turn.

Exercises

1) Start with a figure-of-eight on two 20 m circles.

2) Follow this with three-, four-, five- and six-loop
   serpentines. The more loops in the serpentine,
   the more the horse has to back-track at the
   change of bend. The deeper the change of bend,
   the stronger the suppling effect.

3) Try to ride as many loops as possible through
   the whole arena by back-tracking as deeply as
   you can.

4) Ride tiny loops on the centre line. Each loop
   should go to the quarter line, or be as small as
   you can possibly make it.

5) Ride a figure-of-eight across the width of the
   arena, EXB, and back again.

6) Ride half circles from a long side onto a
   diagonal, and vice versa.

CHAPTER 11

THE TROT

AND ITS EXERCISES

In trot, the horse moves his diagonal pairs of legs identically and simultaneously in a two-time rhythm, with a moment of suspension in between.

RIDER'S POSITION AND SEAT

In rising trot, the upper body leans forward *slightly* while the hips are lifted up and forward at every stride. In sitting trot, the seat is 'glued' to the saddle. All the movement should be in the waist area. This must be completely relaxed, or the rider will bump up and down. Imagine standing on the back of a truck, travelling over a rough track. Your feet must be 'glued' to the floor of the truck while your knees are completely relaxed to absorb all the movement. If there were any tension in your knees, you would be hopping up and down. In sitting trot, your waist area should take the place of the knees on the back of the truck. If you are bumping at all, you will find that you have tension in your waist, or are holding on with your knees. The legs, however, should hang down with no grip at the knees because holding on with the knees has the effect of pushing the seat out of the saddle. (To help the novice rider achieve this relaxation, the ankles should relax, with the feet hanging down.)

Maintaining a sitting trot seems to be extremely difficult for novice riders. Their biggest problem usually is that they become tense as a result of the discomfort of the movement. As soon as tension sets in, the rider's arms and hands will be affected. This, in turn, affects the contact with the horse's mouth. The horse becomes hollow in outline, his stride becomes short and bumpy, the rider loses balance and becomes more tense, and a vicious circle sets in.

Learning to sit to the trot is not difficult, however, provided a rider can learn to relax. A novice rider should adopt the following procedure:

1) Ask the horse to trot very slowly. This will be less disruptive to your balance.

2) Maintain the roundness of the horse's head and neck by 'sponging' the reins.

3) Relax in your waist and legs, and allow the toes to drop down. Do not grip with the knees at all.

4) Feel the left-right movement of the horse's hips and try to 'swing' your hips left-right in rhythm with the horse's hips.

5) Feel your inner thighs alternately touching the saddle as the horse swings his hips.

6) Maintain the relaxation of your arms and hands.

7) As soon as this position can be maintained without any tension setting in, increase the pace a little at a time until the correct forward rhythm can be maintained while you remain sitting comfortably.

8) Initially practise for only a few strides at a time and slowly increase the number of strides until a proper sitting trot can be maintained.

THE GAIT VARIANTS

In training and riding the horse, four forms of trot are employed.

Working trot. This is the natural trot of the horse and is used with the novice horse to establish rhythm, balance, impulsion, strength and a certain amount of straightness. The hind feet step into or slightly beyond the hoofprints of the forefeet.

Collected trot. In the collected trot the hind feet usually step short of the hoofprints of the forefeet. The croup is lowered and the leg motion becomes higher, rounder and more energetic.

Once the working trot has been established and

1) Collected trot

2) Medium trot

3) Extended trot

rhythm, balance, impulsion, strength and an acceptable amount of straightness have been achieved, it is improved to become a collected trot. In collected trot, the quarters become more engaged as the abdominal and hip flexors become stronger and contract more to draw the hindquarters more underneath the horse. Through the contraction of these muscles the hindquarters are enabled to carry more weight, and the hind leg joints have to flex more to carry this weight. The centre of gravity will thus move back, with the result that the forehand will lighten. The neck and head will be carried higher, with the head close to the vertical.

Medium trot. In medium trot the stride is energetic and longer than in working trot, with the hind feet stepping beyond the hoofprints of the forefeet. The horse is allowed to lengthen his frame a little and carry his head and neck a little lower. This allows more freedom of the shoulders.

Extended trot. Power, cadence, impulsion and optimal engagement of the hindquarters are necessary for the extended trot. Since this power and engagement develop from collection, the medium and extended trots should only be attempted once the horse has developed enough strength and collection. The development of collection and extension proceeds more or less simultaneously.

In extended trot, the horse reaches his maximum length of stride with the hind feet stepping well beyond the hoofprints of the forefeet. The rider allows the horse to lengthen his frame and lower his head and neck slightly. There is increased impulsion and thrust of the hindquarters, leading to greater elevation.

FREEING THE SHOULDER ACTION.

A free shoulder action is very important if the medium and extended trots are to be developed to optimum levels.

The biceps and brachiocephalic muscles are the main muscles responsible for moving the horse's shoulder and forelimb forwards. Their ability to perform this task is affected by the ability of the triceps muscle (the antagonist) to relax and stretch. The more the triceps can relax and stretch, the more the shoulder can stretch forward and the longer the horse's stride will be.

The ability of the triceps muscle to relax and stretch is dependent upon the action of its opposing muscles; the trapezius, the rhomboideus and the serratus ventralis. These muscles all lift and hollow the horse's neck when they contract. They are all attached to the upper edge of the scapula (shoulder blade), while the triceps muscle is attached to the lower edge of the scapula. When they contract, they hold the top edge of the scapula forward and prevent the triceps from stretching. When the horse's neck is flexed and stretched down, these muscles have to relax to allow the neck flexors to perform satisfactorily. When the neck extensors relax, they exert less pull on the upper edge of the scapula and therefore allow the triceps more freedom to stretch. It is therefore important to allow the horse to lengthen his frame slightly to attain a longer stride (see Figure 117a and b).

THE AIDS FOR TROT

1) Relax the jaw and neck with 'sponging' rein aids. 'Sponge' the reins throughout the upward transition to avoid co-contraction of the neck (horses tend to balance themselves in transitions by putting their necks in co-contraction). Avoiding co-contraction of the neck will compel the horse to step under with his hindquarters as described in Chapter 1.

2) Contract the seat muscles (gluteals) to bring the hindquarters more underneath the horse.

3) Push the horse into trot with both legs on the girth.

4) Reward with a tickle and relax the leg aid as soon as the horse moves off.

5) As soon as the movement starts to tail off, apply the leg aids again and reward. Do not continually thump the horse with your legs, or

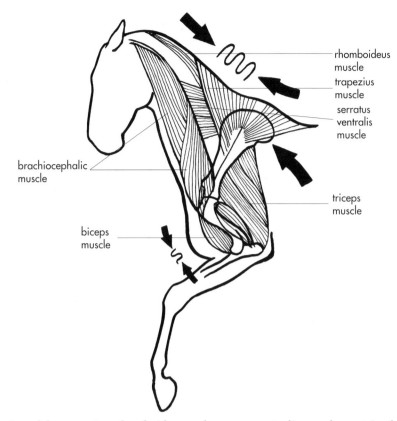

Figure 117(a) Contraction of the trapezius, rhomboideus and serratus ventralis muscles restrict the freedom of the shoulder movement.

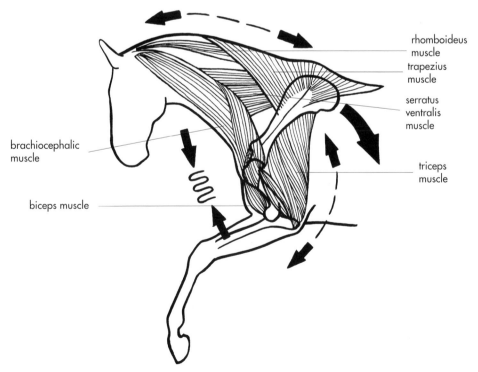

Figure 117(b) Relaxation of the trapezius, rhomboideus and serratus ventralis muscles allows the brachiocephalic muscle to work and the triceps to stretch, leading to free shoulder movement.

he will become dull to the aid.

6) If these aids are not effective, a light touch with the whip is permissible.

LENGTHENING THE TROT

1) Ride in working trot on a 20 m circle, where the horse's balance is less likely to be disturbed.

2) Relax the head and neck by 'sponging' the reins.

3) Push both legs on the girth and simultaneously rise higher out of the saddle. The horse will automatically give a longer stride. Reward him immediately.

4) Allow the horse to lengthen his frame slightly, but do not let him pull the reins from you. This would mean that he is tipping his weight onto the forehand and losing balance.

5) Ride only a few of these lengthened strides and reward the horse.

6) Close your knees in a 'slowing down' half-halt, and rise less. The horse will shorten his stride.

7) Repeat this a few times until the horse responds immediately to the higher rising in the trot and the slight increase in leg pressure. This will not take long.

Should the steps become hurried, half-halt immediately. Do not continually thump the horse with the leg aids or he will lose rhythm and balance. Set him up in the movement and then sit still and enjoy it.

This lesson will be carried over to the sitting trot, when all you will have to do to elicit an extended trot is to stretch your body up and swing your hips forwards, left and right, together with the horse's hip movements.

Exercises in lengthening

1) The first lengthening exercises should be done on a circle. The horse loses less rhythm and balance on the circle, and is less likely to go wide behind.

2) Circle 20 m at A. Ride through the corner to K. Lengthen the trot to V. Half-halt and circle 20 m at working trot. Lengthen from V to E. Half-halt and circle again at working trot. Repeat this procedure from marker to marker.

3) Repeat the exercise above, but lengthen between the two markers, that is circle at C, lengthen from M to B, circle at B, lengthen from B to F, etc.

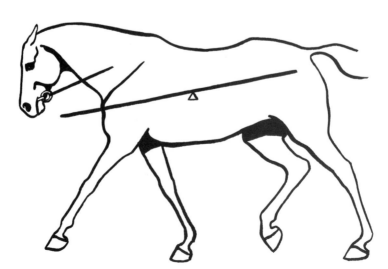

Figure 118 Horse on the forehand and leaning on the rider's hands to help his balance.

4) Lengthen the trot in a 20m circle and then ask for a few strides on the straight. Circle again and repeat. Increase the distance on the straight as the horse's balance improves.

5) Working trot around the short side and start lengthening before the corner (cut the corner). Lengthen along the long side and shorten again as you reach the short side. After a few repetitions, the horse will start to lengthen well without losing balance.

6) Lengthen across the diagonal. Ride through the corner in working trot, turn the horse across the diagonal at K, straighten and balance him, then ask for the lengthened strides. This sequence will prevent anticipation and loss of balance.

TROUBLESHOOTING –
problems in working trot

SHORT, STIFF AND CHOPPY STEPS
The horse has not been allowed freedom of the neck and/or the rider probably has too much contact on the horse's mouth.
Correction
Ride the horse forwards 'long and deep' with very light contact.

HORSE TOO FORWARD GOING
Anxious or unschooled horse.
Correction
Work on a 20m circle. Set your own, dead slow, rhythm with regular knee-closing half-halts. Once the half-halt is performed, the horse should be rewarded and the knee relaxed immediately.

LAZY HORSE, OR HORSE IGNORING THE LEG
The so-called lazy horse is often a horse with slow metabolism. The only reason he is moving too slowly is because he thinks this is what is required. A second reason is when a horse has difficulty engaging his hindquarters.

Corrections
a) Push the horse forwards with the trot aids. If he does not react immediately, touch him with the whip behind the leg. If he then surges forward, reward him with a tickle. Repeat this three or four times. The horse will move off your leg the next time you use it.
b) Canter round the arena a few times, at a strong, forward gait, then return to the trot work.
c) Do as much riding out as you can, at a forward trot or canter.
d) Lazy horses should work around the outside of the arena and in shallow loops rather than on intricate figures.

HOLLOWING DURING SITTING TROT
The rider has become tense, with stiff arms, and is therefore pulling the horse in the mouth at every stride.
Correction
Follow previous advice on sitting to the trot (p. 108).

Problems in lengthened/extended trot

HINDQUARTERS GOING WIDE IN LENGTHENED TROT
The horse has been allowed to shift his weight forwards, and this has led to loss of balance. Once the horse has learnt this and found it more comfortable, he will be reluctant to lose the habit.
Corrections
a) Do not allow the horse to take any weight on the rein. He cannot then shift his weight forwards, but has to stay in self-carriage. 'Sponge' the reins thoughout the movement to prevent him from leaning on your hands.
b) Go back to lengthening on the circle only.
c) Do a lot of work 'long and deep' to strengthen his abdominal muscles and hip and hock flexors and help him to establish balance.
d) Do more work at collected trot to strengthen his hindquarters.
e) Ask for a longer stride in the shoulder-in position (advanced horses).

LOSS OF RHYTHM

The horse has been pushed off balance through the transfer of weight forwards. He has therefore lost engagement of the hindquarters.

Corrections

a) Ask for less length of stride.
b) Set the horse up in the movement and then sit quietly.
c) Ensure lightness of the forehand.

IRREGULAR STEPS

Lack of strength and/or horse not working through his whole body.

Corrections

a) Check for lameness.
b) Do strengthening exercises and more work at collected trot.

'RUNNING'

The horse's weight has shifted forwards and he is trying to keep his balance by moving his forefeet as quickly as he can. He grabs the ground with his forelegs instead of pushing with his hind legs. (He may also be simply in a rush to complete the exercise.)

Corrections

a) Half-halts and more engagement.
b) Walk the horse as soon as he shows any tendency to increase speed, and repeat the exercise until he stops rushing.

c) Ride half-pass a few strides across the diagonal, followed by extended trot on the diagonal.

TOO HEAVY CONTACT

The horse's weight is too far forward and he thus uses the rider's hands to balance himself. This heavy contact prevents lateral suppleness.

Correction

Ask for more engagement.

FORGING

The hind feet touch the forefeet, producing a clinking sound. The horse is on the forehand.

Correction

Strengthening and engagement exercises.

'HOLLOWING'

The rider could be getting tense, and thus pulling on the reins. The horse may be anticipating and trying to 'run off'. Possibly the rider has not prepared the horse by ensuring a light contact in a rounded frame.

Corrections

a) Ensure that you are fully relaxed in the waist.
b) Prepare the horse by 'sponging' the reins and continue throughout the transition.
c) If the horse anticipates, halt and begin the exercise again, with a light contact and a rounded frame.

CHAPTER 12

LATERAL MOVEMENTS

Although the following movements can be performed in walk, and may initially be 'explained' to the horse in this gait, their biomechanical effects of improving engagement are much greater at trot and, except for travers, canter. It is also in these gaits that they appear as test movements.

SHOULDER-IN

The shoulder-in was created by the great French horsemaster, de la Guérinière, in the early eighteenth century. It is an exercise in which the horse moves forwards at an angle of approximately 30 degrees to the track, with an apparent inside bend, which is of similar extent to that observed on a 10 m circle. This apparent bend is brought about by the ribcage being tilted to the outside, the inside foreleg abducting from the body and the outside fore- and hind legs adducting against the body. To maintain the straight movement of the hind legs, the inside hip muscles and the adductors work harder than those on the outside, and carry more weight. The muscles on the inside of the neck and body contract, while those on the outside stretch. The spine, from wither to tail, is more or less straight. The forelegs move sideways while the hind legs (owing to the adduction of the inside hind), move straight. The legs thus move on three tracks: the inside forefoot is placed on an inside track, the outside forefoot and inside hind foot are placed in a straight line on the centre track, and the outside hind foot is placed on an outside track.

REASONS FOR RIDING SHOULDER-IN

The shoulder-in is one of the most important movements in the training of any horse:

4) Shoulder-in

1) It is an important suppling and straightening exercise for walk, trot and canter. The shoulder-in is the most effective way of stretching the muscles on the outside of the horse.

2) It promotes engagement through the inside hind leg, which has to adduct to step under and thus take more weight. This action lowers the hips and improves collection.

3) It improves balance.

4) The aids for shoulder-in are used, in a modified form, for many other movements, such as riding through corners, circles and serpentines, and also in the preparation for, and maintenance of, correct canter. The same aid, with slight adaptations, is also used for travers and half-pass.

HOW TO RIDE SHOULDER-IN

Preparation

1) Introduce shoulder-in at the walk – this is easier for horse and rider, and fewer mistakes can creep in. As soon as the horse understands the aids, and your co-ordination is adequate, you can ride the movement in trot. (Once you are proficient at it, you can use it as an exercise to straighten the horse in canter.)

2) Novice riders may, initially, have difficulty in dissociating the action of their legs and arms. Our leg adductors are used to working in a pattern of movement, together, and that is how our legs have been asking for forward aids all along. For shoulder-in, not only do both legs have to be used separately and differently, but the same applies to the hands also (nearly like a one man band!) It is a perfectly natural re-action, when pushing hard with the leg on one side, to want to pull with your arm on the same side. Such actions are called 'associated movements', but the patterns can be broken with repetition and effort.

Initially, to help you co-ordinate the two different leg actions, it may be necessary to take

your outside leg off the horse. Once you have mastered the pushing effect with one leg only, you can put the outside leg lightly on the horse to prevent his quarters from swinging out.

3) Begin your first few attempts from the corner facing home. Your horse will have natural forward impulsion and will be less likely to become 'stuck', or move across the arena (see Figure 119).

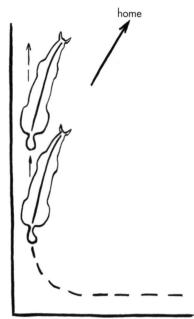

Figure 119 Start the first shoulder-in exercise facing home.

The aids

1) Start to prepare for the exercise before the corner. This will help the horse to maintain balance down the long side of the arena.

2) Put your own body in a shoulder-in position. Turn your hips to the inside (this automatically places the inside leg on the girth and outside leg behind the girth). Put your inside shoulder back and look towards the opposite track at an angle of 30 degrees.

3) The inside leg, on the girth, pushes the horse's ribcage over. Push as though you were pushing your leg right through the horse; imagine that you are pushing a slice of the horse through to

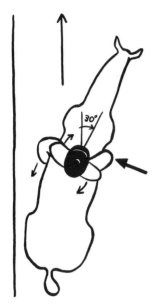

Figure 120 The rider's position in shoulder-in.

the other side. Remember to use your leg with every stride of the horse and relax it again as soon as the horse has moved his inside hind leg forwards. So it becomes a push-relax, push-relax action with every stride. If you should push continuously, your leg would become so tired as to be of no use at all, and the aid would be out of synchronisation with the horse's movement.

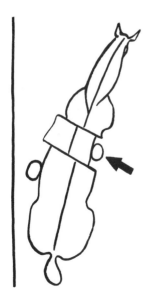

Figure 121 The technique of 'pushing through' the horse with the inside leg.

4) 'Sponging' the inside rein explains to the horse that he should use his inside neck muscles. This creates the inside bend.

5) The outside rein places the shoulder on the inside track by either closing onto the neck or opening away from the neck, depending on whether the angle of the shoulder-in is too big or too small. Use the 'long arm' technique to accomplish this. The outside hand, with a straight rein, can place the horse's shoulder exactly where the rider wants it. If you bring the hand towards the neck until you have the correct position and then hold it there, the horse will keep his own position. If he should give too much angle, open your rein away from the neck, keeping a firm contact, and he will bring his shoulder back to the track. In other words, provided you keep your outside hand exactly over the required track, your horse will keep his shoulder on that track.

6) The outside leg, behind the girth, prevents the righting reaction of the horse aligning his body by moving his hindquarters out.

7) Reward correct movement with a tickle on the neck and a rest period on a long rein. This work is strenuous for the horse and should be done for short periods at a time, or stress injuries to muscles and joints may occur.

Although shoulder-in, as used in competition, is a three-track movement, it may be practised on four tracks for specific reasons. A larger angle has a more gymnastic and strengthening effect on the horse, but be warned – he may lose his collection.

EXERCISES IN SHOULDER-IN

1) Start the exercise as you go into the corner before the long side, or ride a small circle before the shoulder-in.

2) Start on the left rein and ride shoulder-in for a few strides down the side of the arena. Ride a 10 m half circle to the centre line, then another 10 m half circle on the right rein to the track.

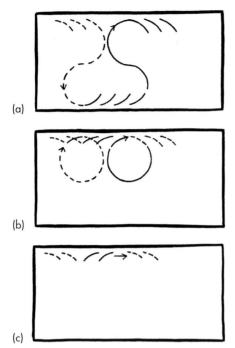

Figure 122 Shoulder-in exercises: (a) Exercise 2, (b) Exercise 4, (c) Exercise 7.

Ride shoulder-in for a few strides on the right rein, followed by a 10 m half circle to the centre line, change rein and repeat.

3) Ride shoulder-in for a few strides, followed by a 10 m circle and back to shoulder-in.

4) Ride shoulder-in, followed by a 10 m circle, followed by quarters-in. Repeat all the way up the long side.

5) Ride shoulder-in up a long side for a few strides, then medium trot across the diagonal.

6) Ride shoulder-in from K to E, turn right at E, ride straight to B, turn left and ride shoulder in left to M.

7) Alternate shoulder-in and travers all the way down the long side.

TROUBLESHOOTING – problems in shoulder-in

TOO MUCH BEND IN THE NECK
This is more than likely caused by pulling on the inside rein instead of only 'sponging' and using the outside rein for the angle. The horse will not come off the track, but will only bend his neck.

Correction
The forehand should be brought off the track with the outside rein.

LEG-YIELD INSTEAD OF SHOULDER-IN
The outside rein has asked for too great an angle and, because the horse's spine cannot bend, the hind legs cannot move in a straight line when at this angle. The quarters therefore swing out.

Corrections
a) Bring the horse back on the track by opening the outside rein.
b) Use more inside leg on the girth and keep the outside leg behind the girth.

Figure 123 When the horse tilts his head he is, in fact, bending his neck in the wrong direction.

TILTING THE HEAD
The horse has lost balance and is using his neck muscles in an attempt to regain it and/or the rider is pulling on the inside rein. This makes the horse tilt his head to the inside because, in fact, his outside neck flexors are active in his attempt to regain balance against the pulling inside rein.

Correction
'Sponge' the reins to relax the neck muscles. Give more support with the outside rein whilst ensuring a soft feeling on the inside rein. Use more inside leg.

TRAVERS AND RENVERS

These two movements are virtually interchangeable. The same aids are used to elicit the same postural reactions from the horse. In both these movements the horse is bent in the direction of the movement. In travers, the horse moves with his forehand on the track while the hindquarters are pushed to the inside of the track. In renvers the hindquarters are on the track and the forehand is to the inside of the track.

REASONS FOR RIDING TRAVERS AND RENVERS

1) They are suppling and straightening exercises.

2) Travers is an excellent preparation for half pass, as exactly the same aids are used. Travers is easier to perform than half-pass because it is performed against the surround of the manège.

HOW TO RIDE TRAVERS

1) Ride a quarters-engaging half-halt as you begin the second corner on the short side.

2) Before going straight on the long side, place your outside leg behind the girth and push the hindquarters to the inside.

3) The outside leg should then push and relax alternately in synchronisation with the horse's steps.

4) The inside leg, on the girth, pushes the ribcage and shoulder onto the track. The forelegs should move straight on the track while the horse looks straight ahead.

5) The inside hand 'sponges' the rein to encourage the use of the inside neck flexors to create a soft inside bend.

6) The outside rein has a firm contact to 'hold' the horse on the track.

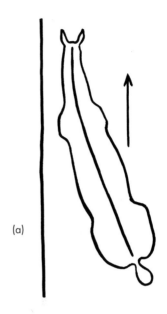

(a)

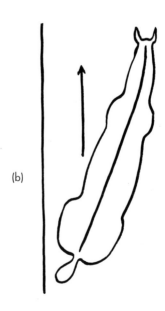

(b)

Figure 124 Travers (a) and Renvers (b).

HOW TO RIDE RENVERS

The opposite aids from travers are used, to keep the hindquarters on the track and the forehand on the second track.

EXERCISES IN TRAVERS AND RENVERS

1) Travers up the long side, circle at each marker, followed by travers between the markers.

2) Travers up the long side, circle at E, followed by travers to K.

3) Alternate shoulder-in and travers up the long side, from marker to marker, with a circle in between.

4) Alternate shoulder-in and travers up the long side, from marker to marker, but with no circle in between.

5) Alternate shoulder-in, travers and renvers.

HALF-PASS

The half-pass is the final product of all the lateral work. The horse moves forwards and sideways, keeping his body almost parallel to the track. The movement should be more forwards than sideways. The inside bend allows the forehand to have a slight lead over the hindquarters. The outside legs cross in front of the inside legs.

This movement is an end product in itself, being used in all the Advanced dressage tests, and it also has the training function of continuing to develop great balance and suppleness.

HOW TO RIDE HALF-PASS

The half-pass is basically travers on a diagonal line. The aids for travers are therefore appropriate for half-pass.

Preliminary exercises

1) Alternate shoulder-in and travers on the long side of the arena.

2) Ride shoulder-in on the line D-E. This will give you an idea of the use of the inside leg on the girth.

3) Alternate shoulder-in and travers on this diagonal line.

Riding the movement

1) Draw an imaginary line connecting the beginning and end of the half-pass and ride travers on this line.

2) Ride an impulsion-producing half-halt to engage the hindquarters and create lightness in the forehand, resulting in freedom of the shoulders.

5) Half-pass

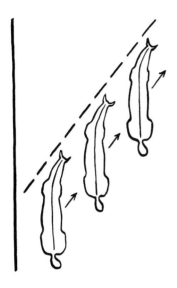

Figure 125 Half-pass – travers on the diagonal.

3) Ensure that there is no tension in the horse's jaw and neck by 'sponging' the reins.

4) The inside rein asks for the inside bend. The horse's head and shoulders should face the marker you are aiming at. This will prevent the quarters from leading the movement.

5) The outside rein pushes the shoulder over with the 'long arm' technique.

6) The inside leg pushes the ribcage to create the inside bend. The inside leg should be quite firm to encourage the use of the horse's inner side flexors throughout the movement. This prevents loss of balance.

7) The outside leg, from hip to foot, pushes the hindquarters over at every step.

8) Impulsion is maintained by the seat and inside leg.

The exercise may also be started from shoulder-fore, because the same initial aids are used.

EXERCISES IN HALF-PASS

Start with a fairly small angle and increase the angle as the horse improves.

1) Ride shoulder-in up the long side, turn down the centre line and half-pass to the track. (The horse finds this easier than from track to centre line.) When reaching the track, proceed in shoulder-in.

2) Ride a circle at K, followed by half-pass to the centre line.

3) Ride shoulder-in down the long side to E, circle 8 m and half-pass to the centre line.

4) Alternate half-pass across the diagonal with a few strides of shoulder-in. This reinforces the inside bend.

5) Alternate half-pass across the diagonal with a few strides leg-yielding to the opposite side. This prevents rushing in the half-pass and improves balance.

6) Alternate half-pass across the diagonal with a few voltes.

7) Half-pass across the entire arena.

8) Counter-changes of hand, where the bend and direction of travel are changed, are the ultimate exercise in half-pass.

TROUBLESHOOTING –
problems in half-pass

HEAD TILTING

The horse has lost his balance and tries to regain it by using his neck muscles for balance. He has, in fact, started using the opposite neck flexors, but is trying to keep the head bent to the inside. Alternately, the horse is not supple enough, with resultant loss of balance.

Corrections

a) Go back to suppling exercises and travers against the surround of the school.

b) Regain balance and inside bend with shoulder-in or more inside leg pressure, then establish more contact on the outside rein while 'sponging' the inside rein.

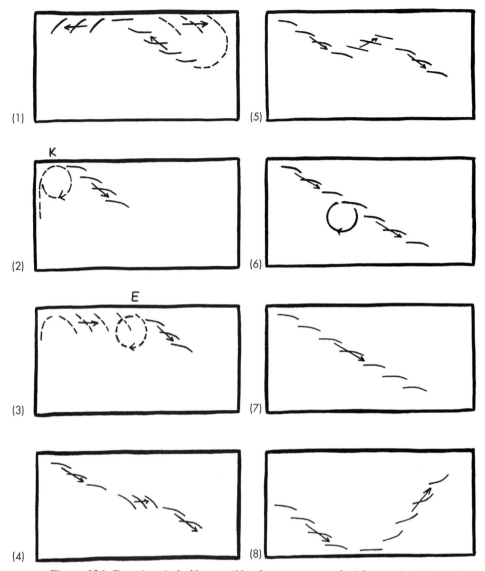

Figure 126 Exercises in half-pass. (Numbers correspond with exercises in text.)

SHORT, HURRIED STEPS
The horse has lost balance and engagement.
Corrections
a) Ride a few half-halts and re-affirm the outside
    rein contact.
b) Alternate a few leg-yielding steps to the
    opposite side with the half-pass.
c) Use more inside leg pressure.

HINDQUARTERS LEADING
The outside leg pressure is too great.

Corrections
a) Push the shoulder over further, with the 'long
    arm' technique. Use slightly less outside leg
    for a few strides.
b) Think 'travers', and point the horse's head and
    shoulders in the direction of the marker you
    are aiming for.

HINDQUARTERS TRAILING
You are not using enough outside leg. Alternatively,
the horse is not supple or engaged enough.

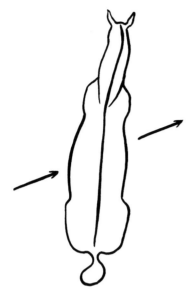

Figure 127 Head tilting in half-pass is an attempt to regain lost balance.

Corrections
a) Go back to practising travers against the surround of the school.
b) Do more suppling and engaging exercises.

LOSS OF RHYTHM
Not enough impulsion, and loss of balance.
Correction
Ride in medium trot and perform a few walk–trot transitions to encourage engagement of the hindquarters and impulsion, then try the half-pass again.

LOSS OF IMPULSION
Loss of engagement.
Correction
Re-establish impulsion and engagement as described above.

TOO MUCH SIDEWAYS AND NOT ENOUGH FORWARD MOVEMENT
The horse has lost balance, or is anticipating the movement.
Corrections
a) Circle 10 m and start the movement again.
b) Alternate half-pass with leg-yielding to the opposite side.
c) Use more inside leg.

TOO MUCH BEND IN THE NECK
You are not using enough inside leg, have too little contact on the outside rein and may not be releasing the inside rein enough.
Correction
The correction is to remedy the rider faults described.

THE COUNTER-CHANGE AND ZIGZAG

More suppleness, balance and collection are required to perform these half-pass movements.

1) Perform the half-pass and reach the track one stride before the marker, ride one stride straight, change the bend on the next stride and start the new half-pass on the third stride.

2) Change the bend of the forehand before pushing the hindquarters with the new outside leg.

When straightening a horse after lateral work, the shoulders should be brought in line with the hindquarters, not vice versa. This will prevent the horse from swinging his hindquarters.

CHAPTER 13

THE CANTER

AND ITS EXERCISES

The canter is a three-beat movement with a moment of suspension after the third beat. It is the most impulsive of the horse's gaits.

The horse canters to the right when the right lateral pair of legs passes in front of the left lateral pair; to the left when the left lateral pair passes in front of the right lateral pair. To clarify this for the beginner you have to imagine that the horse is cut in half through his midrif. When he canters to the right with his forelegs, the right forefoot will be placed in front of the left forefoot, exactly as a person's will if they 'gallop'. Similarly, the right hind foot will be placed in front of the left hind foot. When 'putting the horse back together' the following sequence of steps can be observed: to strike off into canter, the horse stands on his out-side hind foot first; he lifts his other three feet off the ground and then steps onto his inside hind foot and outside front foot simultaneously; lastly, he steps onto his inside forefoot. He then lifts all four feet off the ground simultaneously for the moment of suspension.

The horse must move his centre of gravity back in order to lift his forelegs and shoulders into canter. He needs a powerful surge forward with his hindquarters and therefore has to flex all the joints in his hindquarters and bring his weight back onto them. This frees the forehand to lift into the canter. The weight is taken on the outside hind leg.

The rider's inside leg pushes the horse's ribcage to the outside, freeing the inside foreleg to strike-off, and putting the weight onto the outside legs.

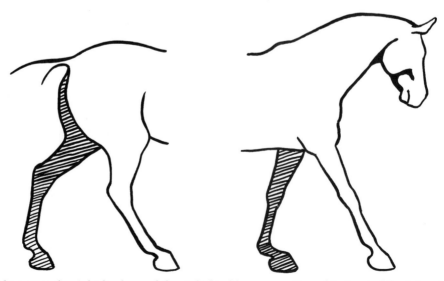

Figure 128 In right canter, the right foreleg and the right hind leg are positioned in front of the left pair of legs.

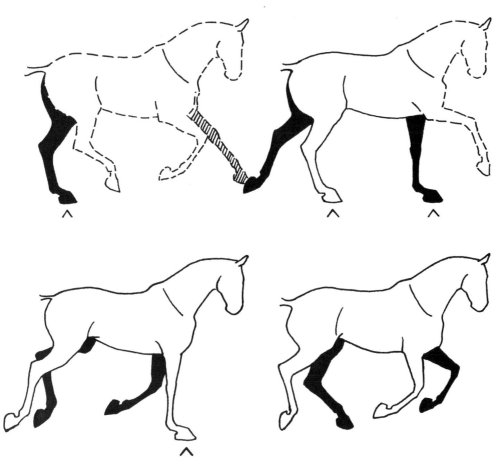

Figure 129 The sequence of footfall in right canter.

This helps with the push from the outside hind. The rider's outside leg moves back and prevents the horse from taking his weight off the outside hind. The rider's outside leg also 'announces' the canter. The powerful surge is brought about by the rider pushing the horse forwards with the inside leg and hip, whilst not allowing the energy to escape through the reins: the rider holds the reins and pushes the horse forward into them. With this amount of energy and the correct aids the horse should strike off correctly.

THE GAIT VARIANTS

The canter is performed in working, collected, medium and extended forms.

Working canter. This is the basic variant in which the horse learns to canter rhythmically, forward and in balance. We use it to establish rhythm, straightness, suppleness and contact. The strides are free and ground-covering, with a moderately arched carriage of neck and head. Once all this has been established, the canter is improved through more engagement of the hindquarters, leading to collection.

Collected canter. In this variant, the hindquarters become more engaged and the croup lowers. The pace becomes slower, with higher and shorter strides. The forehand lightens and the head and neck are more elevated and arched.

Medium canter. The energy from the collected canter is allowed to flow forward into a longer, more ground-covering and energetic stride. The neck is encouraged to lower and thus produce a freer movement of the shoulder (as discussed under Trot Variants).

Extended canter. The energy from collection is released into maximum, ground-covering strides, with a big 'jump'. The horse stays relaxed and under control, and should be easy to return to collection. The horse should not pull the bit from the rider: this would result in long, flat strides. The head and neck are allowed to lower, permitting the brachiocephalic muscle optimum contraction to give lift to the forearm.

THE RIDER'S POSITION AND SEAT

DURING THE CANTER DEPART

1) The upper body should be upright and relaxed, especially in the waist. The rider must not lean forwards during the canter depart, since this will lead to loss of engagement of the hindquarters.

2) The hips should be turned towards the direction of the strike-off. In other words, if the canter is to the left, the hips must be turned slightly to the left. This immediately puts more weight

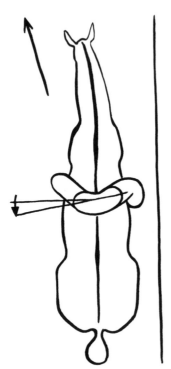

Figure 130 The rider's seat in left canter: the hips are turned slightly, to the left.

into the inside heel, puts the inside leg on the girth and moves the outside leg slightly back behind the girth. The hips and legs are now in precisely the correct position to apply the correct aids. (To help novice riders, I suggest that they look towards the direction of the canter. This automatically turns their hips in the correct direction.)

DURING THE CANTER

1) The upper body should be upright and relaxed.

2) The arms (elbows and shoulders) should hang relaxed against the rider's sides.

3) The legs should hang down, completely relaxed but ready for use. The inside hip and leg will be slightly more forward than the outside hip and leg. This happens automatically as a result of the canter action.

4) The waist should be totally relaxed to absorb all movement from the horse which might otherwise disturb the seat.

To develop this ability, try the following exercises:

1) Walk the horse and remove your stirrups. Open your knees, thus allowing a deeper seat. Make your seat feel very large, or like a bowl of jelly. Relax your waist to allow your seat to move backwards and forwards with each step of the horse. You should now feel your seatbones pressing into the saddle. This is the exact movement you will need for the canter.

2) Put your horse into canter. Imagine that you are cleaning the saddle with your seat. Push down and forwards with every stride (as though you were brushing the saddle). To help you with this, lean back in an exaggerated way. This should give you the experience of the correct feeling of the seat in the saddle.

Once you have mastered this relaxation of waist and legs, you should sit upright again and remain upright for all normal canter work.

THE AIDS TO CANTER

1) Before the aid for canter is given, the horse should be prepared for the movement with impulsion-increasing half-halts to produce the necessary energy for the strike-off.

2) The hands ensure that the horse is relaxed and in soft contact with the bit – he must feel soft on the inside rein. The inside rein is squeezed, either with the fingers alone or with flexion of the wrist. Lateral flexion of the wrist towards the little finger is also acceptable. If the horse is particularly resistant, the elbow itself can be moved back. This action turns the horse's head and neck slightly in the direction of the canter, so that he will be prepared to canter to that side. If there is any tension on the inside rein, he will be using the muscles on the outside of his neck (see Chapter 3), and therefore preparing for a canter to that side. Thus he will undoubtedly perform an incorrect depart. As soon as the head assumes an inside flexion, the rider must release the rein so that the contact becomes completely soft thereby ensuring that, while the horse is bent in the direction of the canter, he is not holding on to (pulling against) that rein at all. (If the horse uses his outside muscles he will canter to the outside.)

3) The outside rein has a little more contact, because the horse will be using the opposite (inside) neck muscles. A firm outside rein prevents the shoulder from moving sideways – falling in.

4) The inside leg, on the girth, pushes the horse's ribcage and therefore his weight to the outside and, together with the reins, puts the horse in the shoulder-in position. This position ensures an inside bend, which indicates to the horse the side to which he should canter. This position lifts the weight off the inside hind and foreleg and allows the horse to step on the outside hind foot and lift all three other feet off the ground in order to strike off at canter.

5) The outside leg, behind the girth, prevents the quarters from falling out. The outside leg, in this position, is only the *announcement* of the canter – the inside leg puts the horse in the position to strike off correctly.

6) The rider leans back ever so slightly and pushes the inside hip forwards to ask for the strike-off. The rider's hips should be turned towards the direction of the canter. The rider's knees must be open, or the horse will not move on.

Provided that the horse is prepared correctly for canter, the final signal may be the rider's own choice: inside leg on the girth; inside hip pushing down and forward or outside leg behind the girth.

These aids should be repeated at each stride to a greater or lesser degree, depending on the amount of collection needed.

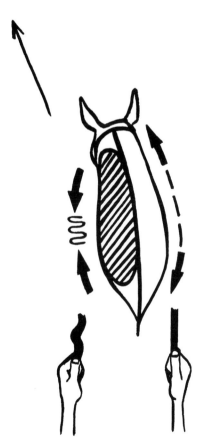

Figure 131 Squeeze the inside rein to ask the horse to use his inside neck flexors in preparation for the canter.

CANTERING THE UNBALANCED HORSE

The young or unschooled horse is often fairly unbalanced in canter. When he is put into canter he will more than likely lift his head and neck, become hollow in outline and canter too fast. The only way of getting him to canter slowly is to allow him to canter on a 20m circle at the speed at which he feels most comfortable. Often, sitting in the saddle makes the horse stiffen his back and lose his balance so you should be in a light seat, off the horse's back, and should stay in this posture until the horse learns to balance, when you should sit down carefully so as not to unbalance him again. Cantering around the outside of the arena usually only encourages horses to canter too fast and therefore lose more balance round the corners.

Once the horse has slowed down a little, start to play with the bit in the same way as in the trot. Explain to the horse that he should round his frame and lower his neck. Do this in rhythm with the canter. Remember to take and let go one rein, then take and let go the other rein and then push both hands forward to make a loop. Repeat the action. Soon, your horse will yield in the mouth, drop his head and neck down and slow considerably into a more balanced canter.

During this work, the horse should not be allowed to break into trot, but should be kept in the canter on the circle until he slows down by himself. He will do this as soon as he has figured out how to control his balance. He will gain balance as soon as he has dropped his head and neck, and become rounded and comfortable on a very light contact, because this brings his hind legs more underneath him.

LOWERING THE HEAD AND NECK

This is done in exactly the same manner as in trot. Make sure that the horse is relaxed in the mouth whilst trotting. Only ask for canter when the bit is lying in his relaxed mouth then, while asking, squeeze the reins alternately to inhibit the balance reaction of the neck. The horse should stay in a rounded frame, but if he hollows and throws his head up, squeeze the reins alternately as explained in Acceptance of the Bit (Chapter 4).

TEACHING THE YOUNG HORSE TO CANTER

If you are an experienced rider, you will be able to teach the horse using the aids already described. An inexperienced rider may have to follow these steps:

First, lunge the horse, lift the rein and give the verbal command 'canter', and push him forward until he breaks into canter. This must be practised on both reins, starting on the horse's 'easy' side.

Once he has learned this command, try it whilst riding him. Initially, you will have to push the horse forward in trot until he breaks into canter with the help of your correct position, seat and aids. Give the verbal command 'canter' as you give the aids to canter. Touch with the whip, if necessary. When the horse canters, it is important to give copious amounts of praise and to stay in canter for a while. Then ask for trot and repeat the exercise on the same lead a few times. Even if the horse strikes off on the wrong leg, he should be allowed to canter for a short time as the concept being taught was 'canter'. The horse will soon associate the word 'canter' with the correct action. (When a trained horse strikes off on the wrong lead, he should be stopped immediately and the command repeated, as this would be a 'canter depart' lesson, not a 'canter' lesson.)

This exercise can be done on a circle, or on the long side approaching the corner. The corner helps to put the horse into canter in two ways:

1) It unbalances him, and his automatic balancing reaction leads him to break into canter.

2) The longer stride in the trot eventually makes him feel uncomfortable. The muscles behind his shoulder start to stretch and the proprioceptive bodies in these muscles tell him that it feels uncomfortable and therefore he

breaks into canter so that the uncomfortable stretch feeling will disappear. The corner, in this instance, places him in the correct strike off position and causes maximum stretch.

Ask for the strike-off in the corner furthest away from the stables, or from other horses. This corner should be in such a position that the horse would automatically want to strike off on the correct lead. In other words, he would be setting himself up for a strike-off towards home. If the first corner fails, the next corner is available immediately. Remember to praise him as soon as he breaks into canter.

These steps teach the horse by associating a verbal sign with what, at this stage, may be an almost involuntary break into canter. The praise he receives for doing the correct action reinforces the concept.

Always start on the horse's 'easy' side and, once this has been mastered, do the same on his more difficult side. Although the canter should be performed equally on both leads to exercise the different muscle groups, initially practise the canter depart on one lead per day to avoid confusion.

Young horses often stop cantering after a few strides. They should be encouraged to keep the canter in order to establish a rhythm. Therefore, if you feel that the horse is about to trot, touch him with your inside leg and if that is not effective, with the whip. If the horse should 'fall' into trot by losing engagement of his hindquarters, he should first be balanced at the trot through half-halts and, only when balanced, asked for a canter depart again.

End the session when you *ask* for a trot transition, not when the horse breaks into trot. This will help to keep him in canter for a longer period the next day.

The more advanced rider need not go through all these phases, being able to teach the horse to canter purely by facilitation of the movement. By using the correct aids in the corner any horse can be induced to strike off into canter, so long as the message is put across very clearly through utilisation of the horse's balance and righting reactions.

PROGRESSION OF THE CANTER DEPART

Once the horse has learnt the canter depart, the process can be improved with the following exercises:

Ask for canter from sitting trot on a 20m circle.

Ask for canter from sitting trot on a straight line.

Ask for canter from walk on a circle.

Ask for canter from walk on a straight line.

TROUBLESHOOTING – difficulty in obtaining correct lead

RESISTANCE TO STRIKING OFF ON ONE LEAD

Most young horses favour cantering to one side. The background reasons for this have been discussed in Chapter 5. In order to canter, the horse will shorten the muscles on the side he is cantering to, and lengthen (stretch) the muscles on the other side. When we ask him to canter to the

Figure 132 The horse will naturally strike off to the side of the shorter muscles due to the stretch reflex.

side of his longer muscles, his shorter muscles will have to stretch. This triggers the stretch reflex and leads to immediate contraction of those same muscles. The consequent discomfort will make him break into canter on the side of the shorter muscles.

Corrections

a) You have to make it impossible for the horse to canter to the incorrect side by manipulating his balance reactions with weight distribution as previously described (The Aids to Canter).

b) If the horse continually strikes off on the wrong lead, try turning your head and looking in the direction of the strike-off.

c) Alternatively, put a pole diagonally across the corner of the school and ask for canter at that spot.

d) If the incorrect strike-off persists, make absolutely sure that the horse has completely released the inside rein and is bent to the inside with no contact on that rein. If the horse has contact on the inside rein he is more than likely bent to the outside. Even if he is only tightening the muscles on the outside while he appears to be bent to the inside he will still strike-off with the outside leg.

e) If he repeatedly strikes off incorrectly, take a fairly strong contact on the outside rein, whilst moving it towards the wither. This will bring the shoulder to the inside and give more of an indication to the horse which lead he should be preparing for.

f) Simultaneously ask for a smaller circle as well as a canter. If the strike off is correct, immediately enlarge the circle again and continue to canter.

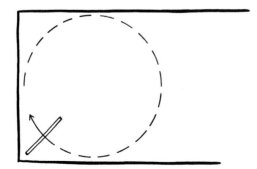

Figure 133 Facilitate the correct lead in the canter with a pole through the corner of the arena.

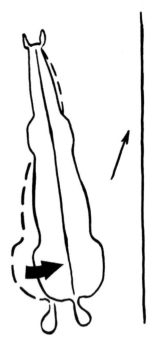

Figure 134 The horse's hindquarters swing out and he thus loses the inside bend.

g) If the horse still makes mistakes, he could well be pushing his hindquarters to the outside in a righting reaction to bring his body in alignment with his head. Although his neck is still bent to the inside, he will have taken the weight off his outside hind leg. His hindquarters are thus preparing for an outside canter. In this instance, your outside leg should be preventing the swing of the horse's outside hind leg.

EARLY WORK AT CANTER

When starting the canter, do a lot of canter work on hacks out, especially up hills and in straight lines. This strengthens the hindquarters and helps to improve the balance of the horse in canter.

To teach the horse to canter straight up the long side without increasing his speed, the canter should be established on a 20 m circle. Once the horse can maintain canter on the circle, he should be asked to continue straight for a few strides to the next marker. Your inside leg should be kept firmly on the girth, with a firm contact on the outside rein.

At the next marker, ride a 20m circle. Establish rhythm and balance on this circle and then ride straight to the next marker. Repeat the exercise. Once the horse maintains the same rhythm on the straight section, he can be asked to canter straight for two markers and then circle again. Repeat this exercise until the horse can maintain a rhythmical, straight canter around the whole arena.

Often, young, unbalanced horses, or horses who have been frightened when learning to canter or have nervous temperaments, will strike off in a canter and then start to 'run away' with their heads in the air. The rider automatically gets nervous, tenses up and starts to pull on the horse's mouth.

This starts a vicious circle, because the horse becomes more frightened and throws his head up in the air and starts running more. Once this has happened, it is extremely important that the rider carries on in the canter, but on a circle, as this will automatically slow the horse down. The rider should take a light seat (virtually standing in the stirrups) and start to 'play' with the reins, squeezing one rein then the other and then releasing both by pushing the hands forwards. This should be repeated until the horse brings his head and neck down.

As soon as the horse's head comes down, he will find his balance and start to canter more slowly.

Figure 135 Bring the horse's head down in early canter work. This will help him to maintain balance.

Figure 136 The young horse finding his balance in canter.

The rider should just sit it through until the horse starts to do this. He will initially go very fast and be very unbalanced, but he will soon find out that in order not to fall over, he must slow down. It is important for the rider to ensure that the horse releases the bit and brings his head and neck down. This brings the abdominal muscles into action, strengthens the back, brings the horse's hindquarters more underneath him and makes him more comfortable to ride.

Horses who are slow and well balanced should be worked around the outside of the arena. They should be pushed forward into a fairly strong canter. This will strengthen the hindquarters and produce a bigger 'jump' in the canter.

THROUBLESHOOTING – problems in early canter work

CANTERING DISUNITED
The horse has lost his balance, is stiff to one side or has a weakness in his hindquarters. This has made him change the leading leg of the hindquarters.

Corrections
a) Stop the canter and ask for a true canter again. If you have done this a few times and he still becomes disunited, give the horse a sharp kick with your outside leg. Give a touch with the whip behind the outside leg, together with the kick, if the kick alone is not effective.
b) Ride on a circle carefully to prevent loss of balance. Ensure that you are on the outside rein and use it to turn the horse ('long arm' technique).

IMPROVING THE CANTER

WORKING TOWARDS COLLECTION

Once the horse has established a rhythmic and enduring canter, start riding canter-trot transitions to encourage more engagement of the hindquarters. At first, when you bring the horse to trot with the downward aids, it is more than likely that he will lose his balance and go on the forehand, as he will

not be able to absorb all his impulsion into the trot. Therefore, ride a series of half-halts as soon as the horse has come into trot, and squeeze the reins alternately so that he does not use his neck to balance with, but engages his hindquarters instead.

To improve the quality of the canter and gain more engagement of the hindquarters, repeat the canter aids lightly at each stride. It should feel as though you are picking up a barrel with your legs and seat at every stride, as when riding an impulsion-increasing half-halt. You have to pick the horse up at every stride and 'catch' the impulsion in the outside rein. This prevents the horse from going faster in the canter. Pushing the horse forward and preventing him from 'running' by means of the reins, produces a better 'jump' in the canter, as a result of better engagement.

One of the most useful exercises in canter is decreasing and increasing the size of the circle. This exercise helps to supple the horse, to engage the hindquarters and to straighten him, and it teaches the horse to move away from the rider's leg in preparation for the shoulder-in. Decrease the circle with the use of the outside hand and the 'long arm' technique. 'Sponge' the inside rein for a smaller circle and give your aids at every quarter circle rather than continuously. Once a fairly small circle is achieved, increase the size of the circle by pushing the horse out with your inside leg on the girth. Use the 'push through' technique as described in Chapter 7.

Alternating transitions from medium to collected canter and back on a circle improves engagement of the hindquarters and thus collection. Shorten the tempo with half-halts and repeated leg and seat aids, to attain more collection.

SHOULDER-IN AT CANTER

Your horse should now be ready for shoulder-in at canter. This exercise is crucial to achieving a straight horse. It is the best suppling exercise at the canter, and it produces great engagement of the hindquarters. The shoulder-in is performed exactly the same as in trot. The outside rein is firm and positions the shoulder on the track. The inside rein produces the bend without any pull on the rein. The inside leg on the girth pushes the ribcage to the outside and the outside leg prevents the horse from throwing his quarters to the outside. Ride a few strides shoulder-in and then circle. Repeat this until you can manage to perform shoulder-in at canter the whole length of the manége.

WALK TO CANTER AND HALT TO CANTER

Your horse should now be ready for the walk to canter transition.

1) Prepare the horse for canter by creating more impulsion with alternate leg aids, but not allowing him too much forward action (rein aids). This engages the hindquarters and will produce the energy needed for the 'jump' into canter.

2) Keep the lightness in the mouth with alternate rein aids.

3) Place your outside leg behind the girth to warn the horse that the canter is imminent, but do not yet give an aid. Although this will be initially a little difficult for novices, the final signal should be given as the horse puts his inside foreleg down. At this moment, the outside hind leg is in the air and the very next step will be the first canter step. The correct timing of the signal will only be possible if the horse is prepared for the movement. This timing will ensure a clean strike-off and prevent the extra little step often seen in walk-canter transitions.

4) Give the canter aids, with extra emphasis on the seat action and clear leg aids. (A quick increase in impulsion is needed.) If necessary, back up the aids with a slight tap of the whip.

5) Hold the outside rein so that the energy goes upward and does not peter out into a trot.

Halt to canter is performed in the same manner as walk to canter. A walk step or two may be allowed initially.

CANTER TO WALK

This is a demanding exercise which can only be attempted once the canter is balanced and fairly collected, with the hindquarters engaged. Also, the horse must have accepted the leg aids for the purpose of maintaining impulsion and collection rather than for acceleration, and the canter-trot transition must be established and balanced.

1) Practise transitions from medium or working canter to collected canter.

2) Canter a 20 m circle. Decrease the size as much as possible and then ask for walk.

3) Collect the canter on a 20 m circle. Ask for a 10 m circle and walk. This automatically increases the engagement of the inside hind leg, and the smaller circle slows the horse down a little.

4) Collect and slow the canter for a few strides. Imagine cantering on the spot. Then ask for the walk.

5) Canter a figure-of-eight across the width of the arena, with a simple change on the centre line.

6) Progress to a transition between E and B, as this is easier than on the diagonal.

7) Ride serpentines with simple changes in between.

8) Finally, attempt this exercise on the diagonal.

9) To perfect this transition, it should also be performed from counter-canter.

The aids for the canter to walk transition
These aids are given when the horse is in the moment of suspension in the canter. When he lands, his outside hind leg lands first, then the diagonal pair, and the next step will be the walk step. The forward walk aid should be given immediately afterwards or the horse will lose impulsion. The aids for the transition are:

First, half-halt to engage the hindquarters.

Then, simultaneously:

Close your knees with as much power as you can manage.

Close your lower leg on the horse to encourage more engagement.

Keep the horse light and rounded with alternate rein aids.

Block the horse with the outside hand by bracing your elbow in co-contraction.

Look up and lean back slightly.

Use your seat by contracting your seat (gluteal) muscles. This ensures engagement and forward action.

Do not relax these aids until the horse takes his first walk step or your transition will peter out into a trot. Once the transition is completed, reward the horse.

The more collected the canter, the easier the transition will be.

TROUBLESHOOTING –
problems in more advanced canter work

CROOKEDNESS IN THE CANTER

Horses are naturally crooked in the canter. This is not the result of their stiff spines, as the same tendency exists in dogs, who have extremely supple spines. The reason for this crookedness lies, rather, in the leading pair of legs. In left canter, for example, the left foreleg leads, as well as the left hind leg. This means that the left shoulder and left hip are slightly more forward than the right shoulder and hip. This natural crookedness is exacerbated on one side of the horse as the result of dominance.

Corrections
a) Suppling and straightening exercises should improve this situation.
b) Ride the long side as though you were riding a circle, on the outside rein.
c) Ride a circle on the short side, then ask for a few straight strides on the long side and circle as soon as the horse loses straightness, or gains speed.
d) Ride shoulder-in at canter.

ON THE FOREHAND
Not enough engagement.
Corrections
a) Ask for more engagement at every stride.
b) Ride canter – trot and canter – walk transitions.

HINDQUARTERS MOVING OUT DURING THE CANTER DEPART
The horse lacks the strength to step under with his hind leg. Alternatively, he may not be straight or supple enough to maintain the inside bend.
Corrections
a) Keep your outside leg firmly behind the girth.
b) Go back to more strengthening and straightening exercises.

FOUR-BEAT CANTER
The horse is not engaged or going forward enough.
Corrections
a) Do more strengthening exercises.
b) Alternate medium and collected canter on a circle.
c) Establish a good working canter before attempting collection.
d) Be certain that you have impulsion in the canter. Slowness does not equal collection.

MEDIUM AND EXTENDED CANTER

Medium canter is used in exercises to strengthen the hindquarters, produce impulsion and engagement and to discipline the horse. Extended canter is mainly a competition movement which shows off the horse's submission, lightness of the forehand and level of engagement.

THE AIDS FOR MEDIUM AND EXTENDED CANTER

1) 'Sponge' the reins alternately to prevent co-contraction of the neck and prevent the horse from putting his centre of gravity forwards.

2) Push him forwards with both legs on the girth.

3) Once the horse has given the longer stride, yield a little with your hands to allow the neck to lengthen. This produces freer shoulder action, the importance of which is described in The Trot Variants (p. 110).

4) The same aids are used for extended canter, but the horse is pushed forwards to his maximum length of stride (ground-covering) with maximum elevation ('jump').

EXERCISES IN MEDIUM CANTER

1) 'Wake the horse up' with medium canter around the whole arena.

2) Alternate medium and collected canter on a circle.

3) Alternate medium and collected canter on the long side of the arena.

4) Alternate medium and collected canter around the arena, with collection on the long side and medium on the short side.

5) Ride medium canter across the diagonal and collect at X.

6) Ride medium canter up the long side, collect at K and walk at A.

7) Ride collected canter on a 20 m circle at A. Proceed to F. Ride medium canter to the next marker. Collect the canter and ride a 20 m circle. Ride medium canter on the straight to the next marker, collect and circle 20 m again and medium canter to the next marker, etc.

8) Ride a 20 m circle in collected canter. Spiral inwards at collected canter and push the horse out again in medium canter.

9) Alternate medium and collected canter during counter-canter. This improves balance.

TROUBLESHOOTING – problems in medium and extended canter

HINDQUARTERS FALLING IN
The horse is not supple or straight enough.
Corrections
a) Do more suppling and straightening exercises.
b) Ride the canter in a shoulder-in position with a strong inside leg and a firm outside rein.

FLAT, LONG STRIDES
The horse does not have enough engagement or roundness.
Corrections
a) Practise more strengthening and engagement exercises.
b) A collected canter with high, rounded, bouncy strides will improve the medium and extended stride.
c) Keep the horse in a round frame, ensuring complete yielding to the hands for more abdominal muscle contraction with resultant arching of the back.

COUNTER-CANTER

In counter-canter the horse canters to the opposite side of his leading leg. Work at counter-canter may be introduced once the working canter is rhythmical, balanced and in the process of developing collection. If it is introduced too soon the horse may lose balance at the working variant, and therefore change lead. Engagement prevents such loss of balance.

REASONS FOR RIDING COUNTER-CANTER

1) This exercise strengthens the leading hind leg more than the true canter would, as the horse has to carry his weight over this leg or he will lose balance. It thus also aids engagement.

2) It straightens the horse by stretching the muscles on the leading side. (The exercise is

completely unnatural to the horse and compels him to use his muscles in a different way.)

3) It is a superb balancing exercise, because the horse has to learn to balance in an extremely unbalancing gait.

HOW TO RIDE COUNTER-CANTER

1) Start with a 3m loop on the long side of the manége and ride in a long curve.

2) Ask for a soft inside bend and ride on the outside rein.

3) The inside leg should remain 'glued' to the ribcage to maintain the inside bend. If this inside bend is lost, the horse may lose balance and change his lead.

4) Your weight should be over the horse's inside leg. If your weight shifts, the horse may, once again, lose balance and change the lead.

5) The outside leg, behind the girth, pushes the quarters over, through the bend.

6) Ease the horse's shoulders over with both reins while 'sponging' the inside rein. If you pull him over with the outside rein, he may lose balance and change the lead. If he shows resistance to the inside rein, he will also lose balance and change lead.

EXERCISES INVOLVING COUNTER-CANTER

1) Start with shallow loops up the long side. Slowly increase the size of the loop until the horse can finally do a 20m, three-loop serpentine.

2) A further development is the three-quarter circle. Ride a half circle in canter to the centre line and join the track in counter-canter at E. Ride around the short side in counter-canter, to X, then ride a 10m half circle in true canter to B.

3) Once the horse has become collected, and performs the 20m, serpentine with ease, he can start circles at counter-canter. A 20m figure-of-eight

with alternating counter-canter and true canter relieves the pressure on the legs and helps him to regain balance after the counter-canter.

4) Slowly decrease the size of the figure-of-eight.

5) Increase the number of loops in the serpentine.

6) Ride a 20m circle at counter-canter; ask the horse to bend from one side to the other without resistance or co-contraction in the neck. Ensure that the contact remains soft. This will automatically make him use his hindquarters for balance.

Once the horse has accepted the counter-canter, all the above exercises should be done with his neck yielding completely to the hands.

The counter-canter may be further improved by the following exercise:

7) Ride a 10m half circle at V, followed by a 10m half circle in counter-canter to P. Ride straight in counter-canter, then ride a 10m half circle in counter-canter at R, followed by a 10m half circle in true canter at S. Continue round the arena in this fashion using all the relevant markers. At all times, endeavour to improve the horse's balance.

TROUBLESHOOTING – problems in counter-canter

CHANGING LEAD
This is caused by stiffness or loss of balance.
Corrections
a) More suppling, straightening and collecting exercises are required.
b) Ensure that your inside leg is really pushing on the girth and that your weight is over the inside leg, and not moving. You must keep the horse in balance, since the horse's natural inclination puts him off balance.
c) Use more outside leg to turn the whole horse.
d) Ease him over with both reins when changing direction.
e) Maintain the soft contact on the inside rein. Do not punish the horse for changing lead. Simply walk and pick up the desired lead again.

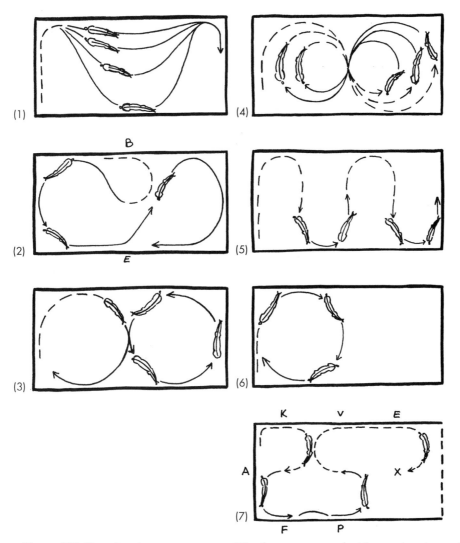

Figure 137 Exercises in counter-canter. (Numbers correspond with exercises in text.)

Punishment can lead to problems when you attempt flying changes – the horse may think he will be punished if he performs a flying change and thus become tense and anxious.

f) Counter-canter to walk transitions will improve balance.

THE FLYING CHANGE

The flying change is a perfectly natural movement for the horse. All horses do flying changes when running free and changing direction. Racehorses may change legs a few times during the course of a race – this protects the tiring leading leg.

The horse does the change during the moment of suspension. The aids should therefore be given an instant before this – at the same moment as you would give your usual canter aid for every stride. During the change, the horse's head and neck stretch forward slightly and the horse lengthens momentarily.

137

PREREQUISITES FOR THE FLYING CHANGE

1) Before attempting the flying change your horse's counter-canter should be clearly established, with good balance.

2) The transitions between walk and canter should be completely established. You should be able to do a specific number of canter strides, followed by a specific number of walk strides (for example, four canter strides, followed by four walk strides, etc.)

3) The counter-canter to walk transition should also be good; transitions counter-canter to walk to canter to walk on a circle should be established.

4) There should be no confusion with canter strike-offs and no resistance in the strike-off, as this would lead to resistance of the bit during the moment of the change, and thus ruin it.

5) The horse should be engaged, energetic, in balance and supple, to ensure a good 'jump' in the change.

THE AIDS FOR A FLYING CHANGE

1) Half-halt to balance and prepare the horse.

2) The outside leg moves back to warn the horse a stride or two before the change. This ensures a better 'jump'.

3) The outside rein takes a stronger contact while the outside leg simultaneously gives the aid, and the hips turn towards the new lead. Remember that the changing of the hips will automatically change the leg position, moving your inside leg forward slightly.

4) The reins yield slightly to allow the 'jump'. Any resistance in the mouth will create stiffness and ruin the change.

5) Half-halt again to regain collection and balance.

6) Reward.

EXERCISES TO TEACH THE FLYING CHANGE

Initially, teach the flying change concept from the horse's 'bad side' to his 'good side' – he will learn more quickly in this way.

1) Ride transitions counter-canter to walk to canter on a 20 m circle a few times. When ready, ask for a change from counter-canter to canter. This method has the added advantage of simultaneously developing balance.

2) Ride a 10-15 m figure-of-eight and ask for a simple change in between the circles. Do this three times. On the fourth attempt, ask for a flying change. Reward and walk. This helps to relax the horse after the change. Then attempt another change. Do not swing the horse in the new direction – this will lead to loss of balance, and destroy the straightness of the movement. (This exercise should only be used to teach the horse the concept as it can lead to anticipation of the movement.)

3) If there is a problem at all, place a pole at the junction between the two circles. The horse will change clean and 'jump' through the change.

Once the horse has thoroughly grasped the concept, the exercise can be taught to the other side. At this stage, the canter should not be too slow and collected, because the change is easier for the horse from a slightly longer stride and frame, and he should go forward into the change to ensure a good 'jump'.

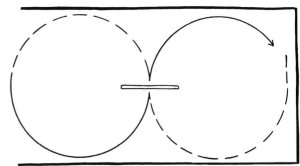

Figure 138 A pole at the junction between the two circles will facilitate a clean flying change.

Once the horse can change from either lead on a circle, you can progress to changing on a straight track through use of the following exercises:

1) Canter on the outside of the manège and turn down the centre line. Ride half-pass to the long side. Ride a few strides straight on and ask for a change. Reward.

2) Canter a 10 m half circle onto the centre line and then proceed back to the track. Ride a flying change a few strides after reaching the track.

3) Canter across the diagonal and change one stride after you reach the track, or at A or C.

4) Canter a 20 m circle. Ride a flying change at the appropriate spot to counter-canter. Initially, do this when facing towards home but, eventually, at any place on the circle.

In these exercises, ride the changes at different markers. If you do them repeatedly in the same place, or as soon as you reach the track, the horse will learn to anticipate the change. (In a test, the change at the end of the diagonal is performed on the last stride before reaching the track.)

SEQUENCE CHANGES

Once the horse is completely trained in single flying changes, he will be ready to start the sequence changes, and will find it relatively easy. The rider however, may find co-ordinating the quick change of aids difficult. The rider with good rhythm will learn quickly. The three- and two-time changes seem to be the easiest, as the former is the waltz rhythm while the latter is a two-step rhythm. The dancers will thus thrive on them.

1) Start by riding two changes along the long side of the arena. These need not be related, but will help to develop quick co-ordination and reflexes. Reward the horse and walk to relax him. Repeat.

2) Once you and the horse have no difficulties in performing two changes, three may be attempted.

3) Now it is only a question of counting and changing. Find the method of counting that suits you best. Each person seems to have a method which helps to co-ordinate their aids with their counting. Some riders prefer to count 'one, two, three, four; one, two three four', with an accent on the 'one'. Others prefer to count 'one, two, three, four; change, two, three, four; change, two, three, four', while some even prefer, 'one, two, three, four 'two, two, three, four; three, two, three, four', etc.

4) At first, start with a fair number of strides between the changes – about seven. This will give you ample time to organise yourself and prepare for the aid. Do a few, reward and walk to regain calmness.

5) Place the outside leg behind the girth one stride before the change, to give the horse a warning. Give pressure with that leg only when asking for the change.

6) Once you have perfected the four-stride changes, attempt the threes and then the twos.

7) When practising the quicker changes ask for only two changes with three strides in between. Reward the horse and walk. Practise this for a few days and then progress to three changes. When the horse does this calmly, you can attempt more, until you can do five or more changes in a row.

8) When you have perfected all these, and can perform them on the quarter line, the diagonal and the circle, you will be ready to teach your horse to change at every stride.

FLYING CHANGE AT EVERY STRIDE

This must be the most exhilarating part of the training of a horse. The rider can literally tell the horse what to do at every single stride! By the time your horse has learnt the sequence changes up to every second stride, he should have no problem with the changes at every stride.

1) Work on the three-quarter line so that the horse does not use the wall for balance. Put your horse in canter and ask for two one-time changes (left, right). Reward him and walk. Resist the temptation to ask for more. Put your horse away and start the changes again the following day.

2) For the next few days, ask for only two changes a few times on both reins.

3) Now ask for two changes twice down the long side of the manège. Reward and walk. You may repeat this a few times, but do not tire or excite your horse.

4) Once the two one-time changes are established, you may ask for three down the long side.

5) After this, ask for five. If the horse does this without any problems you will probably get as many as you want.

TROUBLESHOOTING –
problems with flying changes

ANTICIPATION
Corrections
a) Do not continue to ride changes in the same place.
b) If the horse does a change before the request, walk immediately and ask for canter on the same lead. Continue in counter-canter and ride across the arena to get back to true canter and ask for the change again.

c) Canter across the arena in true canter and change to counter-canter before the short side. Ride counter-canter through the short side and cross the arena again in true canter. Repeat the change to counter-canter. This makes the horse think and wait.
d) Take a three-week break from flying changes. This will take the pressure off the horse. You will find that the work has been consolidated and the horse has lost the anxiety surrounding the flying changes.

SWINGING HINDQUARTERS
The horse is not supple, relaxed or straight enough.
Correction
Do many more suppling and straightening exercises before proceeding with the flying changes.

LATE CHANGE OF HIND LEG
The horse's hindquarters are not engaged enough, he has lost balance, or he has not acquired ambidexterity. If the reins are too short through the change, he will not have enough freedom to change behind.
Corrections
a) Do more exercises to strengthen, collect and engage the hindquarters.
b) Do more suppling exercises.
c) Practise the change over a pole.
d) Make sure that the horse is balanced before the change.
e) Yield slightly with your hands through the change.

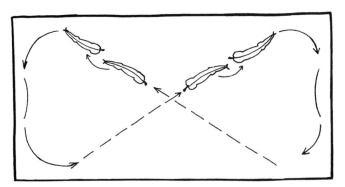

Figure 139 Execute a flying change from canter to counter-canter as the horse reaches the short side.

f) Touch his hind leg with the whip as you ask for the change.

'ABOVE THE BIT' AND HOLLOW
The horse is not engaged enough and is therefore not light enough in the hands.
Corrections
a) Ask for more collection and lightness before the change.
b) Yield slightly with your hands through the change.

THE HORSE BECOMES TENSE
Problem of temperament.
Corrections
a) Do not punish him. Walk and regain relaxation as described in Chapter 4, then start the exercise again.
b) Leave the changes for a few weeks and attempt them again later.

CHANGING HIGHER IN THE QUARTERS THAN IN THE FOREHAND
The horse is on his forehand and does not have enough engagement or collection.
Corrections
a) Do more strengthening and collecting exercises.
b) Ride half-halts before and after every change to encourage more engagement.

GAINING SPEED ON THE CHANGES
The horse is either becoming excited or losing balance and engagement.
Corrections
a) If he does this on single flying changes, do one change and then walk or halt. Repeat this a few times. Your horse will soon associate the change with the walk, and stop rushing.
b) In sequence changes, you can ride a few changes and then walk, halt or do a few changes followed by a pirouette. The horse will then automatically start to wait for the next command.

LOSS OF RHYTHM
There may have been interference with the horse's mouth, or the horse may have lost impulsion or concentration. Also, the rider may have momentarily lost co-ordination or concentration.
Correction
Ascertain which was the case and remedy as appropriate.

THE CANTER HALF-PASS

In canter half-pass the horse moves forwards and sideways in collected canter. A high degree of collection and lightness is required in this movement. This half-pass is an end product of training, and is used for competition purposes.

HOW TO RIDE CANTER HALF-PASS

Half-pass at canter is easier to perform, and presents fewer problems, than at trot. Start in shoulder-fore to ensure an inside bend, and proceed with the same aids as described for trot (p. 119).

1) Ride a half-pass from the centre line to the track.

2) Canter up the long side and half-pass to the centre line. Proceed straight.

3) Alternate half-pass and shoulder-in across the diagonal. This teaches the horse not to rush.

4) Half-pass across the entire arena, ride one stride on the track, followed by a flying change. Alternate the flying change with simple changes and do them at different places to avoid anticipation.

5) Ride counter-changes from centre line to track and back, or from the track to the centre line and back.

6) Ride an 8 m circle on the centre line or track, followed by a half-pass.

TROUBLESHOOTING – problems with canter half-pass

RUSHING SIDEWAYS
Anxiety or loss of balance.

Corrections
a) Ride half-pass a few strides, then ask for a volte.
b) Ride half-pass a few strides, then walk.
c) Ride half-pass a few strides, straighten, then counter-canter.
d) Ride half-pass a few strides, shoulder-in a few strides, followed by half-pass.

HINDQUARTERS FALLING IN
Rider using too much outside leg.
Correction
As for half-pass in trot (see p. 122).

NOT ENOUGH INSIDE BEND
The horse is not supple enough, or you are not using enough inside leg.
Corrections
a) Practise more shoulder-in at canter.
b) Use more inside leg and ask for a soft feel on the inside rein. Use the 'long arm' technique with the outside rein to push the horse over.

CANTER ZIGZAGS

These are ridden around the centre line, with either 4-8-8-4 half-pass strides or 3-6-6-6-6-3 half-pass strides. They must be executed to the same distance either side of, and parallel to, the centre line. The correct bend should be maintained. Once the horse can execute half-passes and flying changes without difficulty, he will not find this movement a problem. The most difficult part of the movement seems to be the rider's co-ordination, and most errors made seem to arise from this.

How to ride a canter zigzag
1) The stride before the change should be ridden straight, to prevent the horse from losing balance. This explains to him that a change of direction is imminent and thus prevents the quarters from swinging or being 'left behind'.

2) Try a zigzag with more strides, and a three-line zigzag initially. This will help you to prepare yourself and get your co-ordination organised. Counting aloud as you canter will help you to organise yourself. Even go so far as counting 'one, two, three, straight, change, two, three, four, five, six, seven, straight, change, two, three' etc. Practise repeatedly until you are quick with your aids, then proceed to the proper zigzag.

This repetitive practice is specifically for the rider. If it is overdone the horse may start to anticipate, which would be detrimental to the movement. Therefore, once you feel confident with your aids, refrain from doing this exercise for about three weeks. This should get it out of the horse's system, and when you attempt it again, there should be no anticipation.

TROUBLESHOOTING –

SWINGING HINDQUARTERS
Not enough preparation for the change of direction.
Correction
Prepare the horse for the change by riding one straight stride beforehand.

THE CANTER PIROUETTE

The canter pirouette consists of some six to eight strides of canter, executed on one spot. This movement is executed slowly in a circle one step at a time, with the hind legs forming the smallest of circles and the forelegs forming a larger circle around the hind legs. The canter should be slow and extremely collected.

The canter pirouette is an Advanced dressage movement; an end product developed through many years of work. The movement requires from the horse considerable strength and balance, which exercises leading to the pirouette help to develop.

HOW TO RIDE A CANTER PIROUETTE

In order for a horse to be capable of doing this movement, he has to be prepared to such an extent that the preparation will eventually lead to the execution of the movement itself. The following exercises should provide such preparation:

1) It is essential that the horse is well versed in the canter half-pass, as the pirouette is virtually a half-pass in one place (large sideways steps with the forelegs and very small steps with the hind legs).

2) Canter a 20 m circle and slowly decrease this to a very small volte and then increase it again. Be certain that the horse's hindquarters do not fall out while executing this exercise.

3) Canter a 20 m circle and ask the horse for quarters-in on this circle. This should be practised until the horse can do it with ease.

4) Canter a half-pass on a decreasing circle.

5) Canter on a 20 m circle. At every quarter circle, canter a stride on one spot. As soon as the horse is able, ask for two strides on one spot and, once the horse is able to do this, ask for three strides on one spot. Increase the strides to about six on the same spot.

6) Walk a small circle with the quarters in, a few steps only, and then proceed with a few steps of canter with quarters in and still on the small circle. Proceed in this manner a few times during a training session. Once this is established, try a few more steps of this canter.

7) Walk in a small circle in a shoulder-in position and then ask for a small canter circle in a shoulder-in position. This exercise will ensure that you have your inside leg on the girth at all times.

8) Your horse should now be ready to do one canter pirouette stride. It is important to ask for one stride at a time, to prevent the horse from swinging his forehand into the pirouette, which leads to the hindquarters becoming 'stuck'. Do one stride on the spot and the next stride in pirouette, then ride forwards again.

Your horse should now be ready to perform a quarter pirouette.

9) Canter in a square, riding quarter pirouettes in each corner. This must be done with control or it will be of little value. If your horse throws his forehand around then go back to cantering on the spot.

10) Canter in half-pass from the wall towards the centre line and ask for a pirouette from this movement. (Be careful not to overdo this exercise, since it can lead to the horse putting himself in half-pass before each pirouette.)

11) Canter in renvers a metre or two in from the track, then ride a pirouette towards the track.

12) Ride shoulder-in, then perform the canter pirouette.

13) Occasionally, ride larger pirouettes to ensure that the rhythm remains constant.

This work is extremely strenuous for the horse, and he should be allowed to stretch from time to time. He will often give an indication when this is necessary. At this stage he should be worked in short sessions.

RIDER'S POSITION AND THE EFFECT OF THE AIDS

1) The inside leg, on the girth, pushes the ribcage to the outside, thus preventing the forehand from falling into the circle.

2) The outside leg, slightly behind the girth, prevents the horse from straightening himself with an automatic righting reaction against the effect of the inside bend. (This righting reaction would make the horse swing his quarters to the outside in order to bring his body into alignment.) The outside leg pushes the whole horse to the inside and into the canter pirouette.

3) The inside hand asks for the inside bend by 'sponging' the rein slightly. The inside rein should be opened slightly to lead the horse into the movement, and closed against his neck if he should attempt to swing his forehand over.

4) The outside hand has a firm contact and brings the horse's head, neck and shoulder towards the inside (the 'long arm' technique.)

5) The rider's outside shoulder moves back slightly to help the outside hand in preventing the horse from throwing his shoulders to the inside. Leaning back slightly may help to produce the correct 'feel'.

6) The seat keeps the forward impulsion of the canter.

TROUBLESHOOTING – problems in canter pirouette

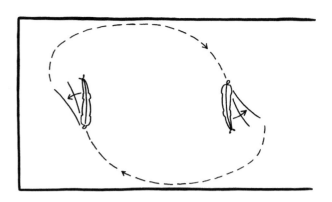

Figure 140 A few pirouette strides executed from the counter-canter can counteract anticipation.

ANTICIPATION

The horse starts to 'throw' his forehand into the pirouette.

Corrections

a) Use a firm outside hand. The inside leg should be pressed harder on the girth, against the ribcage, to push the horse's weight to the outside. Try using only the legs to achieve a pirouette.

b) Ask for two pirouette strides only, then continue straight on.

c) Ride in counter-canter on a 20m circle in the centre of the arena. As you reach the centre line, ask for two or three pirouette strides, then continue in counter-canter on the 20m circle (which will now have a small bulge in it).

HINDQUARTERS 'STICKING'

The horse's hindquarters are not yet strong enough.

Corrections

a) Enlarge the circle and ride definite half-pass steps in a circle.

b) Ride more quarters-in on a slightly larger circle, and do more preparatory exercises.

HORSE BECOMING EXCITED

Corrections

a) Canter forwards, then bring the horse back to accepting cantering a few strides on the spot, followed by cantering forwards again.

b) Give him a three-week rest from pirouettes.

CHAPTER 14

PIAFFE AND PASSAGE

Piaffe and passage are High School movements; end products of training which represent the highest degree of true collection at trot. They are performed mainly in the highest levels of competition dressage and in specialised performances such as those of the Spanish Riding School and the Cadre Noir. Correct work in piaffe produces such quality of engagement that it has the effect of making all other movements relatively easy for the horse and it improves the quality of the other movements. Passage is often seen in horses at liberty in the field, who produce it when they are frightened or 'showing off'. Especially in the former case, however, it may be performed in a hollow outline with hindquarters trailing - features which do not represent the qualities required in the correct school movement.

PIAFFE

Piaffe is executed with optimum impulsion, cadence and consistent rhythm, almost on the spot. Maximum flexion, engagement and power of the hindquarters allow the forehand to lighten; the horse's head and neck are raised, with the head perpendicular to the ground. The toes of the hind legs should rise level with the middle or top of the fetlock of the opposite leg. The toes of the forelegs should be at or above the fetlock of the opposite leg, with the forearms raised to a horizontal level. The horse gives soft, cadenced and springy diagonal steps and is ready to move forwards at any time.

6) Piaffe

Rhythm, cadence and power should never be sacrificed for trotting on one spot, especially during the early stages of training. A slow and high piaffe is difficult to obtain and not all horses have the same talent for this.

THE AIDS FOR PIAFFE

1) The legs give a forward aid *on the girth*. The legs should not be used behind the girth as this area is the key point of control for moving the hindquarters sideways and leg aids given there can lead to swinging of the hindquarters. The leg aid on the girth is the key point of control for forward movement, and piaffe is essentially a forward movement. The legs may be used alternately or simultaneously, depending on which method suits you and your horse best. You may even interchange these methods if necessary. You will soon find out, from your horse's reactions, when to use your legs alternately and when together.

2) The seat is pushed into the saddle to create forward movement and stimulate the hindquarters. Do not lean forward, as this would automatically make the horse move his centre of gravity forwards to compensate for the new weight distribution and thus lose the engagement of his hindquarters, which is so essential for this level of collection. The hips may be used in an alternating fashion in the rhythm of the piaffe. Aim towards eliciting the piaffe from the hip action alone. This will eventually be a less conspicuous aid.

3) The hands 'sponge' the reins to prevent the neck from co-contracting (bracing).

4) The arms, through intermittent co-contraction (bracing) of the elbows, explain to the horse that he should not move off into trot.

TEACHING THE HORSE TO PIAFFE

Teaching the piaffe takes many hours and should be tackled with the utmost patience. Before start-ing the piaffe, the horse should be straight and supple, with well developed hindquarters.

There are three methods of teaching the horse to piaffe:

Method one – in hand. This method makes use of learning through signals and not by learning through facilitation of movement or through 'horse language'. The horse is taught in hand on long reins. As soon as he can piaffe adequately, he is asked to do it with a rider sitting quietly on his back, not giving an aid. The aids are still maintained from the ground. Once the horse can do the movement with a rider on his back, the rider is asked to give the 'aid' simultaneously with those of the handler. This so-called 'aid' is thus only a signal, and not an aid to facilitate movement. For this reason, this method does not fit into the philosophy of this book.

Method two – from collected walk. The walk is slowed down to a half step at a time. You will find that the horse will automatically start to give a higher step with both hind and forelegs. Do this until the horse accepts these tiny steps with no resistance and with good rhythm. He should be light in hand and engaged in the hindquarters. The steps must always be forward and never backward. Should the horse step backwards, he must be pressed forwards vigorously into a strong trot or even canter, brought back to walk, and then once more asked for these tiny half steps.

Once the horse has completely accepted these half steps with good balance, rhythm and lightness, he may be asked for more energy with both legs on the girth, as well as the seat aid. He may confuse this with a trot aid, but your hands should explain to the horse that he should not give long, forward steps. The reins should, however, yield as soon as the piaffe steps are offered.

Method three – from collected trot. This method is the opposite of method two, but quite interchangeable. The horse is asked for a balanced, rhythmical collected trot, which is then brought down to trot half steps. Once the horse accepts the rhythmic trot half steps without resistance and with complete lightness, he can be asked for two strides on the spot or nearly on the spot, but always forward-going. He is pushed forward with the legs on the girth so as not to lose impulsion, but your hands explain to him that he should not move forwards. The hands do not continually pull back, as this will cause resistance, too strong a contact and loss of rhythm. Instead, they block the forward movement and then soften again.

Once the horse has done two steps, push him forward into his half steps again. Repeat this process and gradually increase the number of piaffe steps one by one until you can finally produce fifteen. At all stages, reward the horse whenever he has offered the correct reaction.

Methods two and three may be used interchangeably as some horses learn more quickly from walk while others prefer learning from trot. For an anxious horse the walk method will probably be more suitable while a slow, lazy horse would probably respond better to the trot method. Furthermore, you may find that a combination of these two methods will produce the best results. Asking for piaffe from trot ensures that the horse maintains impulsion, while performing piaffe from walk teaches the horse to 'push the ground away' and thus produce slow, high steps.

EXERCISES IN PIAFFE

Ride the piaffe exercises around the outside track of the manège initially. Begin on one rein and perform a few piaffe transitions and then change to the other rein. Once the horse can maintain the piaffe around the outside of the manège, you may attempt it across the school.

1) Practise walk–piaffe and piaffe–walk transitions.

2) The trot–piaffe transition is the forerunner of the passage–piaffe transition. It is important to perfect the trot–piaffe transition, in balance, before attempting the passage–piaffe transition. Piaffe–trot and piaffe–extended trot transitions will ensure that impulsion is maintained.

3) Transitions from piaffe to passage and passage back to piaffe are very important in the top dressage tests, and should be perfected. The latter is the more difficult to establish.

4) Perfect the piaffe on the centre line. Ride the piaffe in half steps on the centre line until the horse feels secure and does these with ease before attempting them on the spot.

5) Half or full pirouettes at piaffe are popular Kür movements and exciting for the rider to perform.

TROUBLESHOOTING – problems with piaffe

SHUFFLING
This is usually found in horses who have learnt the piaffe in hand. As soon as it is requested from the whipless rider, the horse gives a half-hearted attempt. (It can also be caused by the horse not having developed enough strength in the hindquarters.)
Corrections
a) The horse has not understood the movement correctly and should be taught through the facilitation of movement technique, with a clear reward for the correct action.

b) Do not teach the horse with the whip from the ground. Since the whip is never available during a performance the horse should be obedient to the rider's legs alone. The whip should be used only by the rider in the early phases of teaching piaffe.

c) Ride on a 20 m circle and alternate a more forward stepping piaffe with a very collected and cadenced trot. Once the rhythm has been established, the piaffe may be brought back to one spot.

SWINGING HINDQUARTERS
The horse has not developed enough strength in his hocks to carry his weight. He steps sideways to evade this weight carriage.
Corrections
a) Prepare the horse with more strengthening and suppling exercises.
b) Stay with half steps for a little longer, before

attempting full piaffe again.

WIDE BEHIND

The horse has not developed enough strength in his hocks and is attempting to evade this weight-bearing position by taking too strong a contact and widening his base.

Corrections

a) Do more work on half steps at trot and walk.

b) Ride energetic transitions from half steps to full trot.

c) Ensure that the horse is in self-carriage before you attempt the piaffe.

STEPPING BACK

This is a serious mistake and should be corrected immediately. The horse has difficulty in being in motion on one spot and has to move either slightly forwards or backwards to maintain balance.

Correction

As soon as the horse takes a step backwards, he must be immediately pushed forwards energetically into trot or canter. If you do this a few times, he will keep the forward drive.

LOSING THE DIAGONAL GAIT

This may be a result of teaching the piaffe out of walk. The horse may interpret the request to be for a lateral piaffe, as it is extremely difficult for him to understand exactly what is required.

Correction

Upon the first signs of a lateral gait, push him into a forward trot immediately, then attempt the piaffe from trot. Repeat as necessary. It is essential that the horse understands that it is a trot gait, not a pacing gait, that is required.

LOSING RHYTHM

The horse may not have developed sufficient strength to maintain the movement and thus has a stronger push from one diagonal pair of legs than the other. This leads to a hopping action with the one diagonal pair.

Corrections

a) Be content with a couple of steps of piaffe only, then reward and walk. Once the horse has developed good rhythm with two steps, increase it to three. Continue in this manner until he can maintain rhythm for ten or more steps.

b) If the horse loses rhythm behind, ride forwards in half steps at trot, then attempt two piaffe steps, ride forwards in trot half steps again, and repeat. The horse will gradually develop the ability to sustain rhythm provided that he is not asked for too many steps too soon.

PASSAGE

Passage is a slow, cadenced trot, with a prolonged period of suspension. It has an energetic forward and upward propulsion, brought about by elastically flexed haunches. It is performed in the trot sequence, with a powerful push-off from the diagonal pairs of legs. The steps are high, with the forearm as close to parallel with the ground as possible and the cannon bone perpendicular to the ground. The hindquarters are lowered and engaged, with marked elevation. This allows the forehand to lift and have the same contact and head carriage as in piaffe. The feet lift to more or less the same level as in piaffe. Together with piaffe, passage is the movement with the ultimate collection, submission and obedience.

The horse should be straight, energetic and in rhythm, with no lateral swinging. Each horse has his own style of movement. Although a very high passage is impressive, this, alone, does not indicate quality. The most important aspects of passage are the measured rhythm, energy, cadence and engagement.

THE AIDS FOR PASSAGE

1) The rider's hands ask for rhythmic half-halts at every stride, almost as if 'catching' the energy at every stride.

2) The legs close around the horse to 'lift' him into the hands at every stride.

3) The seat (gluteal muscles) are used, together with the legs, to 'pick the horse up' at every stride, in rhythm with the passage.

7) Passage

TEACHING THE HORSE PASSAGE

Before the passage training can commence, the horse must be straight, collected, engaged, in self-carriage and perfectly balanced. Passage may be taught from piaffe or from collected trot, depending on the talent of the horse and which 'school of riding' the rider follows. Each 'school' has its own philosophy and reasons for training piaffe from passage or vice versa. If your horse appears to show a special talent for passage, start with the piaffe, which would be more difficult for him. If such a horse should first become established in the passage, he may later find difficulty in 'sitting' on the spot with energetically engaged hindquarters.

Passage from piaffe

1) Once the horse can piaffe correctly, passage may be obtained by increasing impulsion with

forward leg, seat and back aids. The hands yield slightly to channel the energy in an upward and forward direction. Throughout the transition, the rhythm should remain consistent.

2) The hands then ask for rhythmic half-halts at each stride to 'catch' the impulsion created by the legs.

3) Ask for a few strides of highly elevated trot steps. Reward the horse and walk before losing the elevation.

4) Progressively increase the number of cadenced trot steps after each piaffe. This will increase the horse's strength and balance to prepare him for the proper passage.

5) Gradually ask for more forward, upward and energetic steps after the piaffe. Use the hands and legs in rhythm with the slow, cadenced

passage steps to create the longer suspension. Do not try to raise the action of the legs too rapidly, as this may cause loss of rhythm and balance.

Passage from collected trot

Prepare the horse by asking for a few energetic trot-halt-trot transitions:

1) Collect the trot and ride a few energetic transitions from collected trot to extended trot and back to collected trot.

2) Decrease the amount of collected and extended trot steps in between the transitions.

3) From the collected trot, ask for an extended trot, but 'catch' the energy in a half-halt with the hands.

4) Continue to give the forward aids together with the rhythmic half-halts of the hands. Continue in this manner, asking for increasingly more impulsion, until you have a good passage.

Exercises in passage

Once the piaffe and passage have been established, the transitions between them should be perfected. Transitions from passage to piaffe are exceptionally difficult, which is why teaching piaffe before passage is preferable. Slow the passage down with half-halts, but keep the impulsion with the driving aids. Work towards half steps initially, and finally piaffe on the spot for a few steps only, then push the horse forwards again into passage. This will prevent the loss of impulsion, which is the biggest problem with this transition.

The following exercises all have beneficial influences on the passage work:

1) Transitions between the trot variants (collected and extended) and passage will improve balance and strength.

2) Circles, figure-of-eight, serpentines and half-passes all improve the horse's and rider's proficiency at passage.

3) Shoulder-in in passage can improve straightness, engagement and, therefore, thrust.

TROUBLESHOOTING – problems in passage

WIDE BEHIND
The horse has not developed enough strength and engagement to carry and push his weight simultaneously.
Corrections
a) Do more strengthening, engaging and collecting exercises.
b) Ride transitions from collected trot to passage and back to collected trot.
c) Ride passage in shoulder-in.

IRREGULAR STEPS
This fault may be caused by inadequate strength or lack of impulsion.
Correction
Ride the horse in collected trot and perform a few energetic transitions to extended trot. Once the horse is moving energetically forwards, you may begin the piaffe and passage again.

STIFF BACK AND NECK
The horse has lost balance and engagement and is bracing his muscles in an attempt to regain them.
Correction
Take the horse back to collected trot to regain balance and then proceed with piaffe or passage.

PART FOUR

<u>FLATWORK TRAINING</u>

<u>AND COMPETITION</u>

CHAPTER 15

THE TRAINING
PROGRAMME

All serious athletes follow a specific programme to develop their bodies to an optimum level for their specific sport. We have to treat our horses as athletes and afford them this same opportunity to develop. With this in mind, we should follow a logical format to develop the horse's athletic ability. This format can be outlined as a series of objectives.

THE TRAINING FORMAT

First objective: relaxation and calmness
Only a relaxed horse can maintain rhythm and only with rhythm does the horse become balanced. No rhythm, concentration, balance, suppleness or acceptance of the bit can be developed before the horse has become relaxed and calm.

Second objective: acceptance of the bit
If the horse has not yet accepted the bit, the rider cannot relax the jaw and neck muscles in flexion. Without this roundness, balance and rhythm cannot be encouraged through the activity of the hindquarters. Acceptance of the bit is all-important for communication and, without this communication, no rhythm or balance can be developed. At this stage the horse may not be able to maintain a steady contact – this takes some time to develop. He should, however, be ridden in a basic rounded frame and should not resist the rein.

Third objective: rhythm and balance
Rhythm is totally dependent upon balance. Rhythm is necessary for the development of all gaits as well as for jumping. Once the horse is in balance, he will have natural rhythm. Only with good rhythm can suppleness be developed.

Fourth objective: suppleness
Suppleness improves balance and rhythm. Without suppleness a horse will never become straight. Suppleness turns the horse into a gymnast and helps to prevent muscle injuries. It is extremely important for jumping and Advanced dressage movements.

Fifth objective: forwardness
If the horse is ridden in rhythm, with balance and longitudinal suppleness, he will automatically take a deeper step to become more engaged in his hindquarters. Without this supple forward movement, the horse cannot become collected, perform Advanced movements or jump effectively.

Sixth objective: straightness
This is closely related to suppleness and develops through suppling and stretching exercises. Straightness is a long-term process and should be worked at continually throughout all training until the horse becomes completely ambidextrous.

Seventh objective: 'on the bit'
The horse can only become properly engaged and collected if he is completely light in hand and reacts to the lightest rein aids. In this way the energy created in collection can be controlled through his own body and not by pulling on the reins. At this stage, the horse should maintain a steady contact on the bit at all times.

Eighth objective: collection

Throughout all the previous phases, the hind-quarters will be gaining strength to prepare the horse for collection. This is the final development in training. The correctly collected horse has become the ultimate equine athlete.

True perfection is seldom attainable in a sport which relies on the ability of two separate individuals. Therefore we may progress, with discretion, to the next phase before reaching perfection in the previous phase. If we should wait for true perfection in one phase, many of us may never progress to the next! Also, the phases are not mutually exclusive – there is almost always some degree of inter-relationship. Therefore, whilst, for example, working on acceptance of the bit you should also be working at improving rhythm and balance and, whilst establishing rhythm, some suppling exercises may be incorporated.

PROGRESSION OF TRAINING

STAGE ONE – BUILDING THE BASICS

1) Teach the horse to accept the bridle, saddle and rider.

2) Training on the lunge.
   a) Teach the horse the voice signals on the lunge.
   b) Teach him the forward leg aids on the lunge. Use the verbal commands together with the leg aids. Start with the walk and halt aids. The halt aid is extremely important at this stage because it forms the basis for future downward transitions and ensures the safety of the rider. A square halt should not be expected at this stage. Obedience to the downward aid should be the aim for now.

3) Training under saddle.
   a) Start by achieving calmness and relaxation, and developing rhythm at the trot.
   b) Once you have established the downward aid, the horse should be taken on hacks out to accustom him to all objects encountered in the open. This will help him to gain confidence.
   c) Establish rhythm on 20 m circles and around the arena.
   d) As soon as the horse reacts immediately to the leg aids, the voice signals may be abandoned.
   e) Teach the horse to accept the bit (the action of your hands). Teach him to follow the action of the bit. As soon as he does this, start asking him to work 'long and deep'.
   f) Once the rhythm has been established at trot, the canter may be attempted. Start on a 20 m circle and on hacks out until the horse can balance himself in a 'long and deep' frame at working canter. Then proceed to working on the outside track of the manège. (Lazy horses can begin canter work around the whole arena.)
   g) Consolidate the canter depart from the trot.
   h) Once the horse has accepted the bit and has established a rhythm, suppling exercises should be started.
   i) The walk–trot and trot–walk transitions as well as canter–trot and trot–canter transitions should now be perfected.
   j) Start doing trotting pole work and little jumps.
   k) Perfect the balancing half-halt.

Much of this first stage work may be established on hacks out to avoid boredom in the young horse.

STAGE TWO – TOWARD STRAIGHTNESS

1) Continue working on suppling exercises.

2) Continue improving downward and upward transitions.

3) Start simple lateral work to improve straightness. Introduce the following at walk and then progress to lateral work at trot:
   Turn on the forehand
   Leg-yielding
   Shoulder-in
   Quarter pirouettes

4) Transitions should become sharper, with more engagement. Repeated trot–halt–trot and canter–trot–canter transitions should start to develop this.

5) More forward activity and impulsion can be expected, since the horse should now be in bal-ance.

6) Teach the rein-back and half pirouette.

7) Continue with trotting poles into jumps, but in-crease the size of the jump. Start jumping small courses at trot. Introduce small combinations and a variety of obstacles.

8) Expect more engagement and a slower canter. Lengthen and shorten the canter.

9) Lengthen and shorten the trot.

10) Ride shoulder-in at canter.

11) Develop the counter-canter.

STAGE THREE – DEVELOPING COLLECTION

1) Concentrate on collecting exercises such as shoulder-in at trot and canter; canter–walk–canter transitions; medium canter to collected canter and medium trot to collected trot.

2) Improve the lateral work; travers and half-pass.

3) Ride half-pass at canter and counter-changes at trot.

4) Medium trot, half pirouette and simple changes should now be perfected.

5) Canter to halt and rein-back to canter transi-tions can be practised.

6) Perfect the individual flying changes.

STAGE FOUR – ADVANCED WORK

1) Perfect collection at trot and canter.

2) Improve the collected and extended walk.

3) The collected, medium and extended trot should be further developed and perfected.

4) Perfect the half-pass at canter.

5) Canter on the spot.

6) Teach the piaffe and canter pirouette.

7) Develop sequence changes and passage.

Throughout all stages, never overface the horse. Once the horse understands the movements and does them calmly, in balance and on light aids, progress to the next stage.

THE SCHOOLING SESSION

The equine athlete should be prepared systemati-cally for his future, whether in dressage or jump-ing. To ensure fitness and health, he should be worked regularly by the rider, because he cannot keep himself fit.

Schooling your horse should be approached with a clear plan. This should include long-term aims such as the time or period you would like to spend at a particular level of jumping or dressage and the time you would like to spend learning a new move-ment. This will vary from horse to horse and de-pend on circumstances such as injury, illness or any other setbacks. Therefore, the plan should not be too rigid. Short-term plans for each schooling session should also be prepared. You may have to deviate from these plans if a new opportunity arises or you come across a problem.

Choose your work area carefully. If your horse does not like working in a manège, he may be schooled when ridden out. Such a horse should be encouraged to work in the manège for ten min-utes before or after the hack, and this should be increased slowly until he can concentrate for half an hour, then up to an hour. Many horses need a variety of work, which should include jumping, hacking and schooling in a manège. We should be aware of the differing needs of horses. Some can be schooled for five days a week, while others prefer fewer days, interspersed with hacking. Lazy horses should be taught to work forwards when ridden out, to avoid confrontation. Anxious and spooky horses may be worked in company with other horses to help them feel more secure. Other horses are happier working alone. While we can, initially, pander to each horse's idiosyncrasies, we should work towards developing his temperament so that he will work with concentration and confidence in a variety of situations.

Regular, short schooling sessions are usually of more value than long, tiring sessions. In general, a young horse should actually be worked in sessions of about ten minutes, with limited demands made on him. This programme should be gradually adapted until the horse can sustain work for about forty-five minutes. Horses in the middle of their training can work for longer periods, while advanced horses will not need to work for too long a period as they have much less to learn. An average riding session should last for half an hour – up to an hour if necessary. Working for a longer period may become counter-productive.

Each schooling session should be divided into three parts: the warm-up, the work period and the cooling-off period.

THE WARM-UP

The warm-up forms the first part of the schooling session. The aim of the warm-up is to stretch and supple the horse's muscles to prepare them for the strenuous work ahead. All athletes have to do stretching and suppling exercises to protect their muscles from injury. Keep the warm-up fairly short to conserve energy for the work period. (For young horses, the warm-up may constitute the whole schooling session, as this is made up of rhythmic, suppling, straightening and forward exercises. Gradually add more difficult exercises.)

Start the warm-up with a free walk on a loose rein to rid the horse of the stiffness induced by his confinement in a small space. Start the horse with a figure-of-eight, with definite changes of bend, at walk. Proceed to walk into the corners, do some quarter pirouettes and leg-yielding. This period at walk allows the rider to practise the lateral aids.

Proceed in rising trot with relaxing, suppling and straightening exercises; circles and serpentines for lateral suppleness and riding 'long and deep' for longitudinal suppleness. Once the horse has become free and forward at trot, ask for canter. At canter, the warm-up should include 20 m circles at the working gait, with a good 'jump'. Ride 'long and deep' with shallow counter-canter exercises, if the level of training permits. (Lazy horses may be warmed up at canter initially to create more forward movement.) Use school figures appropriate to the level of your horse: large figures for novice horses and increasingly smaller figures for advanced horses.

Next, proceed to ask for exercises which will encourage more engagement. Shorten and lengthen the stride at trot and then at canter. Ride transitions and proceed to shoulder-in and travers at trot and finally at canter, until you have a horse who is supple, balanced, relaxed, engaged and going forwards energetically. Your horse will now be ready for more difficult work.

Rest period

After the warm-up allow your horse to rest briefly on a loose rein (and do this a few more times during the training session). It is important to intersperse the work with regular rest periods at walk. This will help the horse to concentrate again, to rest his tired muscles and to stretch his neck muscles down and forward.

THE WORK PERIOD

This should include the following:

Strengthening and collecting exercises.
Consolidation of previous work.
Introduction of new work in preparation for the next phase.

Although a variety of work should be done, you obviously cannot fit all the movements into one session. Decide which movements you need to do and concentrate on those. (You should not ask the horse to perform too many lateral movements at one time, as this causes stress on the joints.)

If problems arise, ride forwards and 'change the subject'. Perform a different movement to motivate the horse to concentrate on your aids and not on the recent problem. The period should be ended on a positive note, with some good work.

THE COOLING-OFF PERIOD

Once you have completed your workout, your horse should be cooled down to prevent muscle spasm and stiffness. Cool him down initially by trotting 'long and deep' on two 15 m circles. Ride one circle left followed by one circle right until he is stretched and relaxed, then walk him around until he has cooled off, and dismount.

CHAPTER 16

THE ART OF COMPETING

The talent for training horses and the talent for competing a trained horse are two different abilities. One rider may have enormous talent for training horses, but not be good at presenting the same horses in competition, while a rider with less 'feel' for training may well be excellent at competing. With hard work and dedication, an ordinary rider can become an excellent rider and trainer, and a less gifted competitor can learn to become proficient at the art of competing.

A dressage competition can be compared to sitting an examination, or being on stage. Exams are always coupled with a certain amount of anxiety, while the ability to act (perform) is a necessary quality in those on stage. All riders are not necessarily good actors, but all can improve their stagecraft.

GUIDELINES FOR DEVELOPING STAGECRAFT

CONTROLLING ANXIETY

The following are a few methods of controlling anxiety:

1) Develop confidence. Learning to believe in yourself and your abilities will decrease anxiety. Have confidence in your horse and learn to 'show him off'. (Confidence can only develop with the knowledge that you and your horse know the work in hand. Therefore, prepare yourself properly for the test.)

2) Learn to relax. There are various relaxation techniques, but the following may be of help:

a) Deep breathing.

b) Remembering to relax your seat and make it 'feel like jelly'.

c) Close your eyes for a moment, cut out all outside stimuli and 'think' relaxation. Take a little time to clear your mind in preparation for the task ahead.

d) Focusing the mind. This is a specialised technique to relieve anxiety and needs practice before the competition. Focus your mind on one phrase such as 'straight entry, square halt'. Repeat the chosen phrase over and over in your mind, in a rhythm. It will eventually be associated with relaxation and, when you are at a competition and find that your anxiety level has risen too high, resort to focusing your mind by repeating your special phrase.

3) Learn the art of role playing. In role playing the person 'acts' as though they were someone else. For example, act as though you were especially confident, or the best rider in the world, even though you may not be.

4) Know your test and visualise all the different parts and difficult movements in it. 'Walk' through the test if necessary. Plan how, and at what point, you would start preparing for each movement. The movement will only be as good as the preparation.

5) It helps to know that most judges are concerned about marking correctly and that most people – including the judges – are not as secure or confident as they seem to be.

6) There are excellent homoeopathic food supplements which help to control anxiety.

CONCENTRATING IN STRESSFUL SITUATIONS

This is one of the most important attributes of a good competitor:

1) Learn to ignore all outside interference – spectators, barking dogs, etc. Try to develop 'tunnel vision' during your test.

2) Concentrate on each separate movement and the following movement only. Try to plan and prepare for your next movement.

3) Should you make a mistake, forget about it immediately and concentrate on the next movement.

4) There is no time to become emotional during a test. Do not become angry with yourself, or your horse if he should make a mistake. This will lead to loss of concentration. The horse has no concept of what a competition is or that he is under scrutiny; he only knows that he becomes anxious in these situations.

5) Concentrate on the task ahead and do not think of winning or losing. This will only interfere with your concentration.

AMBITION AND THE WILL TO WIN

Whether a rider will get to the top or not is up to the individual. The trainer can only correct the training errors, but the determination, self-discipline and will to win are the rider's alone.

Winning the actual competition should not, however be the sole purpose of competing. This will create too much pressure which, in turn, will increase anxiety and affect concentration. The overriding aim should be to ride as well as you can on that particular day. Indeed, there are two main reasons for taking part in a competition, and these may influence a rider's attitude towards a particular competition.

Experience and 'mileage'. It may be necessary to introduce a young horse to shows to give him 'show mileage'. An inexperienced horse may become anxious or excited at shows, and may need to go to a few small ones in order to learn to stay calm. Similarly, inexperienced riders have to gain experience in competitions. They do not necessarily have to be perfect in their work for this purpose. If such riders were to wait for perfection before entering a show, they might never reach a show at all! Instead, they should go to as many competitions as possible to become used to shows and, if appropriate, to give their horses show experience. Once they feel comfortable competing, their aim should change and they should start working towards perfection and winning.

Aiming for the top. Except where novice horses are concerned, riders who wish to reach the top level of their sport will perfect their work at home before entering a competition. These are the experienced and professional riders whose aim is to win prizes and progress to higher levels.

ATTITUDES AND REACTIONS

Self-knowledge of your attitudes and reactions can be very helpful.

Your own reactions. Do you become over-anxious or too relaxed at shows? Is your concentration better or worse at a show? If you know how you usually react at a competition, you can prepare yourself to deal as appropriate with the situation.

Your attitude towards the judges. The judges are there for the benefit of the riders and they try their best to judge correctly. They are, however, only judging brief moments – not your whole riding ability. Therefore, you should not perceive their comments as indicating personal failure, but rather as helpful hints.

Aiming for small successes. Novice riders with little experience may find that the test is entirely too much to concentrate on at once. Concentrate on one area of the test only and try to achieve success in that aspect, for example correct circles. Congratulate yourself on that success and, when you next enter a competition, try to improve another aspect of the test. You will find, after a few of these successes, that you will be able to concentrate on improving the whole test.

HANDY HINTS

PLANNING AND PREPARATION

1) Before you enter a competition, expose your horse to as many different situations as possible: dogs, traffic, different noises, working in company with strange horses, etc.

2) Plan your show programme carefully. Choose those shows which suit your own and your horse's level the best. Smaller and unaffiliated shows are less stressful for novice riders and young horses. Compete at bigger events only when you and your horse have had more experience.

3) You should ride through the test once, a week or two before the show, to ascertain the problem areas. Correct these problems and ride through the test one more time. Any further practice of the test may lead to anticipation on the horse's part.

4) Know the ground your horse prefers to work on. If he works better on firm ground, choose your venue accordingly. Once you are experienced, the horse should be trained to work well on all going.

5) Do all your preparation and packing the day before you travel. This will leave your head clear to think of the work alone.

6) Arrive at the showground in good time – at least one and a half to two hours before the time of your test. On arrival at the show, check your time of riding and whether the show is running early or late.

7) Get to know your horse's reactions at shows. Does he become anxious? Is he better in the first or second test of the day? Does he stay fresh or become lazy after the warm-up? Work accordingly.

8) Watch a few tests to ascertain the condition of the arena – whether there is deep sand in the corners, a waterlogged area, etc.

WARMING UP

While it is extremely difficult to have your horse perfectly warmed up for the test, plan the warm-up to bring him as near to optimum performance as possible.

If your horse is very fit, or has a 'hot' temperament, lunge him for a few minutes, then give him a short break and start your warm-up afterwards.

With experience, you will learn to know your horse's behaviour at shows and what type of warm-up he will need. Some horses need a fairly long warm-up, while others have more sparkle after a short warm-up. Ideally, you should give yourself at least an hour. If your horse is ready earlier, you should dismount, remove his tack and allow him to relax a little. Remount some fifteen minutes before his test to 'wake him up' again. This will prevent dullness and sourness, and also gives the horse the same feeling of tension release he would have after performing a test. In other words, it will make the first test seem like a second test.

Start your warm-up with walk on a long rein and allow your horse to have a good look at his surroundings. Proceed with walking 'long and deep' to relax the horse, inhibit his startle reflex and obtain longitudinal stretching. When the horse is completely relaxed, start with work in rising trot. If he should become tense again, go back to working 'long and deep' on a circle. Work the horse through a compressed daily workout and check, with an extended canter, that all the freshness is worked out of him. Then give him a total break as described above. Do not overwork your horse or try to perfect a movement in the warm-up: you cannot expect the horse to learn new work at a show.

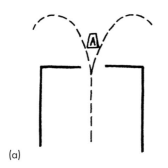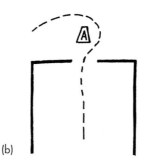

Figure 141 (a) correct and (b) incorrect way to enter the arena.

ENTERING THE ARENA

Endless trotting around the arena will only have the effect of dulling the horse. Walk him around it to introduce him to the surrounding area; the flowers and the judges' boxes. Then ride a few pertinent transitions to ensure that he is on the aids.

Enter the arena on the rein which is easier to control. Ride in front of the A marker to ensure a straight entry. If you should enter behind the marker, you may disturb the horse's balance when you attempt to straighten him onto the centre line. Lock your eyes on the C marker or the judge and ride straight and forward on the centre line. A 'hot' horse should be ridden down the centre line quietly and you should prepare to prevent the tendency of such a horse to step sideways at the halt.

DURING THE TEST

Prepare the horse for each movement carefully to prevent disturbing his balance or losing rhythm and roundness. Never forget that he has no idea what will be asked of him next! Try to ride accurately for easy marks, but do not forfeit rhythm and balance for accuracy: 20 m circles must be exactly 20 m; transitions must be at the appropriate marker.

Try to produce a good last movement down the centre line and halt at the end of your test by riding forward, and once again, locking your eyes on the C marker.

PART FIVE

JUMPING WITH

CONFIDENCE

CHAPTER 17

JUMPING: BUILDING
A SOUND BASIS

To develop your horse's showjumping potential he will have to be trained systematically to become an athlete and an equine gymnast. To develop such ability, he has to acquire the same attributes as his human counterpart:

The ability to relax during physical activity.
Rhythm and balance.
Suppleness and agility.
Forward impulsion and strength (engagement of the hindquarters).
Straightness (ambidexterity).

In addition he will also need:

Acceptance of the bit.
The ability to collect or extend when necessary.
Obedience.

It is therefore important that all showjumpers are trained according to the principles explained in this book. The more dressage training the horse is given and the more control the rider has, the better the horse will jump. The aim of this training is to develop the ability to jump a course with calmness, rhythm, suppleness, balance, engagement and confidence. The horse who is to specialise in jumping will not, however, have to learn *all* the dressage movements previously described. Instead of learning half-pass, canter pirouette, sequence changes, piaffe and passage, he will learn to jump. The jump can therefore be regarded as another 'dressage' movement in the overall training of the horse.

The major difference between dressage and jumping lies in the use of the horse's neck. In dressage, the horse is discouraged from using his neck for balance and is continually encouraged to use his body – especially his hindquarters – to stay in balance. In jumping, the horse should certainly use his hindquarters for balance, but he should also be allowed the freedom to use his neck for balance before, during and after the jump.

The information which follows does not cover all the work necessary to produce an International Grade A jumper but describes how to teach every horse, whatever his absolute potential, to jump with confidence. Most horses can jump a moderate-sized course confidently. Whether an individual horse can successfully attain great heights will depend on his inborn talent. The method of training described will ensure that the horse experiences jumping as a simple, everyday occurrence which should not be feared, but enjoyed. Fear will counteract the boldness needed for jumping, and should not be used in training.

POSITION AND SEAT OF THE RIDER

THE BODY

The forward jumping seat is the appropriate seat to use over a fence, over trotting poles, cavalletti and for gymnastics. This forward seat is necessary to allow the horse the freedom of his neck, to move his centre of gravity forward over the jump and to balance. In addition, it prevents the rider from falling 'behind the movement' and thus disturbing the horse's balance and ability to jump. The exact angle at which the rider should lean forwards (or backwards down banks) will depend on the height of the obstacle and the horse's need to stretch his neck. Furthermore, the forward seat is not static, but can be divided into three stages:

Lift off. The horse rises in an upright position to stretch and jump. The rider leans forward over his base of support (thighs and feet). This will happen almost automatically; the rider's weight should not be thrown forwards, but the rider should wait for the horse to 'come up'. Throwing the weight forwards will disturb the horse's balance and lead to him knocking poles.

Figure 142 The horse comes up to the rider.

Figure 143 The angle between the hip and knee joint closes.

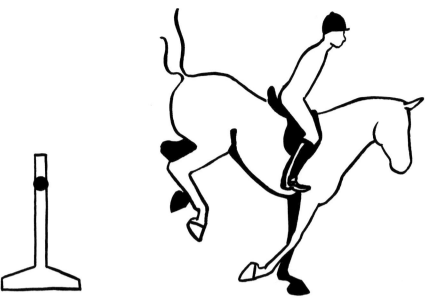

Figure 144 The landing position.

In flight. The rider's seat is pushed backwards slightly and the hip and knee joints close. The sensation may be of the seat being pushed in a slightly upward direction. This will ensure that the rider's back is straight, with the body remaining over the base of support.

Landing. During the descent, the rider should start to re-establish the upright position as soon as possible without pulling the horse in the mouth. This will keep the rider in balance and control for the next obstacle.

While the whole procedure over the jump is virtually automatic, faults may appear and should be corrected.

The position in between jumps seems to depend upon individual preferences. Some riders maintain the forward position throughout the whole course, while others prefer to stay in the saddle with the shoulders slightly ahead of the hips. If the horse needs more engagement or impulsion during the approach to the jump, the rider will have to sit in the saddle to apply seat aids. This will also be necessary when applying half-halts, should the horse become too keen.

THE LEGS AND FEET

The most important factor in the position of the rider when jumping is the ability to balance. To balance successfully the rider's weight should be pushed into the heels through the knees. This will automatically bring the calves against the horse and give more support. Balance is maintained through pressing down on the stirrups with the balls of the feet and keeping the body over the base of support. In this way the rider will stay 'with' the horse. The knees themselves should not grip, as this will block the horse's forward impulsion and will also bring the lower leg off the horse, leading to the backward swing often seen in jumping. The lower leg should, rather, be in contact with the horse, ready to use when necessary. The hips, knees and ankles should remain supple and flexible, to act as shock absorbers and to help maintain balance. There should be a slight inward rotation of the legs, leading to the rider's toes pointing forwards. The stirrups should be fairly short to allow the rider to fold forwards out of the saddle and keep the weight over the horse's centre of gravity.

The pressing down action and balance may be practised in an upright, as well as forward position.

Figure 145 Improving the rider's leg position and balance in preparation for jumping.

Practise by standing in the stirrups whilst trotting and cantering. As the rider's balance improves this forward standing position should be attempted for an increasing length of time. (This is a muscle-developing exercise, and the posture should not be adopted over an obstacle, as it could lead to instability.)

While the rider will not be able to jump effectively without this initial balance, full balance will only develop properly with jumping practice. Over low fences some lack of balance should not significantly damage the horse's jumping ability, but jumping exercises will help to improve the rider's balance and co-ordination.

THE ARMS AND HANDS

The arms and hands should be completely relaxed and move forward with the horse's head during the jump and descent to maintain a consistent and light contact throughout the movement. The hand movement should be towards the horse's mouth in a straight line (the reins being extensions of the arms). This prevents interference with the horse's balance and accidental jabbing in the mouth over the fence. If the rider accidentally falls behind the movement of the horse, the reins should be slipped through the fingers to avoid hurting the horse's mouth. If the rider does not slip the reins, the horse will associate the pain from this experience with the act of jumping and may start to dislike jumping and refuse as a result.

THE EYES

Whilst going over the fence, the rider should look straight ahead. This will prevent leaning to one side, a fault often seen in showjumping. When approaching the fence, the rider should look at the top pole, but also perceive the ground line in order to judge the stride and take-off point. It is important to concentrate on looking at the fence and not to allow any outside interference to effect this concentration. When concentrating on the top pole, most riders and horses will automatically find the correct take-off point through their automatic eye-motor co-ordination and their proprioceptive and kinesthetic perception (see Chapter 6).

TEACHING THE HORSE TO JUMP

PHASE ONE – JUMPING LOOSE

Teaching the horse to jump loose may be compared to teaching the horse new concepts in flatwork by way of the lunge. The functions of jumping loose are:

The horse learns that he should jump whenever an obstacle is placed in his way.

The horse learns to work out his take-off point without the interference of the rider.

The horse learns to jump with balance and agility without the weight of the rider. (The horse can learn to jump before he has reached an adequate level of training and strength for mounted jumping.)

The first few jumping lessons will be easier if the horse has already learnt the concept of taking trotting poles and small jumps in the loose school.

Jumping loose may also be of benefit in exercising a trained horse when the rider is unable to ride him.

Although jumping loose has obvious advantages for the young horse in the early stages of training, it is not a *pre-requisite* for successful jumping. Not all riders have the advantage of a loose school, and many may have to train their horses without this facility. If the horse is trained adequately, he can be taught to jump without the benefit of a loose school.

A complete explanation of jumping loose is provided in *Basic Training of the Young Horse* by Reiner Klimke.

PHASE TWO – GROUND POLES AND CAVALLETTI

Ground poles and cavalletti form the basis of teaching the horse to jump with balance and confidence. They can be introduced fairly early in the training – as soon as the horse has developed rhythm and balance, understands basic forward and halt aids, and simple leg-yielding.

If cavalletti are used for early exercises in walk and trot, they should initially be on their lowest setting. Later, they may be used on their middle setting for trot, but the highest setting should not be used, as it demands more elevation than most horses can manage without losing balance and rhythm. In the following exercises, the term 'ground' poles can be taken to include 'cavalletti'.

Introducing poles at walk

Start with one pole at its lowest level and walk over this from both sides, turning left and right alternately. At first, allow the horse to have a look at it then walk forwards over it. If he should hesitate, allow him to have a good look – this will give him confidence. Once he can walk over one pole calmly, with confidence and without hesitation, another pole may be introduced. Ensure that the distance is correct for the individual horse. Gradually add more poles until the horse walks over up to six in a relaxed fashion, in rhythm and with confidence. Allow the horse to find his own balance and to stretch forward and down in a rounded frame, if he so desires. Bring him in straight down the centre of the poles and allow him to find his own stride. If he makes mistakes he will soon learn, through his proprioceptive sense, to correct his striding. This exercise should not take more than one or two schooling sessions.

Trotting over poles

Once the first exercise has been mastered, you can progress to trotting over the poles. Once again, start with only one pole and, when the horse trots over this quietly and with confidence, add another. Again, gradually add more poles one by one until the horse can trot over four to six quietly, with rhythm, balance and confidence. This should not take more than two schooling sessions. Throughout this exercise stay in the forward seat and allow the horse to stretch his neck forward and down with a very light contact. This will free his shoulder and allow him to take a longer step. Ensure that the distance between the poles is correct for your horse (his hoofprints should be in the centre between the poles). Approximate distances for various jumping-

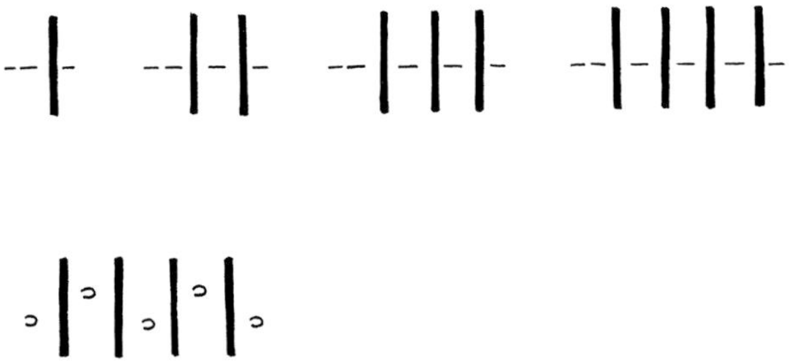

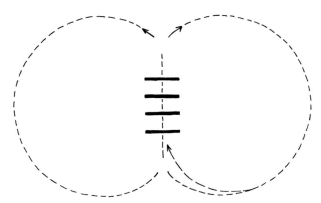

Figure 146 *The first trotting pole exercises. The hoofprints should fall in the centre between the poles.*

Figure 147 *If the horse continually reaches the poles incorrectly, change the curve of the approach slightly.*

related exercises are given on p. 178.

During this exercise, the approach should be straight, calm and with impulsion. Ride the exercise on a large figure-of-eight, approaching alternately from left and right. This will help improve suppleness, straightness and balance. Stay straight for a few strides after the last pole and then continue onto a circle. This will ensure that the horse does not anticipate the turn.

Although, at this stage, the horse should be allowed to find his own stride, this does not mean that you should not try to make things easier for him. Keep him in a rounded frame with a light contact and a rhythmical gait; do not allow him to rush. Concentrate, yourself, on the first pole and not on the curve of the approach. This should be sufficient to bring him to it correctly. If your horse consistently reaches the poles incorrectly, try to change the shape of the curve on the approach. By cutting the corner a little, the horse will often reach the poles in a better position to adapt his stride.

This exercise of trotting over poles should be repeated until you can think about it clearly without becoming tense, and can plan your approach correctly. Jumping has a tendency to excite the novice rider as well as the horse. It often has the effect of blocking the rider's thought processes and judgment. The rider then shows a tendency to think only about getting over the fence, rather than about the planning and correct approach. If the horse starts to rush over the poles, you will have to go back to the exercise of walking over one pole, and progress to trotting once he is calm.

Every jumping session should start with the trotting pole exercise. It serves as a warming-up and loosening exercise. To prevent boredom, these sessions should be short, but the horse should accept this as routine work.

PHASE THREE – GYMNASTIC JUMPING

Gymnastic jumping is the logical progression from the trotting pole exercises. Before commencing this, the horse should be calm and relaxed, accept the bit and follow the rider's hands. He should be obedient to the leg and hand aids, and understand leg-yielding. He should walk, trot and canter in rhythm, with suppleness and impulsion. Gymnastic jumping has the following benefits:

1) It helps to develop the horse's muscular system, especially the hindquarters. He has to push off against the ground, land, and push off again. The abdominal muscles are strengthened through the repeated basculing over a series of jumps.

2) It improves elasticity and longitudinal suppleness through stretching the topline.

3) The horse's reaction time is shortened by the closeness of the jumps. It thus develops impulsion and agility in lazy horses.

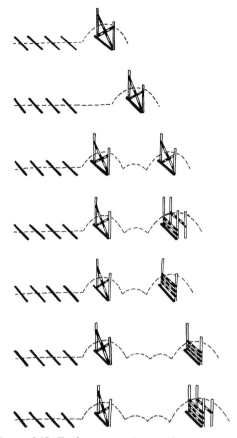

Figure 148 Early gymnastic exercises.

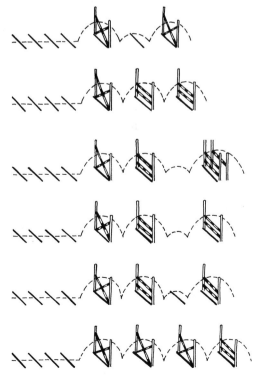

Figure 149 Further gymnastic exercises.

4) It teaches the horse where to take off because the correct striding is worked out for each jump.

5) It teaches the horse to jump with rhythm and balance.

6) It develops confidence, concentration and precision in the horse and rider, because the horse cannot easily run out.

7) Through such exercises the rider can develop a good seat, learn to balance and sit quietly and yield with the hands and thus to jump correctly without the added burden of having to correct the horse. All the rider has to concentrate on is bringing the horse straight to the first jump or pole and retaining impulsion.

The following is a progressive series of gymnastic jumping exercises:

1) Start with four trotting poles and a small cross pole fence (20 cm). At this stage the distance between the poles and the jump should be correct for each horse. The small cross pole is an inviting fence, which improves the horse's bascule, guides him to the centre of the fence and encourages him to jump high. Approach the trotting poles with rhythm and impulsion, but not too much speed.

   This exercise should be used regularly at the beginning of the jumping session. It helps with the warm-up and maintains the longitudinal suppleness of the horse.

2) As soon as the horse jumps the cross pole calmly with rhythm, balance, confidence and a light contact, you may place another obstacle one stride away. This second obstacle can be used to introduce the horse to different types of fence.

3) Once the horse does the previous exercise calmly, progressively add more small fences – but not more than four. The first fence should remain smaller than the rest.

4) Vary the distances between the fences to allow more or fewer non-jumping strides.

5) Vary the shape of the fences to include crosses,

uprights and oxers.

6) As soon as the horse performs these low gymnastic exercises calmly and with confidence, the whole process can be repeated with slightly higher and wider obstacles. Once again, start with only one fence and slowly add more. Adapt the distances in between the jumps as appropriate.

After the last jump, the horse should be returned to trot. If he does not do this with ease, he should be walked or halted, calmed down and then asked to trot again and repeat the exercise. Each exercise should be repeated between three and five times, to maintain the horse's interest. Practise each gymnastic exercise for a few days until the horse is completely at ease with it, then progress to the next exercise. If any problem should arise, go back to the first gymnastic exercise, resolve the problem and then make careful progress once more. The exercises should be ridden alternately from right and left to ensure even development of the horse.

Other points to bear in mind throughout these exercises are:

Although you may help the horse to reach the correct take-off spot for the trotting poles as previously described, do not, otherwise, interfere on the approach.

During these exercises, maintain a forward seat. The leg aids should be used to produce impulsion, because falling back into the saddle to use the seat aids may disturb the horse's balance and rhythm, and could lead to jabbing him in the mouth.

The rein contact should be light throughout each exercise. If the horse begins to take a strong contact, he should be taken back to trotting poles only.

At a later stage, the distances between fences may be varied to train the horse to take shorter strides with more engagement, or longer strides. Do not, however, attempt this until the horse is performing the basic exercises in good fashion, and has demonstrated an ability to shorten and lengthen satisfactorily in his flatwork.

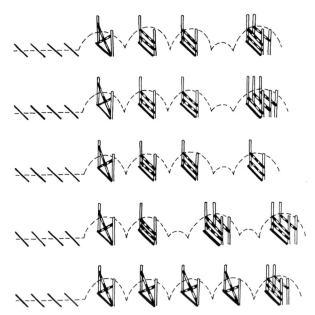

Figure 150 Advanced gymnastic exercises.

PHASE FOUR – INDIVIDUAL FENCES

Although the horse should continue to do a few gymnastic exercises in each jumping session, he should now be confident enough to start small individual fences. Doing this has the following benefits:

1) Both horse and rider learn to jump with more confidence when an obstacle becomes more familiar.

2) Through repetition, the horse learns to see his stride and judge the take-off point. If he makes a mistake he can correct it at the next attempt.

3) The rider learns where to turn to bring the horse to the correct take-off point and can gain experience of seeing a stride.

4) The horse can be taught to change his leading leg on landing.

5) The rider's own position can be worked on more readily than when riding a course.

Start by jumping a small fence (40-60 cm) from trot. Such a fence is small enough to allow the horse to walk over it should a problem arise. Thus, you will be assured that a refusal can be rectified by simply walking over the fence, and the horse soon learns that jumping is easy. Horses who need encouragement should be jumped towards home, follow an experienced horse over the fence, or jump an obstacle with wings. Initially, the approach should be from trot. Trotting has a greater calming effect on the horse, prevents rushing, promotes control and allows the rider more time to correct disobediences and mistakes during the approach. It is also easier to regulate the horse's stride at trot. By jumping these obstacles successfully, the horse develops confidence. Once a fence of reasonable height can be jumped with complete mutual confidence from trot, the horse may be asked to jump from canter.

Early obstacles should be inviting, and help the horse to judge the correct take-off point. They should always have groundlines and be solidly built, for good three-dimensional perception.

1) Start with an inviting cross pole of about 35 cm in height, and jump it a few times in a figure-of-eight formation, alternating between a right and left approach. (A long approach might encourage rushing.)

 Jump from trot and, if the horse canters after the jump, return to trot. However, if the horse breaks into a calm and fairly slow canter before the fence, he should be allowed to complete the jump. Should he canter too fast and become tense, he should be returned to the exercise of trotting poles followed by one jump.

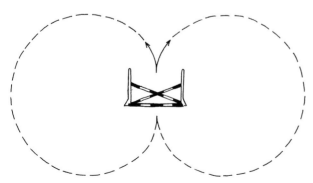

Figure 151 Alternating left and right rein approach to a single fence.

2) When the horse does the first exercise calmly, but with impulsion, introduce a small upright (40 cm). At this stage the horse should be allowed to find his own stride. The less you interfere, the more the horse will try to do this.

 If the horse canters after the jump, ride a few strides straight and then bring him back to trot. Riding straight after the jump will prevent anticipation of the turn and crookedness over the fence. Use the voice, leg and hand aids to re-establish a balanced trot.

3) When the horse can jump the cross pole and upright calmly and confidently, small parallels and spreads may be introduced. Keep the height of 35–40 cm, with the width not more than 40–50 cm at this stage. The back pole of an oxer should be slightly higher than the front pole to allow the horse to see it.

4) Gradually increase the height of the individual fences one notch at a time, once the horse is jumping them with confidence. Do not attempt a fence you are not confident about – put it down a few notches and then jump it.

5) Now it is time to introduce a great variety of small obstacles, which should all be jumped from trot. Oxers, spreads, ditches, logs, banks, etc. should be introduced. Once the horse is at ease with small examples, the size can be increased gradually.

PHASE FIVE – JUMPING A BASIC COURSE

When your horse can jump individual obstacles with confidence, it is time to introduce him to a small three-jump course at a height of some 40 cm. The height of this course will be lower than the individual fences he has become accustomed to. Once again, he should be trotting into the fences but, if he breaks into a controlled and balanced canter, he should be allowed to proceed. When he stays calm throughout the small course, more fences can be added one by one until he can jump a course of eight or so with complete confidence.

Throughout the course, he should be allowed to find his own stride as, at this height, an incorrect take-off point will not have serious consequences. If he becomes excited, calm him down and lower the fences, or revert to a previous phase.

At this stage his flatwork training should include 10m circles, leg yielding, transitions at canter (lengthening and shortening); he should be accepting the bit and working towards collection.

The first fence of the course should be inviting and easy, and the rest should be far enough apart to encourage rhythm and balance. A variety of fences should be introduced to prepare the horse for the different obstacles he will encounter at shows although, at this stage, all should have groundlines. When a new fence is added, allow the horse to inspect it before attempting to jump.

When the horse can jump such a course with confidence from trot, he may attempt it at canter. Start with only three fences and add more when he jumps with confidence and control. Rhythm and balance should be re-established after each jump, as necessary. Once the horse can canter such a course in good style, the fences can be made higher, one notch at a time.

So far as riders are concerned, novices often become too anxious to think clearly and plan their approach to the fences. Should this happen, more practice over individual fences is required, followed by a simple three-jump course, to promote clarity of thought and concentration on the job at hand.

PHASE SIX – INTRODUCING COMBINATIONS

Since combinations will have been introduced in the gymnastic exercises, doing them on their own should not present a problem, so long as the horse has been trained to lengthen and shorten his stride on command. At the first stage, only simple doubles are required, with the correct distances between the elements.

1) Start with a small cross pole to a small upright, with two non-jumping strides in between. Trot into the first element, but allow the horse to

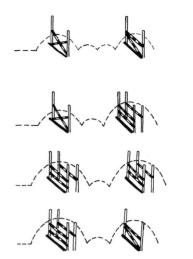

Figure 152 Progression in jumping a double.

canter in between elements.

2) As soon as the horse masters the two-stride double without rushing and with correct striding, change it to a double with one non-jumping stride.

3) Slowly increase the height of the elements, but keep the combination lower than the single fences your horse is jumping at this stage.

4) Introduce as many variations to the combination as possible, with correct striding between elements. For example, jump upright to oxer, upright to upright, parallel to parallel and parallel to upright.

The most important part of riding a combination is the first element. If your striding is correct for this, it should automatically be correct for the second element, provided that you have measured and planned the combination correctly. At this stage, the striding should suit the horse. A take-off pole may be placed in front of the first element to ensure that no mistakes are made. When the horse jumps this simple double with ease, the take-off pole may be removed.

If you make a mistake at the first element, you will have to try to correct it before the second. At low levels, this should not present a problem, but over bigger fences it will be much more difficult to correct. If the horse takes off too far from the first element, push for a longer stride in between the elements. If he gets too close to the first element and jumps big, shorten the stride to the second.

REFINING THE JUMP

Having looked at the basic processes of teaching the horse to jump, we should now consider further those factors which, given due attention, will lay the foundation for further progress.

THE APPROACH

The approach is the most important part of a jump. A correct approach virtually ensures the successful execution of the jump. The approach should be planned with concentration and calmness. Look for the easiest direction and line that will bring your horse to the correct take-off point.

Novice riders often make the mistake of not showing the horse the fence early enough. The rider should start to look for the next fence as soon as the previous one has been negotiated. On coming round any corner, the horse's head should be pointed towards the fence while the rider's legs guide the horse's body, in balance, towards it. The horse should be brought to the centre of the fence with calmness, balance, impulsion and engagement. This will have the following advantages:

1) It helps to bring the horse to the correct take-off point.

2) The horse will have the facility to lengthen or shorten his stride if necessary.

3) It gives the horse more power from his hindquarters to jump higher and thus clear the fence.

4) It improves the horse's balance during the approach and landing.

5) Lack of engagement and impulsion can lead to refusals and knock-downs.

Ride the horse in balance with the correct bend through the turns (for this purpose the horse should be trained in shoulder-in). The head bent to the outside and the shoulder 'falling in' can often be seen at showjumping competitions. This is the result of the horse bending to the outside through his body. This will certainly unbalance the horse and lead to rushing. A strong inside leg and 'sponging' with the inside rein should prevent this incorrect bend.

Be careful not to unbalance the horse through an illogical approach. This is often seen when a rider has the choice of passing in front of, or behind, another fence in order to reach the one required. The same bend should be maintained up to a fence. Passing in front of the intervening fence will result in the bend being correct; passing behind it will result in having to change bend to take the fence required. When changing bend, the horse may be in counter-canter for a few strides and may therefore lose balance.

Try to avoid long approaches. The horse may start to rush, lose his collection or lose impulsion. He will have too much time to plan a refusal. Riding from a curve or circle will have a calming effect on the horse. Note, however, that *too* short an approach can lead to a refusal or running out before the fence.

Rushing should always be avoided. If it happens during schooling revert to previous exercises and re-establish calmness.

LANDING

The landing should be straight, calm, in rhythm and balanced in order for the horse to be prepared for the next fence. Riding straight after the jump teaches the horse not to lean to one side over the fence, or anticipate the turn. If balance is lost, the horse should be rebalanced with half-halts.

If the horse rushes on landing, he should be returned to trot and walk as quickly as possible. Calm him down, and pick up the trot again. If he is difficult to slow down, a small circle may help, but this should only be used in the early training. Young horses may lose balance after the jump, and increase speed in an attempt to regain it. As the horse develops strength in his hindquarters, he will be easier to slow down. Use your voice, leg and hand aids to slow him. Continuous pulling with both hands together will just make the horse resist and rush more.

CHANGING LEAD OVER A FENCE

The easiest way to teach the horse to do this is in a figure-of-eight over a single fence. If the horse is jumping from the left and turning to the right, the following procedure should be used:

1) During the jump, the right rein (new inside rein) should be 'sponged' or opened to encourage the lateral neck flexors to contract on the right side of the neck. This gives the horse an indication of the new direction.

2) The left rein (new outside rein) is brought closer to the neck with the 'long arm' technique.

3) Look to the right and turn your hips and upper body slightly in that direction.

4) The left leg (new outside leg) gives the canter signal behind the girth, but should not push the horse over – this could lead to crooked jumping.

5) If the horse should still land on the wrong leg, he should be brought to trot and given the aid for the correct canter depart, before proceeding to re-take the fence.

Repeat this exercise a few times on both reins over the same fence and your horse will soon understand and follow the correct lead from these aids.

TEACHING HORSE AND RIDER TO SEE A STRIDE

Unfortunately, not all horses and riders possess a natural ability to judge the correct take-off point. In most cases, however technique can be improved. The process of arriving at the correct take-off spot is usually a team effort. The horse learns to see his stride, while the rider develops an instinctive

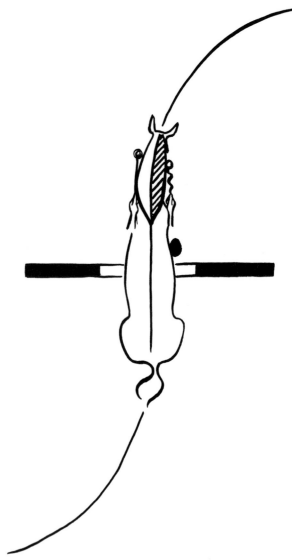

Figure 153 Change the direction over a fence by 'sponging' the new inside rein to encourage the new bend. Keep the new inside leg against the girth to prevent loss of balance.

ability to arrive at the fence correctly. These processes are the result of the development of the horse's proprioceptive sense, and the eye-motor co-ordination of the rider. (This is the same ability as knowing where to stand to catch a cricket ball or return a tennis ball. A rider who is unable to develop this skill will only be able to jump at low levels.)

Ideally, the horse should find his own stride to reach the fence correctly, with little interference from the rider. Since no rider can always be perfect at every obstacle it is important to teach the horse to see his own stride. Nevertheless the rider should, where necessary, be *able* to help the horse to reach the correct take-off point. When practising jumping off a correct stride, the fences should be kept low until the horse jumps consistently correctly.

EXERCISES TO HELP THE HORSE

All the gymnastic exercises already mentioned will help both horse and rider to develop the ability to see a stride. Other specific exercises are:

1) Repeatedly jump a small upright, parallel and spread (in that order) in a figure-of-eight shape. Jump the same fence until the horse reaches the correct take-off point consistently. Allow him to find his own stride. By repeating the exercise you will, in addition, be able to work out the exact curve to follow to bring the horse to the jump correctly.

2) Place take-off poles at the correct distance from the fence to bring the horse to the correct take-off point. Initially, put the pole one stride away then, once the horse has gained enough experience with this, move it two strides away. Proceed in this manner until you can place a pole four or five strides away from the fence.

3) To teach the horse the correct striding between two jumps, poles may be placed at intervals, corresponding to the horse's stride, in between them. Remove the poles one by one until the horse takes the combination correctly.

The best way to help the horse to find his stride however, is to train him to have balance, rhythm, suppleness and engagement, which will allow him the ability to lengthen and shorten his stride when necessary to reach the correct take-off point.

EXERCISES TO HELP THE RIDER

It is extremely important for the rider's eye to be 'glued' on the top pole of the fence. This will help the automatic perceptive reactions (eye-motor coordination, proprioceptive and kinesthetic senses)

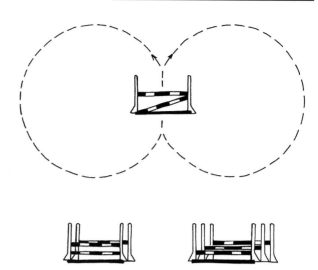

Figure 154 Jumping different individual fences on a figure-of-eight to encourage the horse to find his own stride.

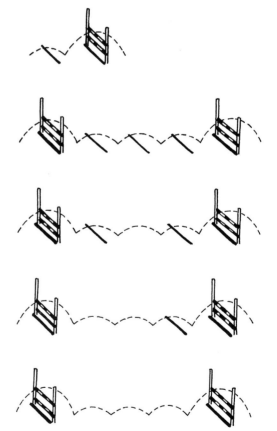

Figure 155 Using placing poles to establish striding.

Figure 155(a) Using a marker on the ground to help find a stride.

to ascertain the correct take-off point. The following exercises can assist the development of the rider's 'eye':

1) Place a marker on the ground, canter towards it and try to place your horse in line with the marker. Repeat the procedure until you are consistently correct.

2) Repeatedly jump a single small fence and try to say aloud when you are one stride away. When you are consistently correct, try to do the same when two strides away. Repeat this when three, four and five strides away.

3) When jumping a fresh obstacle, try to count the strides aloud from four or five strides away.

Schooling sessions over fences should be kept short to retain the horse's interest. Ten to fifteen jumping exercises per session should be ample. The lesson should include gymnastic jumping, single fences and a small course. Teach the horse that jumping is a part of the daily routine, not something to become excited about. He may be asked to jump a very small fence, every day, after a hack out or a flatwork session. Jump him over small logs and ditches on his trips out and school him in between the fences in the jumping paddock.

Most of the problems that may occur in the early stages of training can be corrected by lowering the fences, dealing with the basic problem and then increasing the height very slowly.

DISTANCES

At the early stage of training, the distances between trotting poles, gymnastic grids and fences should be suitable for the individual horse. The distances which follow will give an approximate idea of where to place the poles, cavalletti and fences. They should, however, be adjusted if they prove to be incorrect for the horse concerned. Once you have found the correct distance for your horse, measure it, and keep the information for future reference.

Trotting poles and cavalletti
Walk: 0.8-1.1 m.
Trot: 1.2-1.5 m.
Canter: 3.0-3.5 m (the smaller the jump, the shorter the distance).

Gymnastic exercises
Last trotting pole to first small cross pole: 2.5-3 m (bounce); 5.8 m (one stride).
First small cross pole to upright: 3 m (bounce); 6.5-7 m (one stride).
All following jumps in gymnastic grid: 3.5 m (bounce); 6.5-7 m (one stride).

Combinations
Total distances between elements:
One non-jumping stride: 6.5-7.8 m.
Two non-jumping strides: 10.2-11 m.
Three non-jumping strides: 14-15 m.
Add approximately 3.5 m for each extra non-jumping stride at canter (3.5-4.0 m is the average non-jumping stride in canter).

In all cases, the exact distances depend on the length of the particular horse's stride, the height and width of the jumps and the types of fences. From an upright, the wider the following fence is, the shorter the distance between. This is because the horse needs to take off close to a spread. Thus, the distance between an upright and a spread will be the shortest. On the other hand, if the first fence is a parallel, the distance to the second will be longer the more upright it is.

Take-off poles
In front of a jump:
Trot into an upright: 2.5-3 m.
Canter into an upright: approximately 3.5 m.
Canter into an oxer: approximately 4 m.
In between jumps, they should be placed at intervals of approximately 3.5 m, to reflect a non-jumping stride.

THE JUMPING COMPETITION

PREPARATION

The horse should be introduced to many different

obstacles at different venues before entering his first show. Preparation should include a trip to a show without actually competing. Introduce him to strange objects, strange noises and to being with other horses. As soon as he is calm in these circumstances, he should be jumped over the lowest level at a practice show. Only enter competitions once your horse jumps calmly and with confidence at home.

At first, compete at low levels to ensure that the horse has a positive experience at shows. Once he jumps with complete confidence you may move on carefully to bigger courses.

THE WARM-UP

This does not have to be too long. Long warm-ups are tiring and the horse needs energy to jump a course. Loosen up in walk, trot and canter. Work for suppleness first and then start to ask for more engagement. The horse should be obedient to half-halts, halts and the forward aids.

Once the horse is warmed up you should jump him over a few practice fences, which should be lower than the actual course. The horse has already learnt to jump and you should not try to teach him at a show. Too many practice jumps will tire him before he enters the arena. Take the first obstacle from trot and, if the horse does this without difficulty, repeat it from canter.

Plan your warm-up to include a short break before entering the arena. This will help the horse conserve his energy for the course.

WALKING THE COURSE

This should be done carefully and thoroughly. First, memorise the course, then walk it exactly as you plan to ride it. Check for unlevel ground as you walk.

Study each obstacle for hidden traps. Check the take-off and landing areas for holes, slippery approach, hard going etc. Plan how you will ride each obstacle according to what you have noticed. Plan your turns toward the fences to ensure that your approach is straight and at the centre of the jump.

Check the position of the sun. Horses do not see well when heading towards the sun and shadow in front of a fence may effect the horse's ability to see his stride.

Pace the distances through combinations and between related fences and decide how many strides your horse will need to jump effectively. (You will have to know your horse's stride and how to adjust it for difficult distances.)

Having completed your walk, visualise how you should tackle each obstacle, then watch a few other competitors and identify the tricky areas. Check the fences most often knocked down. Especially, watch how the combinations are ridden and plan accordingly.

At an appropriate moment, check on the jump-off course and plan accordingly.

RIDING THE COURSE

Once you have entered the arena, walk around the fences to acclimatise your horse to the arena and the spectators.

When the bell rings, pick up canter on the appropriate lead for the first fence and ride a circle to bring your horse in alignment with it. Then ride through the start.

Try to maintain an even rhythm throughout the whole course. If the horse speeds up, ride a few half-halts. If he is lazy, push him forwards. Ride with determination to jump the course. This will give a novice horse confidence.

When riding past or away from the entrance, be prepared for a young horse to slow down or try to slip out of the arena! If a fence is placed close to the entrance, but facing away from it, the young horse should be pushed forward to avoid a refusal.

After riding through the finish, return gradually to walk, tickle (reward) the horse and only then leave the arena. If necessary, walk past the exit first to prevent the bad habit of rushing out of the arena.

CONCLUSION

Recently I overheard a riding teacher instruct an enquiring pupil to stop asking questions and to do as she was told. 'There is a system of riding,' he maintained, 'and you have to follow the system.' This attitude, which is by no means uncommon, has prevented riders throughout the world from thinking and experimenting. What is more, it has inhibited the scientific development of our sport and is probably the prime reason it is still enshrouded in mystery and myth.

I hope that this book will encourage both a greater understanding of the art of riding and the development of a more scientific approach to equitation. The prime motivation behind it was to remove some of that mystery and myth which surround the training of the horse and to enable all riders to understand and learn the art with ease.

I have tried to explain how to communicate with a horse in a language he can understand clearly. Together with communication, there are a few other important factors to consider when training the horse. We have to realize that the horse has very limited thinking (cognative), motivational and communication skills. When training becomes difficult and frustrating, when the horse does not seem to be understanding and we feel we are not coming closer to our goal, that is when we have to respect the fact that he is only a horse. Most of the horse's evasions arise from his misunderstanding the instruction, be it through anticipation, anxiety, apprehension, stubborness, lack of intelligence or whatever other reason. Many riders are also guilty of using the horse as a vehicle to promote their own ambitions and goals. They leave the horse little choice in the matter. This is why the rider and trainer should develop utmost patience in their handling of the horse.

Everything new in riding seems to be measured by whether it is 'classical' or not. We should rather take from the classics that which is effective and has stood the test of time and build on this with what has been proven in modern scientific research. We have to search for the truth; the truth in the classical methods, the truth in modern research, and blend the two. We should always be prepared to experiment in order to find effective ways of communicating with the horse. If we do not try new and different approaches, we will never find the truth.

BIBLIOGRAPHY

Betrix, Gonda, with J. Attwood-Wheeler, *Jumping to success*, Southern Book Publishers (Pty Ltd. 1991).

Blake, Henry, *Talking with horses*, Souvenir Press Ltd. 1976. *Thinking with horses*, Souvenir Press Ltd. 1977.

Bobath, Berta, FCSP, *Adult hemiplegia: evaluation and treatment*, William Heinemann Medical Books Ltd. 1970.

D'Endrödy, Lt.-Col. A.L., *Give your horse a chance*, J.A. Allen (2nd edn) 1978.

Frandson, R.D., *Anatomy and physiology of farm animals*, Balliere Tindall 1981.

Getty, Robert, CMV, Ph.D., Sisson and Grossmans' *The anatomy of domestic animals*, W.B.Saunders Co. (5th edn) 1975.

Goody, Peter, *Horse anatomy*, J.A. Allen 1988.

Herberman, E.F., *Dressage formula*, J.A. Allen 1989.

Jackson, Noel, *Effective horsemanship*, Michael Russell Ltd. 1967.

Jousseaume, André, *Progressive dressage*, J.A. Allen 1987.

Klimke, Reiner, *Basic training of the young horse*, J.A. Allen 1985.

Loriston Clarke, J., *The complete guide to dressage*, Stanley Paul & Co. Ltd. 1987.

Oliveira, Nuno, *Reflections on equestrian art*, J.A. Allen 1976.

Paalman, Anthony, *Training showjumpers*, J.A. Allen 1978.

Podhajsky, Alois, *The complete training of horse and rider*, George Harrap & Co. Ltd. 1967.

Popesko, Peter, Prof. DMV, Dr. Sc., *Atlas of topographical anatomy of the domestic animals, Vol.1*, W.B.Saunders Co. 1977.

Seunig, Waldemar, *Horsemanship*, Doubleday & Co. (2nd edn) 1972.

Smythe, R.H., *The horse structure and movement*, J.A. Allen 1975.

Swift, Sally, *Centered riding*, William Heinemann Ltd. 1985.

Wells, Katherine, Ph.D., *Kinesiology*, W.B. Saunders Company 1966.

Winnett, John, *Dressage as art in competition*, J.A. Allen 1993.

INDEX